How I Lost My Mother

How I Lost My Mother

A Story of Life, Care and Dying

LESLIE SWARTZ

Published in South Africa by:
Wits University Press
1 Jan Smuts Avenue
Johannesburg 2001

www.witspress.co.za

First published 2021

http://dx.doi.org.10.18772/12021036949

978-1-77614-694-9 (Paperback)
978-1-77614-695-6 (Hardback)
978-1-77614-696-3 (Web PDF)
978-1-77614-697-0 (EPUB)

Project manager: Alison Lockhart
Copyeditor: Alison Lowry
Proofreader: Alison Lockhart
Cover design: Hybrid Creative
Typeset in 11.5 point Crimson

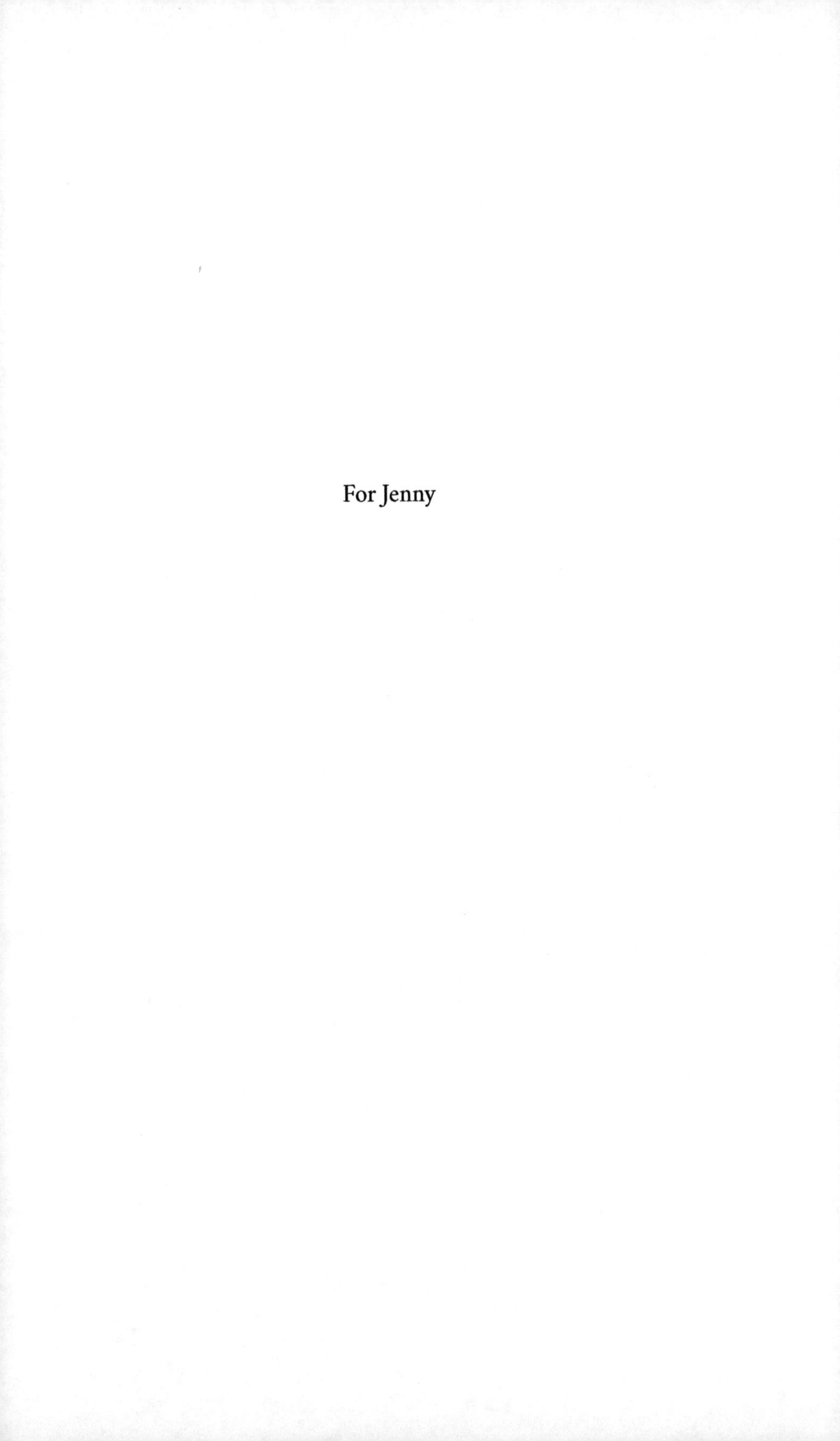

For Jenny

I know a few things about Father's past, and what I don't know, I've made up.

Anne Frank, *The Diary of a Young Girl*,
entry of Thursday 8 February 1944

How do I tell her story? When does it actually begin? When does that dying begin?

Michael Ignatieff, *Scar Tissue*

He once called her his basil plant; and when she asked for an explanation, said that basil was a plant which had flourished wonderfully on a murdered man's brains.

George Eliot, *Middlemarch: A Study of Provincial Life*

Contents

Introduction

This book is, in its heart, my version of the story of Elsie Swartz, born Cohen, who lived from 1925 until 2011. Elsie was my mother. She was born in Johannesburg to immigrant Jewish parents, was considered clever at school, but never completed high school. She married my father, Alfred Swartz, in 1951, and they moved to what was then Rhodesia, shortly after they were married. My elder sister Jenny (born in 1952) and I (born in 1955) grew up in what was then Salisbury, before our family returned to South Africa in 1966. Jenny married and had two children (she is now a grandmother) and moved to Australia. I married (twice), have two children and live in Cape Town.

My father was physically disabled (not a word he himself would have used) from birth and died rather young, at the age of 62. He was an engineer, fond of sport, despite living with impairments and pain, and very happily married to my mother. Elsie, for her part, worked as a shorthand typist most of her life, until retirement, following her husband from cement factory to cement factory, wherever his job took him. She was deeply affected by the impact, on his life and hers, of his mother, my grandmother, and his aunt Leah (who preferred to be known as Lea), Granny's younger sister; both were demanding and difficult older women.

Ten years ago I published a book titled *Able-Bodied,* which dealt with my father's life and its impact on me. Although that book had elements of memoir, it was also a chance for me, as an academic who works in disability studies, to write and think about issues of disability rights and access in southern Africa. This book, similarly, is about my mother, but it is also about other things. Like my mother before me, I am interested in all sorts of things. I am interested in what care is and how we care for one another; I am interested in memory and how we remember; I am interested in identity and how we become (and create) who we are. At different times, I discuss all of these things in this book and I invite you, the reader, to take a bit of a circuitous journey with me.

Most of all, writing this book has for me been an act of love – for my mother and what she gave me, but also for my family, and especially my wife and my daughters and my sister. I don't know (does anyone?) how to be a proper son, father, husband, brother, grown-up person. Writing this book, for me, has been part of the ongoing journey to try to find out.

Leslie Swartz
Cape Town
August 2020

Part I
Finding

1 | The Weeping Rose

Getting old is difficult, my mother used to say, but the alternative is worse. She should know. When she was 17, Elsie's father dropped dead in front of her. She never forgot what she called the sound of a death rattle. As the baby of the family by many years, she was the only one of her siblings still living at home with her parents and she was also the only one who was there when her father died. In addition to that, she had been living for months in a house in which her parents were not speaking to each other and communicating, if at all, through her. After his death, Elsie told her older siblings about this state of affairs, but they would not believe it. She was alone, with her own mother, Paulina, with the secret, the one who made things up.

Years later, when her mother died, Elsie was far away, living in Rhodesia with her husband and two young children. Paulina died a few months after the death of her only son, Hymie, who died young, in his 40s. Whereas both her husband and son had died of heart attacks, Paulina was said to have died of a broken heart. Elsie flew to Johannesburg for the funeral but she was not really part of things. For the rest of her life she railed against the fact that when Paulina's possessions from the old house were distributed amongst the siblings, nothing was set aside for Elsie, who was too far away. Years later, when she saw the jardinière she had loved as a child cracked and in poor shape on the stoep of a cousin's house, she fumed. Not only had she been forgotten, but the memories she had were disrespected too.

When I think of my mother's life and death, her suspension between those two poles – too close when her father died, too far when her mother died – seems to me to tell another story. Elsie was the afterthought in a big family: her siblings were Cecilia (known as Tilly), Ida (known as Ada), Hyman (known as Hymie), Annie (known as Hannah), and last of all Fanny (known, appropriately enough, as Babe). Ten years later, as a mistake and an afterthought, along came Elsie (known as Elsie). They couldn't even find another name for her. She heard told that when her mother was pregnant, her father had said he would forgive her and the child if it was a boy. We all know how that turned out.

Although the house in Abel Road in Johannesburg was quite empty by the time Elsie was 17, it had not always been so. As with many immigrant families, children and relatives were many and space was tight. Elsie never forgot sleeping three to a bed with two grown sisters, having her little pillow jammed between two pairs of big girl feet. This nugget of information proved useful to me in my first job after qualifying as a clinical psychologist. It's a bit hard to credit it now, but my boss in a psychiatry research unit was fond of explaining that the reason Black South Africans lived in overcrowded conditions was that culturally they liked being close to one another. I would snort and point out that my mother, Jewish like him, had grown up in an overcrowded house, but that as soon as the family had any money, the birds flew the cultural nest and started to live, so to speak, like white people.

With all this pushing and shoving for space, where was the room for little Elsie? In addition to all the siblings there was a changing cast of relatives staying in Abel Road, among them cousin Bernie Apfelstein and his mother, who was, as they say, a bit slow. The story was that Auntie Minna had been raped by a Cossack during a pogrom and that Bernie was the child of this rape. When Bernie was about five years old, kind relatives got the money to get Auntie Minna to South Africa from Lithuania. The journey was via London, and for five days Bernie disappeared in London. Nobody knows where he was (he did not remember any of this) and nobody knows how and where he was united with his mother, who had never been to London, could not speak English and didn't have the intellectual skills to set up a search party. I quibble now with some of the detail of the story – was it London or could it have been Southampton? – but none of this matters much in the telling and the feeling.

My grandfather, Jacob Cohen, never made a living, and the family moved around a bit – from one house in Abel Road, then to the neighbouring town of Edenvale, then back to a different house in Abel Road. Jacob tried his hand at many things, including, for some time, a bicycle shop, which looked like it might work but didn't. In his heart he had always dreamed, impossibly, of becoming an architect, and in fact he designed the Lyndhurst house where his daughter Hannah and her family lived for many years. After Jacob had had his fingers burned a few times, he was approached by his cousins, the Cohen brothers, to go into a new business with them. It would be a kind of general dealer, selling things for only a tickey, sixpence or a shilling. Wise by then to the history of all his failures, Jacob turned them down, and the Cohen brothers went on without him to launch what was to become OK Bazaars – 'Where Africa Shops', as the brown paper carrier bags said at the Salisbury branch of the chain where we used to shop years later.

Two stories, images really, Elsie told of her mother Paulina stick in my mind, and give me a sense of connection to this grandmother I never really knew (she died when I was three and we were living in Rhodesia). The first is of Paulina in later life, reading newspapers. Despite being uneducated, she could read English, Yiddish and Russian, and she read the newspapers from cover to cover. Literally. As Elsie told it, Paulina would read the Johannesburg *Sunday Times* from the first page to the last, reading every article and every advertisement – everything.

As her daughters got older and married, they brought sons-in-law of rather different stripes into the family. Ada married Louis, whose life traced the classic arc of the wildly successful immigrant. An impoverished newspaper-seller in Russia as a boy, Louis managed to get to South Africa, where he made a living as a rag-and-bone man. Later on he became an auctioneer and he died a millionaire whose investments, among others, were gold mines. He was the arch-capitalist and Zionist, making lots of money and positioning himself as a (genuinely) generous philanthropist. By contrast, Elsie's eldest sister, Tilly, married Harry who, like her father, just could not make a living and struggled through life. Tilly married much later in life than her siblings. This was, people said, because she had the bad hip and the terrible limp and what kind of a man would want her, after all? Eventually, she found and married Harry, and had a long childless marriage with him (because she probably couldn't have children, poor thing). Through some illness, which I suspect could have been diabetes, and before dying young, Harry lost a leg. I remember going to see him in the hospital shortly after the amputation on one of our visits to Johannesburg. I must have been about five or six, and I was terrified of this bewhiskered old man who grabbed so powerfully onto my wrist as my mother encouraged me to make small talk with him. Harry had been a failed worker and not much of a catch himself, but he was also a dedicated communist – politically the exact opposite of what the patriarch and benefactor Louis became.

For Paulina, family loyalty was everything. Although I remember nothing of her, from Elsie's telling I see Paulina clearly in my mind's eye, her grey hair in a bun, with newspapers spread out in front of her. For Louis, she read the *Zionist Record*, and for Harry the *Daily Worker*. Both from cover to cover. Fair is fair, and family is family.

The second clear picture I have of Paulina is from around the time when Hannah got married to Mike. Family lore has it that Babe was the beauty in the family, but when I look at old family photographs it is Hannah who strikes me as quietly beautiful, serene and unaware of quite how striking she is. Hannah and Mike had been given a dinner service for their wedding, which arrived in a crate with sawdust and newspaper for padding. Having had to move from house to too-small house throughout her marriage, Paulina knew that the best way to deal with mess was to get rid of it straight away. So as Hannah unpacked the delicate china cups and plates, Paulina threw the detritus of paper, wood and sawdust straight into the anthracite-burning Aga stove. Soon a series of loud bangs was heard from inside the stove, as well-wrapped crockery which Hannah had not even laid eyes on exploded in the heat.

When I picture this scene, and get the sense of the acrid smell of anthracite in my nostrils, I locate Paulina and Hannah not in the Abel Road house where this must have happened, and which I never saw, but in the only other place where I had ever seen an Aga stove at work. This was in Hannah's Lyndhurst house, the one designed by her late father and where Hannah and Mike and their children lived for many years. On holidays from Rhodesia and, later, from 'the country', wearing our contradictions of country bumpkins and intellectual sophisticates, we would visit my mother's older sister at this perfectly square house with a red-soil driveway around it and rows and rows of pear trees behind it. Lyndhurst was already officially a part of Johannesburg, but it seemed like more a part of the countryside than even the dorps we lived in. Part of this came from the fact that the house was next to a small general dealer similar to those we would see at the side of the road when we travelled across the country. There was even a big sign outside for Three Trees Tea. The implied clientele was poor and rural, who would not have had easy access to other places to buy supplies.

Uncle Mike had inherited this store from his family and he ran it for many years, with Hannah's help. On weekends, and when we visited, Mike would sit on the back stoep next to the anthracite-smelling kitchen drinking tea in what I was told was the Russian style. He would pick up a sugar lump (this was the first time I had seen sugar lumps), wedge it firmly between his teeth, and strain tea through the sugar as he drank. Hannah served tea seemingly endlessly. I remember the back stoep changing over the years from being open to the elements to being enclosed with a glass widow and a flimsy glass door; I remember the lacy tablecloth being replaced with another one, which was also lacy but made of easy-to-wipe plastic. Through these changes, through me and my cousins growing older, it felt to me that Mike remained seated, waiting, as men did in that time and place, for the next cup of tea or the next thing to eat. I remember Hannah moving backwards and forwards, backwards and forwards, between the Aga and the stoep, tending to Mike and to all of us. Hannah, I now realise, was for me the link between my modern, undomesticated mother and her past. Hannah had the stock pot boiling on the stove long after everyone else had modern electric stoves; the Aga burned day and night, summer and winter, warming the house when you needed it, making it unbearable in summer, and always stinking of anthracite and women's work.

Hannah was the one who made kreplach ('Who makes kreplach today?' I hear my mother ask, rhetorically), latkes and kichel. She was the one who put all the old-time things in the food – the cow intestines in the kishkes (I couldn't face them), the chicken feet in the chicken soup. My mother used to tell me of Fridays before Shabbos when the slaughterer would come to decapitate the Sabbath chicken in the back yard, the headless bloody chicken continuing to totter around till dead and ready for plucking and the pot. Well, here were the feet in Hannah's soup. To me, chickens in their natural habitat were encased in plastic in a freezer at the grocery store. My world, though populated with insects, lizards and snakes, so much part of the Rhodesian landscape, had moved on from this. When my mother was at work, I used to spend hours trying to catch the flies that congregated against the glass of the 1950s style picture windows and French doors at our house in Salisbury, but I was not so uncultured as to suck on chicken feet and sugar lumps. Snobbery is as snobbery does.

There was another way in which visits to Lyndhurst were trips into a past my mother either never had, or had escaped. Mike sat, and Hannah served, and as they got older, the boys of the family learned to sit while Hannah served them too. What kind of a woman was this? What kind of men were these, who knew what they wanted and knew who would get it for them?

For over three years, Hannah would pick me up from my boarding school and take me to Lyndhurst to spend what, for me, would be a wretched Sunday out, despite all the kindness shown to me. Hannah and the whole family were remarkably kind to me, and I never heard or sensed a word of complaint against this alien interloper, child of the foreign laatlammetjie sister living in some Godforsaken somewhere and allowing her children to endure hostel life.[i] Week after week the white Cortina would arrive at the hostel punctually and off I would go into this time capsule of extended family kindness from which my mother had broken but also longed to restore. I misfitted back into a world she had never fitted in herself. Why I see this as a trip back in time I am not quite sure, as there were parts of it, like my cousin Stanley's sticker and matchbox collection – along with what I suspected was his weed smoking, which I would never dare to do – that were much more up to date and appropriately 'teenagerly' than I could ever hope to be. Stanley was the tearaway rebellious boy of his family, terrible at school in everything except maths, at which he excelled, girl crazy and not scared of the fast life. Although he was only a year older than me, Stanley was much more grown up than I was.

It was through the lens of the visits to Lyndhurst (147 Johannesburg Road, to be precise) that I got the strongest sense of my mother's family and childhood and all the ways in which she, and we, didn't quite fit in. But also, it must be said, did fit in – just as snugly as a little girl fitted her pillow in between the feet of her sisters. As the laatlammetjie, Elsie got in the way of the blooming development of her teenaged sisters. When I see her in my mind's eye demanding bribes from her big sisters to get out of the way when their gentlemen friends came calling, I see this happening in the lounge of 147 Johannesburg Road. When I hear her little-girl voice telling big sister Tilly's best friend, 'Tilly says you dress like a boerite' and then getting a klap, a sharp smack, from Tilly, 18 years her senior, I see this all in that same lounge.[ii]

---

i 'Laatlammetjie': The lastborn, afterthought child after a long break with no children – literally, in Afrikaans, 'little lamb who came later'.

ii 'Boerite': A Yiddish construction of the Afrikaans word 'boer', literally meaning 'farmer' but in South Africa generally meaning 'Afrikaner'. The word boerite, which has three syllables (boer-it-e), denotes an Afrikaner woman.

Elsie was bookish and clever, and she was also a budding scientist. She had heard that cats always fall on their feet. Not content to take this information for granted, and ever the empiricist, little Elsie spent hours picking up her beloved cat and throwing the animal off the balcony of the Abel Road house, carefully changing the angles at which she threw the cat down. She clearly did not want the cat's falling on its feet to be an artefact of the angle of the trajectory, or of random sampling variation. As she used to tell it, many hours were spent in this exercise of cat-tossing. I can reveal both that the cat, in general, and certainly more often than can easily be explained by chance, did fall on its feet; and that though I have to make some architectural adjustments in my mind, the veranda of the Abel Road house is recognisably a version of 147 Johannesburg Road's front porch.

On one of our holidays to Johannesburg, before my boarding school days, Jenny and I were with Auntie Hannah, Uncle Mike and their family having lunch when the meal was interrupted by the phone ringing. Hannah could be heard in the adjacent passage trying to get off the phone as quickly as possible: 'Tilly, we're all fine. We're having lunch. Got to go.' Hannah returned to the table and was just sitting down when the phone rang again. Tilly. 'Sorry,' Tilly said, 'but I forgot to send love to the children.' Wonderful, mad Tilly – the eldest and the eccentric, the one with the funny hip. She was the one who tormented my mother the most of all the sisters, but her eccentricity and lack of fortune allowed much to be forgiven over the years. And my mother, the changeling youngest, the cuckoo in the complete family nest, was the one who went on to marry a man with a limp and a funny hip, a man very different in all sorts of ways from Tilly and the others, but in another way oh so similar and familiar. I had not thought of this before, but it was almost as though slightly dotty Tilly and unwanted little Elsie, children of the same family but of a different generation, bookended the old-time respectability of the others – Ada, the intellectual who married well; Hannah, the capable home-maker; Hymie, the boy, which would have been enough, who also became a lawyer and a wealthy man before he died too young; and

Babe, the great beauty and sportswoman. All were a credit to the Cohen dynasty, but Tilly and Elsie probably not so much.

The telephone Tilly interrupted us with twice that holiday mealtime was one of those large black Bakelite jobs with a dial, which took some effort to use. It sat on a little telephone table in the passage next to two Johannesburg phone books (one Yellow Pages, one White Pages, though I am not sure it was called 'White Pages' back then – it was just the main phone book).

On the wall was a gilt-framed print of Vladimir Tretchikoff's Weeping Rose. This was when Tretchikoff was still largely considered kitsch, if not beneath contempt, long before his work swept back into favour; and certainly before the variety of options a quick online search will tell you are available. You can own a Weeping Rose (and many other Tretchikoffs) print of various sizes (framed or unframed), or have it as a fridge magnet, a cosmetics bag, a wall clock or a cushion cover – each item proudly emblazoned with the words 'Made in South Africa'. There are yoga mats too. Should you feel so inclined, you could do your Downward Dog face to life-size face with Tretchi's blue-faced Balinese Dancer, but I digress ... At the time of which I am talking, a framed Tretchikoff print was something you would have paid good money for and would probably have thought about quite a bit as something beautiful to have on your wall.

The faux Axminster blood-red floral floor runner, hard to see in that dark passage, was also probably carefully chosen, although both the carpet and the print could, of course, have come from Louis' 'mart' – Rand Auctioneers. By selling what was left of respectable homes and lives to those wishing to buy good quality but at less expense, Rand Auctioneers was how Ada's formerly Peruvnic husband had established his fortune and his role in the family.

I am not quite sure why it is this passage – this nondescript dark tunnel linking the various rooms in the house – that seems to speak to me most vividly of 147 Johannesburg Road and the world my mother had come from, why it should feel to me the true authentic real thing of her past, but somehow it does. The house, designed as it was by my grandfather, was built long before the advent of fancy-pants passages like 'breezeways', the pride of the Spanish Period of homes of Johannesburg's rapidly expanding northern suburbs in the 1970s. I think my attachment to this passage stems both from that 'love to the children' extra phone call from Tilly, and another series of entanglements involving her, Hannah and all the rest of us. These are what I have come to term the Ben Black Concealments.

Ben Black, I think, was a distant cousin of some sort. In any event, he was the sort of person whom our extended family believed we should be looking after in one way or another. Maybe he was a landsman – a person whose progenitors came from the same shtetl as the one our family came from in the old country. He married a blonde little boerite much younger than himself. What did she see in him? It certainly couldn't have been his looks because he didn't have any; and he was also deficient in the money department. Maybe she thought all Jews were rich? Well, she'd learn the truth about that fast. Regardless of this, family is family and obligation is obligation, so the Cohen sisters had to be nice to him. There were just two problems with this. First, they didn't really like him, and the little boerite just complicated matters. (What was there to say to her?) Second, Ben Black had the nasty habit of driving all the way to Lyndhurst unannounced and just rocking up there for tea on a Sunday afternoon. (Hadn't he heard of the telephone? What kind of person was this?)

After being ambushed a few times by Ben and the boerite, the family got wise. Through a complicated lookout system, the arcane details of which I cannot recall, Tilly sounded the warning. Venetian blinds were rapidly pulled down and the whole family congregated silently in the passage. The crunch of car tyres on the circular driveway was followed by a rapping on the back stoep door. We remained silent. After a few tries of knocking on the back stoep door, there was the crunch-crunch of footsteps walking round to the front of the house. Then came the fusillade at the front door and hushed whispers in the passage ('Hannah,

I saw him peer through the windows to check if we were home, can you believe it?'). Eventually, we'd hear the car engine start and the car drive off. By this stage, though, the coast was by no means clear. Knowing Ben Black and the boerite, they were quite capable of turning back and trying again. After waiting a bit longer to make sure they weren't coming back and we could all relax, everyone returned to their Sunday afternoon pursuits – the wireless, newspapers, baking, naps.

With the passage of years I may have some details of the Ben Black Concealments slightly wrong, but of the central fact I am very sure. As a teenage boy I stood with at least three grown adults (Hannah, Mike and Tilly) hiding from a potential visitor and his boerite wife. What stopped Hannah and Tilly (I suspect that Mike was a reluctant participant in this drama) being clear with Ben Black about when they would and would not be at home to him and the boerite? I can hear Tilly's voice in my head: 'You can't be rude. Poor Ben Black – I would never want to upset him.' Cold-faced and clear-eyed logic tells me that it is probably rather upsetting to know that people you just want to visit for a cup of tea, Russian style, are holed up against you next to the Tretchikoff like homesteaders in a tacky Western hiding from the marauders. This is probably even more upsetting than learning from your relatives or friends that they do want to see you but on their own, more predictable terms. But to face Ben Black with this limit was clearly too much. To look a man in the eye and say to him that he is not always welcome could hurt him, and could also hurt those doing the looking in the eyes. Worse than this, it could give the game away about our feelings about the little boerite. Ben Black, poor man, had to marry whoever would take him. Thank God this didn't happen in our family.

The house at 147 Johannesburg Road, Lyndhurst, is long since demolished. Nowadays, of a Sunday, you can attend the Alleluia Church Ministries service in the large building on the site, led by Pastor Shepherd Gwenzi. Both Abel Road houses in Berea had themselves long since made way for flats and flyovers. But it is in the Lyndhurst house partly where my memories of my mother and my memories of her memories live on. The Cohen family lived on, then, and now dispersed far and wide, but anchored there.

Number 147 Johannesburg Road is also the place where I first remember seeing my cousin Pamie, Hymie's younger daughter, and the cousin to whom I remain the closest, both physically (our houses are walking distance apart) and emotionally. Lucky me to have Pamie so close to me now in Cape Town; lucky for Elsie that Pamie was so much with us at the end. Pamie is now what would be called an old lady by any standards, but when I see her sitting cross-legged and slim on our couch it is hard to think of her as 77. When I first saw her all those years ago, she was a young woman in a black mini-dress with black lace stockings, sitting on the lap of her impossibly handsome fiancé. I don't remember saying a word to her back then – I was an awkward boy and she this urban sophisticate. Now we are both old people thinking about the past. Time, time, time.

2 | Be sociable

Every day when we came home from school my sister Jenny and I would sit at the huge desk in our parents' bedroom and finish our homework. Our mother was often still at work but she insisted on this, and it was a habit we did not resist.

Elsie worked half day as a shorthand typist and secretary at the cement factory where my father was chief chemist, but sometimes the days were longer. Jenny and I were looked after by live-in domestic workers – a nanny/housekeeper and a gardener. All white people in Rhodesia had servants, usually more than one. When I travel to other African countries these days and I see how many servants my academic colleagues have, I think of how colonial traditions of master and servant are alive and well. There was certainly no question in our house about who would cook, clean and look after us while our parents worked. I don't remember a single other school friend whose mother worked outside the home, but they all had servants. Elsie accepted having domestic workers as natural, and she was kind but not disruptive of the power relationships. To be fair, though, she was not one for laziness. Years later when a cousin was having marital problems and she got to know something of his domestic situation, she discovered that this young then-childless couple lived in an easy-to-run flat, that the wife who was causing all the trouble did not work outside the home, and that the couple employed a full-time maid. 'What does the wife do all day?' Elsie wanted to know. Her answer to her own rhetorical question was the tight-lipped 'Well, I suppose someone has to watch the maid.'

There were those amongst the friends, and their parents especially, who disapproved of my mother's working ('No wife of mine will do that, I tell you for sure'). I don't remember feeling anything other than proud of the fact that Elsie worked. It was something that set us apart from others, and she enjoyed the work, that was clear. And I think I came to see that she needed it, but more about that later.

Jenny and I were good at entertaining ourselves. Although we played a lot with the next-door kids (among them my best friend, Bruce), I spent hours and hours reading, resisting my mother's entreaties, when she was home, to go outside and play in the wonderful Rhodesian climate. The bush across the road from our house was a place for making houses and playing some fantasy games (often based on books we'd read), but climbing trees, along with huntin', shootin' and fishin', were never really for me.

Doing my homework, I would sit not on a chair but on the kist, sideways on to the huge desk. With its brass fittings and ball-and-claw feet, the kist was heavy, solid and seldom opened. Most of what was inside it, or most of what I remember anyway, came from Granny, my father's mother, who lived with us on and off in Salisbury. This included the best quality embroidered tablecloths, sheets and suchlike. With visitors far and few between at our outpost so far from Johannesburg, there was seldom any need to bring these out. My father was an only child, and anything likely to have been inherited from Elsie's mother had been snapped up in Johannesburg by her sisters, so Elsie had to (chose to) accept the yield of her awful mother-in-law's at times rather awful fancy-work. When the kist was opened, there was the smell (it remains with me) of naphthalene moth balls. Life in the (sub) tropics was a constant battle against insects, snakes and so on, and moths and putzi flies would make short shrift not only of the good linen but also of your skin. It was only much later that I learned that the scientific name for putzi fly is *anthropophaga*, Greek for 'human eater'. We knew many stories of people who had not ironed their clothes properly after taking them off the washing line, leaving the putzi fly eggs in the material to hatch into maggots that feasted on their flesh.

This time – the early 1960s – was the age of all sorts of labour-saving devices, including the advent of drip dry. According to the Oxford English Dictionary, an article in *Woman* magazine in 1953 declared: 'With this permanently pleated nylon nightie ... you just ... rinse out, drip dry, and you don't even think of ironing.' Similarly, and also according to the Oxford English Dictionary, in 1964 *Modern Textiles Magazine* informed their readers: 'There are a number of competing processes now being offered ... with claims of permanent creasing, permanent pressing, permanent shape retention, etc.' The putzi flies of Rhodesia clearly cared nothing for *Woman* or *Modern Textiles* and thank God we had servants to iron everything thoroughly and naphthalene for the rest. Granny was a formidable darner of jerseys, which were routinely chewed by moths, but as with all things, prevention tended to be better than cure as her darnings were, shall we say, robust and vigorous, and clearly visible to the naked eye at 100 paces. Granny was a great one for malapropisms and language errors. She insisted that it was always a good idea to take your clothes to a good tailor to have them, as she always put it, 'visibly mended' – so beautifully 'visibly mended' that you would never ever know they had been mended at all. In the case of Granny's darning, 'visible mending' was no grammatical error but a sad and irrevocable proof both that the moths had got there first and that we could not afford to replace damaged clothes.

Jenny and I would sit at the desk in our parents' room, at times looking out of the picture window, with the garden outside, the hawthorn hedge marking the end of the property and the jacarandas behind the hedge by the side of the gravel road with the bush beyond. The four jacarandas had been planted by Elsie (well, Elsie would not have planted the trees herself – she would have supervised the 'garden boy' doing the planting) as her nod to being here in Africa. She loved jacarandas, which are actually native to South America and the Caribbean but turned Johannesburg purple every spring and continue to do so, and the saplings gave Jenny an opportunity to do a school project over a period of months. For weeks my sister studied the trees and the insect life around them, and even constructed what she described in her Osmiroid blue ink in her project as a 'rain ~~gus~~ gauge'. Even Jenny's deletions were precise and beautiful to look at.

Although she had no choice but to establish a garden from scratch because we were the first inhabitants of our house on a new estate carved out of the Rhodesian bush, my mother was very clear that real devotion to gardening was definitely not a Jewish thing. But 'the yoks love it,' she would say. According to some sources, 'yoks' is a term for non-Jewish hooligans, but to us it referred to non-Jews in general. Generic, but a bit more disparaging than the neutral 'Gentile'. My mother was anything but yokkish in her approach to gardening, going for sensible rockeries and gravel driveways while neighbours sweated to raise perfect roses under the African sun. But Elsie loved trees – especially the jacarandas and the bauhinia she planted. On a visit to what by then had become Harare one year I went to look at our old house. Predictably, I suppose, the house of my childhood seemed to have shrunk in size over the years, but what was shocking was the huge size of the jacarandas. We had had a sunny garden with the jacarandas beyond, but now the whole house and garden were in deep shade, shrinking, it seemed, from the sun.

The view from my parents' bedroom was the view of a frontier. The cement factory where my dad worked, and which had occasioned the building of the housing estate, was six miles out of Salisbury along an impossibly rutted and treacherous red road, especially difficult to navigate in the rainy season. Beyond that, as far as we knew, was only bush. When John Lennon asks us to imagine 'above us, only sky' and comfortingly tells us 'this isn't hard to do' (thereby implying that it is in fact very hard), I want to say, 'John, I grew up at the edge of things, with no street lights and a huge sky above, and the terrifying bush beyond – maybe I should not be imagining too much.' The very kist on which I sat and did my homework, when it was still in West Nicholson, where my parents had lived in the very early days of their marriage, had hidden a large snake sleeping in the cool inside for who knew how long.

The country idyll, which my wife Louise speaks about so amusingly as a cultural trope, was not something Elsie sought or wanted. She didn't want to be a bumpkin; she was a city girl interested in the world, and would not somehow revert to pre-industrial shtetl-type making gardens and milking cows. Life on the frontier, although it came with all the luxuries of a brand-new house with American kitchen and parquet and lino floors, was hard and not always such fun. The impossible, heavy furniture of the time has now become 'desirable' – from Kist Company you can now buy various versions of Executive Kist, including a Super Executive Kist, or a Maiden and Groom Kist, all now suitably Africanised for an emerging new elite. But for Elsie the kist was the ungainly container in which you tried to maintain the shreds of your linens and your respectability against the ravages of a tough environment, of creatures great and very small.

There was also the dust to deal with. As a result of spectacularly bad planning, especially given the amount of free space available, the housing estate we lived on was situated downwind of the cement factory, and everything on the estate was covered in grey cement dust. Trees became green only when it rained, and it rained much less often than we would have liked. Despite our living in the African bush, things were not bright and luxuriant as you might expect. Colours were muted by the grey patina of dust over everything.

Added to this was the isolation. There weren't many Jews in Salisbury; even fewer of these were liberal religiously and part of the fledgeling Reform movement in Rhodesia. We lived miles away from where the action was – on this satellite settlement that existed solely as a compound for the cement factory employees. I suppose there must be some chicken and egg questions about my parents' isolation and where we ended up living – I am not really sure which came first. In any event, my parents very seldom went out in the evenings and had few house guests, apart from Granny and her even more formidable younger sister, the dreaded Auntie Lea.

Once my beautiful and much older cousin Glenda visited with her friend Audrey. They were two young ladies on their way on an overseas adventure and had a stop-over in Salisbury. Audrey had the longest fingernails, painted pink, that I had ever seen. She could cut into an apple with her thumbnail. This visit must have been some time after the visit of Glenda's younger brother Stephen, along with mutual cousins Shirley, Jack and Stanley (Hannah's children). That visit took place soon after Babe's husband Alec, and Stephen and Glenda's father, died very young from lung cancer. He had had a reputation as a sportsman and as something of a roué, and he was a very heavy smoker. Stephen was a few years older than me, a teenager, and lost, angry and difficult during the time he was with us. My parents did their best to provide him some respite from the world that had betrayed him by killing his father.

Apart from these visits from cousins, and one visit to the airport to see my eldest cousin Dinky (Ada's daughter), her husband Syd and their children on their way to London where Syd, who was a doctor, would specialise, I remember very few other visitors. The exceptions were various members of my father's extended family, some of whom lived in Southern and Northern Rhodesia. Then there were the Sapersteins, who arrived on our doorstep with a suitcase, having fled something or other in the Belgian Congo, a hushed story of the barbarians at the gate, but also in other tellings something to do with a business deal going bad. Not much else. No passing traffic – we were the end of the line. So you can imagine the excitement the very occasional sound of the ice-cream man might cause. Ringing his bell, he would cycle his little cart over the bumpy miles from civilisation all the way out to the cement works estate. Such a visitation was probably even more welcome and exciting to us than to children elsewhere and Elsie always gave us money to buy an ice lolly or ice cream. The Lyons Maid brand was the only one on offer. My particular favourite was the new Mivvi, advertised on television with the jingle, 'Two in one! Two in one! Two in wonderful Mivvi!' The Mivvi combined both ice cream and water ice (pineapple water ice was much better than strawberry) so you got the best of both two-in-wonderful worlds.

The only other people who came calling were insurance salesmen (boring) and – the best treat of all – Encyclopaedia Britannica salesmen. I loved encyclopaedias and longed to have a full Encyclopaedia Britannica set at home. I assured my parents that I would read every word, which, given the amount I read, was no idle promise, but what I loved most were the beautiful pictures and the mock-up of how our own set would sit handsomely in situ. The Britannica never materialised, but I did have a growing collection of How and Why Wonder Books. One very special single-volume children's encyclopaedia, bought from Barbours in the centre of Salisbury, turned out to have some pages missing. When we went to return it we were given a brand-new copy *and* we were allowed to keep the old defective one, which meant I got to cut pictures from it for school projects. I was mortified when a teacher commented that I should not cut pictures out of books. It was unthinkable that the goody-goody I was would dream of defacing an intact book.

My parents tried, and to a degree succeeded, at living a good colonial life. New cement factory building a new country, which they hoped would be more liberal than the South Africa of their birth; wonderful climate; tea and biscuits served by pleasant domestic workers; golf for my dad and bowls for my mother. Nice neighbours next door, and joint trips with Auntie Myra to Mrs Garrett the dressmaker. Mrs Garrett had a dachshund so fat that its stomach wheeled about on a little trolley, which delighted me. In those days nobody worried too much about animal (or human) obesity and health – you were given your cards and you played them. Elsie was, through no desire of her own, to be part of this group, part of a club of patriotic White Rhodesians who smoked as many cigarettes as they possibly could, tobacco being a key crop for the economy. After her father had died in front of her when she was 17, Elsie had been given a cigarette by a kind adult, with the reassuring promise, 'This will calm your nerves.' It did indeed calm her nerves, and Elsie became a teenage smoker.

So much social life revolved around cigarettes. The standard (and welcome) gift one could give anyone was an ashtray. Ashtrays came in every conceivable shape and form, ranging from small, delicate, one-cigarette jobs made of glass blown by artisans in Italy, through heavy glass ashtrays embedded in small replicas of car tyres (Christmas gifts from tyre salesmen and service stations), to elaborate metal faux verdigris pots standing on three legs. This last was a desirable piece of furniture in itself! Then there were sets of ashtrays thematically linked, the tobacco lover's equivalent of flying ducks going up the wall.

The ashtray that, for some reason, fascinated me the most, was not in Rhodesia but in the house of Auntie Babe and Uncle Alec on Pretoria Street in Johannesburg. They had a split-level, ranch-style home with a huge swimming pool. Proudly displayed in their lounge was an oil painting of their two beautiful daughters, Glenda and Hazel, and elsewhere was the painting of cousin Stephen, the little prince. Amongst all this opulence, the thing that impressed me most was the ceramic wall tile ashtray in the guest toilet. The tiles in this little room were fashionably light blue-green in colour. If you sat on the toilet, just to the left of you was a tile just like all the others, but with a seamless ceramic protrusion in the shape of a small ashtray. This was the day of labour-saving devices, and of the housewife's friend (and, indeed, of the Stepford Wives and the Feminine Mystique), but the sheer labour-saving convenience of grown-ups being able to sit on the loo and have a place to put their lit cigarettes down really appealed to my sense of wonder. There may well have been two reasons for my romance with the ceramic wall ashtray. The first had to with my disgust at my great-aunt Lea's habit of (unsuccessfully) flushing her half-smoked cigarettes down our loo in Salisbury. There was invariably a butt floating in the toilet water, and the rank smell of cigarettes in the small toilet room was constant. In Auntie Babe's house, by contrast, any smoker could put their butt aside and take it up again after making use of the facilities. And that shiny green room never stank of stale cigarettes, or of anything else that I can remember. The other reason I remember that little room in Pretoria Street so well, and hence the clever little ashtray, I think, was that Babe and Alec had what I am sure most people found to be a witty toilet cover with a cartoon on it. The cartoon was of a goblin emerging from a green toilet bowl. Hilarious, you may agree, but I found it terrifying – especially when I had to flush the toilet, expecting that the goblin would threateningly emerge at any second from the noise and the foam.

In addition to tobacco, copper was especially important to the economy of Rhodesia, and also to what was then Northern Rhodesia (Zambia). In Rhodesia, a dual expression of true patriotism was the display and use of copper ashtrays. There was a wonderful shop in the Linquenda Arcade which sold copper gifts almost exclusively, and many of the gifts were ashtrays in various sizes. They also sold huge copper fire-screens with a flame lily design, that being the national flower. Later, with the ascent to power of Ian Douglas Smith as prime minister, and the Unilateral Declaration of Independence (UDI) in 1965, a range of desirable copper likenesses of good old Smithy himself were added to the range of stock, as well as copper tea trays with the new Rhodesian flag.

As liberals strongly opposed to UDI (a rare breed in White Rhodesia), but also as a better class of people, my parents sneered at such nationalist kitsch. But they did like a good ashtray. On their return from a trip to America, they brought me and Jenny some small gifts, which included troll dolls, never been seen in Rhodesia before, as far as we knew, and for themselves a small porcelain ashtray with a drawing of a hapless fat boy on it wearing an inappropriate hat and looking as miserable as sin. The cartoon was not dissimilar in style to that of the goblin toilet cover in Babe and Alec's Johannesburg home, which was the last word in modern taste. The caption to the ashtray cartoon was: 'Now that you're older, go play in the street.' The ashtray was proudly displayed in the small entrance lobby of our house, much to the delight of my parents and the few adults who visited. As an eight-year-old with feelings, I was far less impressed. I had fantasies of smashing the damn thing but was much too good a boy to do it. My parents would have said I shouldn't take the ashtray joke so seriously, that it wasn't meant personally, but I knew better; and a part of me knows better still. Babe and Alec's goblin was one thing in all its strange mystery, but my parents' wish to be rid of me felt like something altogether different.

Cigarettes were everything in Rhodesia at that time, and along with alcohol the central things that kept white settler society together. My parents were never big drinkers. Although my mother would gamely down a ginger square cocktail to be sociable, she didn't really like it too much. The most important way to be sociable in Rhodesia was very clear from the advertisement for the cigarette brand I remember most clearly: 'Be sociable – have a Matinée'. The box was yellow with brown and grey corners, and looked very sophisticated. I am not sure if it was Matinée cigarettes – it may well have been First Lord – which had the slogan 'Do have one of mine' (a version of the 'Have one of mine' slogan of Old Gold cigarettes in the USA), but First Lord cigarette boxes, like many others, were displayed in advertisements with three cigarettes emerging invitingly from the box. By sharing cigarettes, especially those showing sophistication and old-time military or maritime greatness, people like my mother could ensure that they could be part of things. Not that she didn't feel too Jewish, too urban, too literate, too ugly and incompetent for the frontier. Many of the residents at the housing estate on the cement works were working-class British people transported from drab post-war greyness to this paradise of blue skies, safety and, above all, cheap Black labour. My mother deplored how poorly these people treated the help, not that she did not have help herself. But decency and her relatively elevated status as wife of the chief chemist (and, effectively, deputy manager) of the factory required her to be civil. She was not going to get drunk with them in the pub, but she would surely sit and smoke with them.

There were some people to whom Elsie felt closer, apart from Auntie Myra and Uncle Cecil next door. There was the brilliant but drunken Mac McKenzie, who had clearly failed at an engineering job in his native Scotland because of his love of whisky, and had somehow ended up working in 'this Godforsaken country in the middle of nowhere', as he put it. Mr Mac's wife was long gone ('She schmeitzed long ago,' said my parents), so he lived with his mother, Mrs Mac, just as formidable as Granny.[i] Where Mr Mac's bloodstream was probably 90 per cent

---

i 'Schmeitzed': buggered off.

whisky and 10 per cent First Lord nicotine, Mrs Mac's was 70 per cent whisky and 30 per cent nicotine – she had a bit more control, but not much more. Mr Mac would drive my mother to bowls along the bumpy Arcturus Road on a Saturday afternoon, and Jenny and I sometimes went along. Not surprisingly, and despite the sparse traffic on the road, one sunny Saturday afternoon Mr Mac managed to slam his Morris Oxford into an articulated truck. None of us was badly hurt, luckily, although Mr Mac was far too pickled to care very much. Nowadays I find it hard to believe that our anxious and ridiculously protective mother allowed us both before and after this accident to be driven around by the town drunk, but those were different times. One had to be sociable and not cause upset. Between aunties Tilly and Hannah, and Elsie's putting us in mortal danger for the sake of peace, we were learning some important life lessons.

An important figure in our lives at the edge of the edge was the dapper Dr Levy, our GP. It was a long bumpy ride to get to him but he and my mother became close, and when it was required, he would drive the miles out to see us for our illnesses and ailments. Dr Levy always had a very white shirt and always wore a bow-tie. His hair was kept very neat. He must have been about 40 when he finally married. Six weeks later we were at his rooms for a clinical consultation and the marriage was over. As he was examining me, he talked over me to my mother.

Dr Levy: 'She wanted everything pink. Not just the lounge pink, but all the furnishings pink, the sheets pink, the bedspreads pink, the curtains pink, everything pink. Elsie, I couldn't. I couldn't go on like this.'

Elsie: 'You're a hundred per cent right, a hundred per cent.'

After the consultation, my mother could hardly contain herself. 'What kind of a person gets divorced after six weeks of marriage because his wife wants everything pink?' she said as we got into the car. 'That's not a reason. For God's sake!'

She could not wait to tell my father of this folly. And he of course agreed that Dr Levy, whom they both loved, and who was so important to the care of our whole family, was the very opposite of 'a hundred per cent right' on this matter of the heart. With the wisdom of about 60 years' hindsight and some professional experience, I can see that Dr Levy was very obsessional or gay, and most probably both. In his case, as in so many others, I am almost certain that it was not all about the pink, however much he might have wanted it to be. I don't know, of course, what Dr Levy thought of my mother's hundred per cent backing of his story, and he certainly remained a supportive and caring professional to us all. But here's the lesson in this: when Elsie tells you that you are a hundred per cent right, you had better watch out. Come back, Auntie Tilly and the Ben Black Concealments. All is forgiven.

3 | Goodwill

It's hard to know when things started to go wrong. In matters of the heart and mind this is probably always the case. How far back do we go? In the field of schizophrenia we know, for example, that symptoms usually start in late adolescence or early adulthood. Although childhood-onset schizophrenia does exist, it is rarer than the adult form and the disorder is usually thought of as mainly a disorder of adulthood. Many people who develop schizophrenia do well until their teens, but schizophrenia is increasingly seen as a neurodevelopmental disorder affected by childhood circumstances – we know that people with schizophrenia are more likely than others to have experienced child abuse, for example. Some research and theory push the trouble even further back – way back, to intrauterine experiences. When we start to think about anxiety and trauma, there may well be precipitating events, but there are also those who research our species' evolution over very long periods of time, trying to understand how the brain of today replays what we learned as an evolving species of ape. Or earlier, and earlier.

Elsie's nerve problems were much more mundane, and much more easy to overlook, than anything as serious as schizophrenia. But nevertheless, she suffered. And, if we take a broad view of research, the reason Elsie suffered, and suffered so badly, with anxiety was probably all because she was a mammal. I am aware as I write this that this statement may well be discriminatory against fish. Crustaceans and even trees, which we now know do communicate with one another, may in their turn object to being left out of the puzzle. To reframe: Elsie suffered because she was alive. And in her case certainly, she was alive because she suffered. On a global or cosmic scale, if we try to compute the incomputable, she did not suffer that much – no pogroms, death camps or being on the wrong side of colonialism and apartheid. None of that. But hers is the life I want to understand. When I wrote my first memoir, *Able-Bodied,* which looked at my relationship with my disabled father, a number of people, with varying layers of disapproval, said to me that they missed a fuller engagement on my part with my relationship with my mother. Didn't I care about her enough to write about her? Was our relationship so distant? The secret, of course, was not that I didn't care enough – I cared too much. So much that it was and is hard to think about and impossible not to think about. And a big part of why I cared was that things went wrong.

We might have been at the edge of the known universe with winds of change threatening to blow our houses down, but White Rhodesia was the suburban dream. Fabulous climate, hope for the future (if sanity and white privilege would only prevail), wide open spaces, labour-saving devices in the form of appliances and, crucially, a plentiful supply of cheap labour. The lady next door (in the usage of the day we called her Auntie Myra, although we were not related) embodied much of this. She was blonde and beautiful – her sister was a former Miss South Africa – and could make anything from ginger beer to marshmallows encased in elaborate icing baskets with tiny, tiny edible flowers. She knew how to drink a cocktail. Elsie was not immune to this glamour, and on one occasion she and Myra bought almost identical sundresses – white, with shoestring straps and a full skirt. The pattern on Myra's was bottle green and that on Elsie's was purple, but this was the only difference. Another difference between these two women was that while Myra spent hours making pig's ears and blancmange, pork loin simmered in beer, and pigs in blankets, Elsie left the cooking to the servants and the baking largely to her mother-in-law, whose lofty impression of her own confectionary skills was somewhat out of proportion to the heavy sweet things she produced. I did love Granny's jam tarts but they were made with pastry so heavy that just one of them could probably have sunk the Titanic.

Elsie had a reasonably well-thumbed copy of the green-covered Goodwill Book, as we called it. This book, which was put together by the Yeoville branch of the Johannesburg Women's Zionist League, was first printed in 1950, two years after the formation of the state of Israel, but also two years after the National Party came to power in South Africa. Many of the Nats had had links with Nazis, and national socialism and apartheid shared an interest in eugenics.

When the Nats unexpectedly came to power (with less than 50 per cent of the white vote), Elsie was working for the Jewish Board of Deputies in Johannesburg. She remembered going in to the office and shredding document after document, the fear being that Jews, like Blacks, would be vulnerable under National Party rule. This fear turned out to be unfounded, but it tells us something about a climate of fear experienced by Jews, many of them refugees themselves or children of refugees, and living in the shadow of the Second World War. When I was in psychotherapy with a Jungian analyst of Irish origin, my Jewish hackles went up when he almost casually told me that from a collective unconscious point of view it is not surprising that Jews as a group are a bit paranoid. He may well have had a point. I love the informal summary of the script of every Jewish holiday: 'They hated us, they killed us, let's eat!'

So Elsie had it from all sides. As a white woman in the colony, she needed to up her cake-frosting skills; as a Jewish woman she needed to up her game in the kugel and tzimmes department. Good Jewish girls were supposed to learn 100 ways to pack flavour into your gribenes at their mother's knee, next to the Aga stove. I suspect that by the time Elsie was born, Paulina had had quite enough of this, thank you, and that Elsie spent rather more time reading and experimenting with cats than did her older sisters. She didn't know much, and in many ways didn't care.

I can't really explain my own fierce and sentimental attachment to the Goodwill Book. I have had a copy of the 5th (1969) edition for as long as I have lived away from my parents' home, and I was pathetically grateful to find a copy of the 1954 edition (the one I remember from Salisbury) for sale on the internet for an outrageous amount of money. Nothing was going to stop me getting hold of a copy of that one. Part of my pleasure at reading the Goodwill Book is, admittedly, perverse and cruel. It gives me an enormous thrill in particular to read the modern and up-to-date addition to the newer versions. The section in question is called 'Fat Free Foods For Fitness', and the Goodwill Book tells us: 'This section has been contributed through the courtesy of MRS. ADA HALPERIN, author of "COOKING AND BAKING THE FAT-FREE WAY".' I have managed to hold myself back from purchasing a copy of 'COOKING AND BAKING THE FAT-FREE WAY' from Amazon.com …

Ada's 'Fat Free Foods For Fitness' section certainly brought the old Goodwill Book up to date, but it may not quite have delivered what was offered on the box. The first recipe is for the very exotic, and I am sure, delicious Chilean Fish Soup (so modern and international – you've come a long way from Yeoville, baby). The very first ingredient of this very first recipe is, and I quote, '1 cup Sunflower Oil'. Similarly, should you want to make Chicken Supreme, you will need 2 tablespoons Sunflower Oil, and for Crumpets you will use, along with 2 tablespoons Sugar, 1 tablespoon Sunflower Oil. In summary (and I have done the research), there is not one single Fat Free Food For Fitness recipe that is in fact fat free. What the Goodwill Book achieved in terms of alliteration, clearly it lost in accuracy.

So, I can make knowing jokes about the Goodwill Book (don't get me started on First-Aid for the Newly-Wed in which Mrs. Newly-Wed is addressed by that name and welcomed 'into the ever increasing ranks of housewives') but fun though this is, if I am honest, it is easier for me to do than to think about another reason I feel such tenderness about the Goodwill Book. The early 1960s was long before the age of glossy celebrity cookbooks with beautiful photographs, and I don't remember having any other cookbook in our house apart from this one. Elsie's copy, I always thought, would have come from her mother or from her sisters, and represented a link with them. I also imagined a link to the ladies of the Yeoville branch of the Johannesburg Women's Zionist League, and especially to Violet Wittert, Hanny Seeff and Gertrude Harvey Cohen. These three women, in my mind anyway, represented everything of Jewish South African women's success in the 1950s and 1960s. Indeed, the *SA Jewish Report* of 7–14 February 2014 has an item headed 'Trusted cornerstone of a Jewish kitchen', in which the book is described as a 'Taste of Nostalgia':

> The first edition of the iconic South African International Goodwill Recipe Book was published by the Yeoville branch of the Johannesburg Women's Zionist League in October 1950 and edited by Gertrude Harvey Cohen. The anthology of tried and tested recipes, flower arranging and other domestic tips became the cornerstone of survival in the kitchen and dining room for young Jewish wives through the generations and is currently in its seventh edition.[1]

I imagine Gertude, Hanny and Violet as competent Jewish women married to successful Johannesburg Jewish men, with the skill and time to devote to drawing the community together through a cookbook with the tastes of home and the rules of womanhood. I have never met any of these women, but I would put money on their having done good works, donating money and time to the underprivileged, and having a nicely filled Blue Box in their homes. A Blue Box was (and is) a money box into which people drop coins to send to the Jewish National Fund (JNF). As the JNF puts it on their website: 'Every Jewish home has a Mezuzah. Every Zionist home needs a Blue Box.' I imagine Gertude, Hanny and Violet having children and grandchildren who are doctors, lawyers and accountants, none of them married out of the faith and all with children of their own, cooking really fat-free foods for fitness but on special occasions making latkes for the children, or peppermint crisp pudding, the staple of 1970s Johannesburg Jewish suburbia. It takes great self-control for me, the googler-in-chief, to stop myself from spending hours tracking down Gertrude, Hanny and Violet and what I imagine to be their illustrious mainstream Jewish families (I confess to having had a little peek on ancestry.com ...) because this is not the point, or not the point of this story anyway. Gertrude, Hanny and Violet are, in my mind's eye, these competent creatures who know who they are. They know what it means to be a modern Jewish woman. They can rustle up a kischke, express their opinions, manage the staff, and throw together a book that becomes an icon to a community. And makes money for the Zionist cause to boot.

My mother, the talented, quirky woman that she was, was nothing like them. There she was at the Godforsaken end of the known universe, married to a handicapped man who worked in cement for a company run from Britain by a bunch of upper-class anti-Semites. What did she have to offer the community or the Zionist cause?

If the Goodwill Book kept Elsie linked to the world she had grown up in, the Yeoville, Berea and, later, the Lyndhurst world, it also in no uncertain way told her, and repeatedly, how far away she was from what good members of the community did. They stayed put for one thing. I can see Elsie poring over the Goodwill Book with a look of agony on her face as she tries to hit upon a new dish she can have the servants prepare for the family. Though Date Pinwheels and Stuffed Monkeys beckoned as part of the repertoire of biscuits Mrs Newly-Wed should ideally offer to Honoured Guests, Friends and Family, Elsie reverted to producing, yet again, her version of Crunchies (page 11, recipe supplied by Helen Aron). As a boy, I so wanted my mother to be able to follow the complex instructions of the steps to be followed, with accompanying indecipherable (to me, anyway) illustrations, in making biscuits of intricate designs (page 27). I wanted her to make the checkerboard sandwiches, involving layered deconstruction and reconstruction of store-bought loaves of white and brown bread (page 151). I was particularly captivated by the handsome full-page black and white photograph (page 23) of a large oval tray boasting about 60 biscuits of many different types, from pinwheels to macaroons to almond fingers. The caption below this photograph said it all:

1. TIME 2. PATIENCE 3. IMAGINATION
THE RESULT!

No such luck. No 60 different types of biscuits in our family.

When it came to being a good Johannesburg Jewish wife, Elsie had none of the three core ingredients and THE RESULT! for her was something less palatable and more complex than a wonderful tray of perfectly crafted delicacies.

Added to all this was the tyranny of her mother-in-law and Auntie Lea. There were laws (too many of them to count, too painful to be relived in full) in the relationships between Granny and Auntie Lea and the rest of us. One of the laws was that Granny, and only Granny, was the wonderful cook and baker, so capable in all things domestic. As I sit here, older now than both Granny and Auntie Lea themselves were at the time, I can confidently tell you that in reality, although Granny had 1. TIME in spades (I think a lot of the poison she spewed had to do with crushing boredom), she was seriously lacking in the 2. PATIENCE and 3. IMAGINATION departments. But not lacking in asserting her skills and Elsie's incompetence. In fact Granny was a pretty terrible cook and baker and Elsie, in terms of talent and imagination, was actually far more skilled. The reality did not much matter in this scenario. More important was what Granny and Lea knew in their vicious old bones to be true, and made sure that we did too.

The sources of Granny and Auntie Lea's tyranny over my mother and over all of us were complicated. The first thing is that they were just horrible people, with Auntie Lea being especially horrible. It was not for nothing that Auntie Tilly – the same Tilly who could not bring herself to tell Ben Black and the boerite not to visit, and who phoned back to apologise for forgetting to send love to the children – took one look at Auntie Lea and dubbed her the Buchenwald Chicken, a name that has stuck over the generations. These were women of almost mythical malice. I am not making this up.

After *Able-Bodied* was published, a second cousin of mine, Ari, whose grandmother was the eldest sister of Granny and the Chicken, got hold of and read a copy. Ari is much older than me, and his grandmother, in contrast to her younger sisters, was a sweet and kind woman. Ari lived in Northern Rhodesia and then in Israel, and now in the USA, where he has spent all of his adult life, and I had very little to do with him growing up. I can count on the fingers of one hand the number of times I have seen him face to face, but Granny, and the Chicken, especially, spent quite a bit of time going to see his family for various extended holiday visits. When Ari read *Able-Bodied,* which starts (as do so many of our family stories) with an account of these monstrous women, one of the first things he did was show the book to his therapist, saying, 'See! I did not make these terrible women up! They were no fantasy – they were real!' When he told me this I, too, took comfort, because they were so awful and so awfully powerful that there is no sensible way to think about their power and why, in different geographical locations, people were subjugated by it.

A second source of the tyranny of Granny and the Chicken was the fact of my father's disability and his health problems and pain, which dogged him from childhood into adult life. The clear narrative was that this sickly, disabled boy had caused his poor mother no end of pain and misery, and the rest of her life was payback time. And we were the ones (or some of them) who would have to do the paying. Our own difficulties and challenges, such as they were, in having a disabled husband and father, counted for nothing in the great accounting of things. We would forever have to try to pay back for all my Granny had had to go through. All of us, including the source of all the trouble – my father himself – kept paying. But it would never ever be enough. The books could never balance.

The third source of the power of Granny and the Chicken over my mother and over us was something less tangible but, I think, just as important. We were such an isolated family, far away from Johannesburg, the only Jews for miles around, the only liberals, stuck at the end of the rutted Arcturus Road and the end of the world, living at the outpost of the outpost, seeing few people and hardly going out. My parents held no truck with the overt crude racism of most of the white people around us, but would never have dreamed of making friends with the Black people (treating them well – yes, but treating them as equals, not really thinkable). And many of the people at the cement works were in any event themselves far flung from where they had come from, away from families and familiarity. In enclosed spaces, in echo chambers where there are few voices, the loud voices become louder and louder. For us, and for Elsie especially, the power of Granny and Auntie Lea grew because there were so few countervailing voices and forces.

And then there was the issue of obligation and the right thing to do. Elsie often described going to Bulawayo to meet my father's family, after he had proposed to her but before the family had approved the wedding. She was confronted with four women seated on a large settee – Granny, Auntie Lea, another of their sisters, and a woman closer in age to my mother, who was my father's cousin. According to Elsie, and I find this chillingly believable, the four women initially said nothing. They just sat and scowled at her. Then followed a series of aggressive questions, all of which made it clear that this woman – uneducated, without money and, let's face it, no oil painting – was not good enough for Alfred Swartz and his family. Elsie returned to Johannesburg intimidated and frightened, and not a little angry. Her mother, Paulina, said to her, 'You have to understand this mother. She lost her other baby in infancy. She had to care for this boy with all his physical problems. She is a widow with nobody else in the world apart from her son. If you want to marry this man, you must understand that you will have to look after this woman for the rest of her life. That is what you are taking on.'

Elsie made her choice. She married my father. I have no doubt at all that this was the right choice as they were unusually happily married. But she took on the responsibility for caring for this old battleaxe and her poisonous sister, and she cared for them both until long after my father had died. She did what her mother had told her to do, but for this she, and we, paid the price.

While researching for this book, I spent some time looking at books produced by Jewish families about their ancestors and heritage. I read quite a few of them. One such book has a cover picture of a smiling extended multi-generational family, all in glowing colour, superimposed on a background of sepia photographs of previous generations. An inscription on the front of this handsome hardcover reads: 'Remember where you come from so you will know where you are going.' The back cover has a quotation in Hebrew and in English from Devarim (Deuteronomy):

> Remember the days of old,
> Consider the years of many generations,
> Ask your father and he will tell you
> Your elders and they will inform you.

When I got over my punctilious irritation at the lack of a comma at the end of the third line of this quotation, I started to do a bit of quick research about the source of the quote.

In their official version of the Torah, the Jewish religious organisation Chabad renders this quotation as follows: 'Remember the days of old; reflect upon the years of [other] generations. Ask your father, and he will tell you; your elders, and they will inform you.'[2] So far so good. But look at the verse before this one: 'Is this how you repay the Lord, you disgraceful, unwise people?! Is He not your Father, your Master? He has made you and established you.'[3] This puts a slightly different spin on why it is so important to reflect on the past and to know about previous generations.

The economy of remembering is brought into even sharper relief when at the click of a twenty-first century icon, we can turn on the interpretation of these words by the renowned eleventh-century Jewish sage and biblical commentator, Rashi. Rashi leaves us in no doubt that these are not the sentimental words of a benevolent father wanting his children to remember a glorious past. According to Rashi, verse 6 is clearly about all the bad things the Jews did to God, despite his generosity to them; and the injunction to 'remember the days of old' at the beginning of verse 7 should be understood as an instruction to remember 'what God did to past generations who provoked Him to anger'. Even more bleak is Rashi's interpretation of verse 8, which follows the one that was quoted. This verse begins, 'When the Most High gave nations their lot ...'. To you, me and I am sure to many of the family in question, this may seem quite innocuous, but to the sage Rashi, this means: 'When the Holy One, Blessed is He, gave those who provoked Him to anger their portion, He flooded them and drowned them [that is, that was their lot].' Not so good, I'm sure you will agree.

I have no doubt at all that the multi-generational family book was lovingly compiled, with the very best of intentions, and I found many of the writings by family members about how wonderful their grandparents were heartfelt and touching. I feel churlish and even a bit arch reading things into a book that was not written for me, but written by and for a family I don't know – a loving act of remembrance, celebration and identity. I think it is good that there are books like this, and I would imagine that this very book did some good and will be cherished by many.

But books like these are also doing three things that I struggle with, and I think Elsie struggled with her whole life. The first thing they do is tell us in no uncertain terms who's in and who's out – who's one of the Chosen People and who isn't. Even more broadly, I think, it is quite possible to be one of the Chosen People but not to feel like you are one. Elsie was very clear that she was Jewish, and that meant a lot to her, but whether she felt chosen, in her family, in her religious group, in Johannesburg, in Salisbury, or in any other place, is a different matter altogether.

The second thing books like these do is tell us clearly how to continue to be chosen. I find myself rebelling quite strongly against the idea of a straitjacketed future guided by the glories of my familial past. This is not because I don't feel proud of many achievements and people in my family's past (including my poor old mum), but because I think who we are would be diminished rather than enhanced if we framed ourselves only, or primarily, as vessels through which the wisdom and glory of the past flows into the ever-better future. When I read books like these, even though this was never the authors' intentions (they don't even know me), I see a set of instructions on how to live and how to be in the world. I see the list of requirements and prescriptions at which I have failed, my family has failed, and I have failed my family.

The third thing that books like these do is to Not Mention the War. Ongoing difficulties and insoluble problems are not really spoken about at all – problems are admitted but, they are overcome. The difficulties fit the trajectory of adversity providing an opportunity for growth and doing better in the future. I don't know any of the people in these books and I don't know their stories. But as I looked at book after book with their glossy pages and dipped into their interesting tales, I was reminded of Elsie rolling her eyes as only Elsie could roll her eyes at the (unpublished) memoir written by her sister Babe.

In many ways, Babe was the golden girl of the Cohen sisters, admired for her beauty, her sporting ability and her equally sporty, dashing and rapidly upwardly mobile husband. Elsie was seen as a poor comparison. Although Babe's trajectory was interrupted by the very early death of her husband and her unhappy marriage some years later to a gambler and a drunk, she maintained her lustre, and like many others, I was dazzled by her and adored her. But Babe's life story, written in later life, infuriated Elsie, focusing as it did on all the good things in her life and skimming over or leaving out altogether the difficult or bad bits. It was Babe's right to write her story in any way she chose, but Elsie was irritated and dismissive: 'That's Babe – she never could face reality.' Part of Elsie's irritation, I think, was with the mere fact that Babe had written a memoir at all, that her sister had the confidence to write her version of things and then put it out there for everyone to see. If there is any tragedy in Elsie's life of privilege, it lies somewhere in her not becoming a writer. Was there nothing Babe could not have or do?

Beyond the thwarted ambition and the sibling rivalry, though, I don't think there is a question that Elsie had real objections to Babe's Not Mentioning the War. If there were wars, Elsie believed they should be mentioned, even if she did not always fully succeed at talking about difficulties herself. But in her rejection of the rose-tinted spectacles, what made Elsie so different from Babe, and from all her sisters? Some of the difference was generational – she was so much younger than all of them – but I think there is something more here, and I think it has to do with the constant struggle as to where to place herself.

In my work in disability studies and psychological assessment, I often have to grapple with the really tough question of 'can't do' as opposed to 'won't do'. A person who is absent from their work a lot, and who doesn't complete tasks can often drive co-workers nuts and get the label of lazy. In my experience, it is generally (though not always) the case that people would prefer to do well at work than not to, to get things done and to feel valued in their team. But they may not have the skills to get things done, they may be depressed, they may lack confidence – there may be a million reasons, none of them laziness, why people cannot at this time do what they are supposed to and want to do. It's so hard to disentangle what is seen as a moral failing from life struggles. And of course no thing that we do is ever determined by one thing, and we all do (or don't do) things with a range of causes and motives and reasons.

In writing about how to write about a good Jewish woman (which Elsie was) and her off-kilter Jewish-ish family (which we are), I am reminded of (and am comforted by) Philip Roth's wonderful novel *The Ghost Writer*, the first of his Zuckerman novels. Zuckerman, like Roth himself (and who among us can get all these identities, 'true', and 'false', and everything in between, straight?) rose to fame with a book that was scandalously irreverent about the Jewish community. In the novel, Zuckerman's father sends Zuckerman's manuscript to Judge Leopold Wapter, described as 'perhaps the city's most admired Jew' after two other luminaries, one of whom is a famous rabbi. Wapter writes a long letter to Zuckerman, which starts as follows:

> Dear Nathan:
>
> My familiarity with your fine family goes back, as you must know, to the turn of the century on Prince Street, where we were all poor people in a new land, struggling for our basic needs, our social and civil rights, and our spiritual dignity.[4]

If this is not an echo of Devarim 32:7, I don't know what is. Wapter concludes his long letter to Zuckerman with a postscript advising him to see the Broadway production of *The Diary of Anne Frank*, and appends a list of ten questions for Zuckerman, which interrogate his (Zuckerman's) right to call himself Jewish in a host of ways. Each and every one of these questions feels completely familiar to me, and in my head I can hear people like my mythical construction of a sage Jewish grandfather, desperately disappointed in me. I never had a grandfather – both my grandfathers died before I was born – but I do have my very own 'cop in the head', to use the words of Augusto Boal. Boal was a Brazilian theatre practitioner and founder of Theatre of the Oppressed, and he knew a thing or two about how we all internalise and elaborate on our own oppression, and silence ourselves in response to voices we have had put into, and have allowed to be put into, our own heads. The stronger we are, the more we can look our own cops in the eye and the more free we can be of them, not that we can ever really get away. And some, if not all of us, do try to run. Off Elsie ran to Rhodesia with the cripple husband her family was scared would die young and leave her a penniless widow. But she did not get away – and getting away, here's the rub, was both the first and the last thing she wanted.

When I think back about my mother with such intense love, loss and admiration, part of what I admire and miss is the fact that she was never one for a hagiography, for a book trumpeting her (or anyone else's) brilliance, morality and wisdom. I learned from her not to trust stories like this, and I am glad I don't. But what was the price of all this? Would Elsie have had all the scepticism, would she have rolled her eyes so often or so expertly, if she had not struggled, if she had not been aware in her bones of how unwanted she was as a child, if she had not, later, fallen apart in some ways? If she could have chosen, what would she have wanted? The canny intelligence she had to accept nothing and question everything? Or an easier life as a wanted child, a life being a pillar of Johannesburg society, maybe a contributor to the Goodwill Book; a life in which 1. Time, 2. Patience, and 3. Imagination would have yielded THE RESULT! of a glowing mainstream life? It's so easy to pontificate shallowly about how struggle and sadness make us all better people. Sometimes it's true, sometimes not. Some suffering has no meaning, no purpose and no redeeming value. But when I think back on Elsie and my fierce love for her, a love forged itself in my own struggles, I know that some of why I love her so much is for what became of her through having to try to cope with all sorts of difficult things. When we say we love someone 'warts and all' we imply that we overlook the warts for the more beautiful bits. For me, though, Elsie's warts, and all that remained of them, were the source of the love rather than the impediment to it. She would never be, as my Granny would put it about other people (and certainly never about Elsie, definitely never about Elsie), a Wonderful Woman, or So Capable or, even, a Professional Woman. For me, it was her misfitting that made Elsie – her ability to write a memoir of her own, but at the same time her complete inability to do a Babe in the memoir department; her wanting to learn but knowing in her bones how stupid she was, her power held in brutal check by the clear and certain knowledge of her own dullness. I wish that she had not had to struggle quite so much and quite so profoundly (although even in her struggle there was little drama), but without that I would not be me and I would not love her in quite the same way.

4 | The trouble with nerves

In the colonies, where blonde women were home-makers and fully able to bottle the fruit growing on their abundant trees in their lush gardens, rituals were important. Among these was the absurdity of the full turkey-and-all-the-trimmings Christmas in sweltering summer heat, but smaller rituals like birthday parties were also important and a good opportunity for these women to demonstrate to other mothers their organisational and confectionary skills.

I was born on 2 November 1955 in the little hospital in Gwanda in what was then Southern Rhodesia. If you think Gwanda is the middle of nowhere, think again. At around the time of the transition of Rhodesia to Zimbabwe in 1980, the census estimated that the population of Gwanda was smaller than 5 000 souls. Nevertheless, to our family it was a big centre to West Nicholson (now Tshabezi), where my father worked as a chemist at the corned beef factory. There was no hospital in West Nic, so I was delivered by Dr Osborne in Gwanda. When I was six weeks old we moved to Salisbury and the world of cement.

The day I was born was so hot that the mercury in one of the thermometers at the hospital burst. As had been the case with Jenny's birth three and a half years earlier, Elsie was far away from her own mother and her family, in labour at the edge of the known world. There was a major advantage to my having been born on 2 November, though. In the Rhodesian colony, the celebration of Guy Fawkes night on 5 November was a big deal, and every year we learned in school about gunpowder, treason and plot. For some years, my birthday party was celebrated as part of the communal Guy Fawkes fireworks and bonfire night celebrations involving all the white employees of the cement works. I loved it. Nothing could be better than a party in the hot Rhodesian night with a bonfire and a fireworks display; and every boy who came to my party got his own set of sparklers and jumping jacks to light. The lights and the danger of having to stand back while brave dads (my dad included) lit the fuses on rockets jammed into used cold-drink bottles were exciting, and made for very successful birthday parties for this rather poorly socialised young fellow.

My parents were really clever (and kind, even to themselves) to institute the Guy Fawkes parties, not least because I had what I considered a rather sad history of birthday parties. For one of my birthdays – I think it was my sixth, late in the year in which I first attended school – I did not have a birthday party at all. This was not negotiated with me and would certainly not have been my choice. I can't remember if my previous parties had been disastrous (which is not entirely unlikely, given my social awkwardness and being the weed that I was), but even if they had been, the decision of my parents not to give me a birthday party was certainly a big deal. It was unheard of not to have a birthday party and I knew it. My sister, whom I adored but with whom I had my fair share of rivalries, had all her parties. What happened with my party? Why didn't I have a party? I ask this question primarily on my own behalf. A birthday party is a silly, trivial thing in the grand scheme of things, especially considering the lives of most children in the world, and most children in Rhodesia at that time, but birthday parties held huge significance in middle-class children's lives. They still do, apparently. A common form of cyberbullying these days is for girls to invite most girls in their class to the parties, and then to post pictures on social media of everyone enjoying themselves, partly with the aim of shaming and humiliating those girls who were not invited. In Salisbury, at the cement works estate, furthermore, it would not have gone unnoticed amongst other parents (and certainly not by Auntie Myra and Uncle Cecil next door) that I did not have a party.

If my mother felt inept at making marshmallow baskets and toffee apples, this decision not to hold a birthday party for her only son could only make her more excluded from the dream of competent colonial happy families. Something, clearly, and in plain sight of us all, was up.

When I put my own, embarrassingly still hurt, feelings aside, part of me wants to applaud my mother for this. There is a part of me that is admiring of her courage to thumb her nose at what was expected, to break a rule so clearly and publicly. But so many feminist texts, and so many discussions of women's frailty and self-harm ask the question, 'Did she fall or was she pushed?,' or other versions of this, like 'Did she jump or was she pushed?'

I did have a dad and I guess he could have intervened, but – sorry to be gendered about this – birthday parties were women's work, and his not insisting that I have a party, even though he might have wanted to, could well have been an act of care towards his struggling, fragile wife.

Elsie was not a self-harmer in the sense of self-cutting, overdosing and such things but, like all of us, and in the case of not holding a birthday party for me, she did things to hurt herself and to hurt others. How do we know why people get hurt, hurt themselves, hurt others? Whom do we blame? Is the (hurtful) act of bucking convention an act of triumphant assertion of independence, a thumbing the nose at restrictive respectability? Or is it an act of desperation? Did she jump or was she pushed?

With Elsie, as with so many other people, we cannot know and she probably couldn't either. Maybe the question is wrong: maybe she jumped *and* she was pushed. All too often, it is people with power who freeze the stories of others with less power into narratives the powerful people control. As a psychologist and disability researcher, I guess I have been doing this all my life with other people's stories. And I am doing this to my own mother. Did she push or did I fall?

Maybe I am making too much of the non-party for my birthday, but this story has a context. When I started school, I was the youngest boy in my class. I did not know a single child in my class on our first day. Our school year followed the calendar year, and I turned six in November, after the birthdays of my classmates. From the beginning I did well at school, so my being young was no academic impediment, but I think I was far too young, compared to my classmates, to manage properly the social demands of being at school. This was made worse by my very obvious physical problems. I was very poorly co-ordinated. I could not catch a ball, could not stand on one leg, could not cut out shapes neatly, could not colour within the lines. My ineptitude at all this was made worse, if anything, by my strengths in reading and arithmetic, because teachers just could not understand, and were often exasperated by, the contrast between my being the boy who came first in class and my also being the boy who could not (would not?) do the most basic things, things an average four-year-old could do.

Many of the skills I did not have, and still struggle with to a degree, were ones I gratefully saw being lovingly taught to my daughters when they were in pre-school. For reasons that were impossible to discuss (and I tried), I was never sent to pre-school – in those days we called it nursery school – so I arrived at big school, the youngest boy in the class, thin and weedy, never having been to nursery, and never having interacted with large groups of other children. My best friend next door, Bruce, who was my age, went to nursery school, but because his family was Catholic, he went to a Catholic one; there was never any discussion of my going along with him. So off he went in the mornings and I stayed at home.

My sister Jenny, three years ahead of me at school, had gone to nursery school and had loved it, so my parents knew what it was all about. I don't know how I spent the mornings with my parents at work, Jenny off at big school and my best friend next door at nursery school. The only thing I remember clearly was trying, unsuccessfully, to catch flies against the glass, listening to the radio a bit, and following the maid around as she did her work. I was perfectly safe and very well cared for. I loved Mitzi and she, like many women before her and after her to this day, looked after me with a tenderness that went way beyond the demands of any job.

My parents must have made an active decision not to send me to nursery school. There may have been many reasons for this. Perhaps they made an assessment that I was too puny and too emotionally immature to handle pre-school – they had good reason to worry that I would be bullied. But they were not unintelligent people. If the possibility of bullying and my emotional immaturity were their primary concerns, I would imagine that they would have thought that keeping me at home for two years, while my peers were part of the developing rough-and-tumble of nursery school life, would hardly miraculously prepare me for 12 years of schooling with these same peers. What was going on?

When I asked Elsie, and I asked her a lot over the years, why I was not sent to nursery school, her answer was always the same. 'We couldn't send you, because there was petrol rationing, and there was no way we could get you there.'

Petrol rationing was a huge issue for us. It was instituted around the time of the country's Unilateral Declaration of Independence (UDI) in November 1965 (we left Rhodesia in March 1966, partly because of UDI). Because the cement works was so far from schools and shops – from all amenities – and because there was no public transport apart from school buses, which did not cater to pre-schoolers, we were hit hard and the rationing added to our isolation. There was only one problem with my mother's justification for not sending me to nursery school. Petrol rationing was instituted in 1965, and my nursery years would have been 1959 and 1960. I've wondered a lot about this over the years, and I still do. I certainly raised it with my mother many times, and each time she said that the reason for not sending me to nursery was petrol rationing. Each time I would point out the time discrepancy, and each time she would vaguely acknowledge this and change the subject. I don't really know why I did not pursue this question more vigorously with her, especially as in general one of the things I held, and hold, most dear about my relationship with my mother was that we could fight like hell and come out of fights closer rather than further apart.

Maybe I was too hurt and angry to pursue things. I know it is ridiculous, some 60 years later, to hold onto something, but I thought, and still think, my parents could have done more. They could have done what all the other parents did – help me to socialise and grow up, not keep me at home as they did.

My father was unusually respectful to women and open and proud of their emancipation. Unlike a good Rhodesian man, he was pleased rather than humiliated that Elsie worked outside the home – he told everyone how good she was at her work. Interestingly, though, I have never blamed him for the decision not to send me to nursery school. Heaven knows, I am not shy to blame my father for a whole lot of other things, so this is not part of a pattern of gendered forgiving on my part. If there is one lesson we can take from the worst forms of psychoanalysis, it is that it is always Your Mother's Fault. I don't think this sexist legacy is why I attribute the decision to my mother. I think what she did to me has something to do with what was happening to her. I could be wrong, but I'm the one writing this.

So: if it wasn't petrol, and it wasn't (in a crude sense) Freud, what the hell was going on? My parents, and my mother in particular, prided themselves on being educated, enlightened and liberal, which they were. My mother's parenting bible was none other than Benjamin Spock's *Baby and Child Care,* and she often quoted to me his advice that parents should be 'friendly but firm' with their children. I can't tell you how far this philosophy was from the 'beat them till they submit' style of, it seemed to me, most parents in our orbit. Although both my parents hit me (it didn't work), I was miles away from the many boys and girls who would come to school proudly displaying a range of welts and bruises, usually caused by terrifying fathers wielding sticks, straps, belts, shoes or whatever else came to hand.

Modern Dr Spock, as I read him, would have supported the role of pre-school experience to develop competence, confidence and social skills in children. It is true that the famous first line of Spock's book was 'Trust yourself. You know more than you think you do', aimed to increase the confidence of anxious parents. Crudely, I guess, we could say that Elsie trusted herself and did what she thought best. It was certainly easier not to have to arrange for me to be schlepped miles to and from nursery a few times a week. But Elsie was not cynical or selfish, and she was certainly not unthinking.

I feel I may be making too big a deal of my no-nursery mystery and the silence around it. Part of me wants to stop making such a matzo pudding out of it and, to mix oral metaphors, sometimes a cigar is just a cigar. Maybe it was just easier to have me at home, and that trumped everything. But this simple story feels all wrong to me – there was just too much at stake in this for my mother, and too much at stake in it for me. For me, what makes most sense are two interleaving stories, or maybe they are the same story. The first part has to do with protecting me. I was clumsy, effeminate and very, very thin. When I was an infant, Elsie took me to see a paediatrician on one of her trips to Johannesburg and the paediatrician boomed, 'This child has malnutrition – you must feed him!' I think it made things all the more humiliating that the paediatrician was a woman. Elsie had been struggling with breastfeeding. I was put on formula and I thrived, but I remained very thin until I turned 40 (and from then on, the rest is the daily struggle with corpulence). Elsie was afraid I would not cope and, as was the case with Stephen Spender, 'My parents kept me from children who were rough.' Maybe if I waited a bit longer I would grow out of it. I didn't, but my mother did keep worrying about my frailty. Later, when I was at school and beyond abysmal at games, she drove me every week to a gym in the centre of Salisbury. Gyms in Salisbury in those days were hardly the pumping lycra palaces full of people that they are now. The gym was a few dingy rooms in a depressing office block with heavy and terrifyingly dull grey weights, attended solely by enormous musclemen clearly wanting to get more enormous, really not the fashion of the day, and I found them frightening and freaky. The gym owner, as big as all the others, would help me perfunctorily to try to lift a few of the lighter weights for a little while and then allowed me to sit and read the magazines that were there or a book I had brought along until my mother arrived to take me home. As far as bulking me up went, these gym visits were an unadulterated failure, but the gym owner was kind, and I think it helped Elsie to know she was trying her best to help me. All this extra effort once I was a bit older seems to me strangely in contrast with my not getting the basics of a nursery school experience.

The second thing, and for me the crucial thing, which surreptitiously had started to creep into our lives was the fact that for Elsie, coping was becoming more and more difficult. I don't know whether she had post-natal depression or whether things started before that. She was certainly, as she told us, very worried through both her pregnancies as neither she nor anyone else knew whether my father's physical impairments could be passed down to the next generation. As it happened, they were not, and Jenny, in fact, turned out to be a talented dancer and athlete.

Elsie had a lot to cope with. She was out in the colonies in a strange place, far away from her family and with almost no Jewish people around except her truly awful mother-in-law and aunt by marriage, who were demanding, difficult and downright cruel to all of us. My father was a good man, who loved her and treated her with great tenderness and care when she needed him most, but having had a life of being bullied by his mother and aunt, he wanted out. His out was a combination of long working hours (which he had to put in) and weekends spent on the golf course, leaving Elsie to cope with two young children and Arsenic and Old Lace, as a relative had dubbed the two old ladies. It was too much, and Elsie started falling apart. Not dramatically, not so many people could see, but enough to make ordinary tasks of middle-class parenthood, like getting your younger child to a nursery school he would probably have hated initially, too much to face.

I don't have too much of a chronology of how things unfolded, but trips to Dr Levy increased, and Elsie was put on barbiturates and, later, Librium. For the rest of her life, she would tell anyone and everyone that barbiturates were marvellous drugs, and that if she had had anything to do with it, they would never have been taken off the market because

Librium was okay but not nearly as good. For me, she did not fit the stereotype of the woman who'd go 'running for the shelter of a mother's little helper'. A few years later, in my last years of high school, when we were back in Johannesburg, I devoured an orange-backed copy of Betty Friedan's *The Feminine Mystique*, which had been published in 1963. I was a not unpretentious teenager at the time, wanting, together with my classmates, to be a hip intellectual. I was reading (as we all were) *The Greening of America* by Charles Reich, alongside the Friedan book. *The Greening of America* was a manifesto for the coming age of the rise of the counterculture. It was exciting for us all to come of age with that promise, and I can't help saying now that whatever the flaws might have been with Reich's work, I confess to feeling desperately sad that the kind, green future that he had good reason to be rooting for has been replaced by an apocalyptic nightmare, now on a planetary scale. My wife Louise and I often ask each other what Elsie would have thought of Donald Trump and we shake our sad, sad heads, not that he is the only reason that *The Greening of America*, which was a serious book, now reads like a fairy tale.

My attachment to *The Feminine Mystique* was, however, uniquely fierce, even compared to the reactions of my female classmates, who liked the book but not in the fierce way I did. Some of my insistence on loving this book was, I am ashamed to say, somewhat disingenuous – there is no question that I was trying to impress our very beautiful science teacher, who proclaimed herself to be a feminist. This was part of it, but for me the real appeal of *The Feminine Mystique* was that it gave me words for my feelings about Elsie. Introducing the book, Friedan describes what she famously terms 'the problem that has no name' – the creeping malaise of post-war middle-class American women. Many of them were highly educated but found themselves constricted by the grip of gender roles. Their gender required them to devote their lives to ministering to the needs of their husbands and baking cookies for their children – sacrificing themselves in the service of men, and of the next generation.

In crucial ways, Elsie was nothing like these women. She had not had every advantage, and was not highly educated and, unlike everyone else around us, she insisted on working outside the home, something I was really proud of. But she did have a problem and it didn't have a name. Some of it would have had to do with her following her man to the colonies, and taking on the soul-destroying work of trying to act as a buffer between him and his poisonous mother and aunt. She was so much out in the world – a competent, working woman, a woman who had opinions, a woman who, like her mother before her, devoured the news and loved to discuss politics. But she was also, in crucial ways, completely alone. I feel so sad about this, and I wish I could have helped more – but that, in some ways, is part of the problem.

Things slowly got worse. Elsie started having what she called 'giddy spells'– episodes of dizziness and shakiness. With the knowledge I now have as a psychologist, I can tick off in my head a list of the autonomic symptoms of anxiety, and I can also see the classic picture of that nineteenth-century condition, now completely out of fashion diagnostically, of neurasthenia, a protean mixture of physical and mental symptoms often characterised by weakness, exhaustion and pains of various kinds. As George M Beard, the psychiatrist credited with coining the term 'neurasthenia', wrote in an 1889 publication, though, 'each case of neurasthenia is a study of itself', and Elsie's story is a story in itself. She started having panic attacks during which she was convinced she would die. Nobody in our world had the vocabulary that included the concept of panic attacks; the diagnosis of what we now call 'panic disorder' entered the diagnostic system only in 1980. In the current version of the Diagnostic and Statistical Manual of Mental Disorders, the key symptoms of panic disorder are: palpitations, pounding heart, or accelerated heart rate; sweating; trembling or shaking; sensations of shortness of breath or smothering; a feeling of choking; chest pain or discomfort; nausea or abdominal distress; feeling dizzy, unsteady, lightheaded or faint; feelings of unreality (derealisation) or being detached from oneself (depersonalisation); fear of losing control or going crazy; fear of dying;

numbness or tingling sensations (paresthesias); chills or hot flushes. Elsie had every single one of these symptoms, and some of them, like palpitations and fear of dying, she had in spades. Part of me feels really angry that the diagnostic wisdom and relatively easy ways of treating panic attacks came just too late for Elsie, but on the other hand, trust Elsie to be ahead of her time.

Dr Levy did what he could, and he did a lot. He diagnosed her with low blood pressure, and low blood pressure, though generally not bad for your health, can indeed, as the Mayo Clinic puts it, cause 'dizziness or lightheadedness, fainting (syncope), blurred vision, nausea, fatigue, and lack of concentration', all of which Elsie had. From here followed years of Elsie piling salt on absolutely everything she ate in an effort to get her blood pressure up, including on apples, oranges and bananas (like me, she loved fruit). She tried other things and was open to advice. She was addicted, as was the whole of White Rhodesia, to cigarettes. Cigarettes had been calming her nerves since she was 17, but as the news on the health effects of smoking became more prominent, she worried that smoking might be affecting her symptoms. This was the golden age of the cigarette holder, which not only looked elegant but also, it was said, could allow you to continue to smoke as much as you wanted but would filter out all the bad things. My mother accumulated an array of these, my particular favourite being a very smart tortoiseshell one, in the production of which, I hope, no actual tortoises were harmed. Given when the holder was bought, mind you, I cannot be sure. Somebody told Elsie, or she read it somewhere, that if you pricked the sides of a cigarette just above the filter, this would also mitigate the toxic effects, so she tried that as well.

She didn't want to feel what she was feeling and she was open to anything. There was at the time one psychiatrist in Salisbury and she did consult him, but what was happening to her was so all-consuming, so changeable, and so debilitating that it was never clear if this was a disease of body or mind or, indeed, of the soul. Of course it was all three, and we now know that bodies, minds and souls are all part of one another.

For a time Elsie took to her bed. Sometimes huge fires would rage in the veld opposite our house and I remember on one occasion sitting on her bed, looking past the desk where we did our homework, past the grey hedge, at the terrifying flames high in the gum trees across the way. We had good reason to be scared, but it also felt that in some sort of cosmic way, the flames and the fire were linked to what was happening in that bedroom, dimly lit by a bedside lamp and the Rhodesian bright day turned abruptly into darkness. I could see my mother, lying in bed, and me, sitting on the edge of the bed, reflected in the lamp light in the plate-glass window, with the fire, red and angry against the darkening sky. The fires told a story of what was happening to our family, and what was happening inside my mother. There seemed to be no boundary between the inside and the outside. Years later, I learned the marvellous-sounding word 'palimpsest', which according to the Oxford English Dictionary is 'a parchment or other writing surface on which the original text has been effaced or partially erased, and then overwritten by another; a manuscript in which later writing has been superimposed on earlier'. When thinking back on that scene, which is so clear in my mind, I think of it as a kind of visual palimpsest of images: a sick woman and her son in a darkened room illuminated only by a side lamp, reflected in plate-glass, superimposed on a background of blackness and of fire. We were safe from the fire but vulnerable to it, but the fire was in us too, the boundaries between inside and outside frighteningly permeable, as were the boundaries between me and my fragile mother.

My father was wonderful to her. One day he arrived home with a large box – he must have somehow (and so unlike him) taken off work to make the long hot trip into the centre of Salisbury to get it. I can see him with that twinkle in his eyes slowly taking the item from the box, teasingly slowly. It was a pale blue Philips portable radio (imported all the way from the Netherlands) with white and brass trim and beautiful rounded corners. The strap was made of white rubber or plastic, and the radio was indeed portable, although by today's standards, of course, it was huge, clumsy and bulky. I can still feel the imprint on my hand of the basketwork covering of the front of the radio where the speaker was – nothing felt better than pressing my hand gently to the radio and feeling the vibrations made in concert with the voices or music. I loved that radio. One reason was that a kind relative from Johannesburg (I don't know who, but I think it was Auntie Ada) had sent me the child's equivalent of a radio crystal set some time before. Largely on my own (the instructions were easy, clear and directed at young children), but with some help from my father, I had assembled a very odd-looking radio, which actually worked. Through earphones you could hear the crackly and seemingly underwater sounds of the BBC and what was to be known as the Rhodesian Broadcasting Corporation (RBC). So I knew something basic about the transistors and resistors that went into radios, and I marvelled at the idea that transistors and resistors not unlike those I had used had been fitted into this beautiful radio. I marvelled, as well, at the miraculously clear sound that emanated from this small, pale blue box. The sound, of course, was of laughingly poor quality by today's standards, but astonishingly better than the sound produced by my home-made job, and better than the huge, wood-encased Bush radio that sat in the lounge.

My second reason for loving this pale blue Philips radio with its basketwork front was that it was, more than anything, an act of love and care from my father to my mother. Compared with many of my friends' parents, mine were embarrassingly frugal. As an example, for many years the dull plain red carpet that covered the parquet floor of our lounge was so threadbare we were in danger of tripping through the large hole that had worn in it. This was, believe me, no shabby chic or the faded gentility of people with old money, the kind of people I came to know only when I moved to Cape Town for university. At some stage the hole in the carpet was clumsily sewed together in a manner in which, if Granny had said it, had been 'visibly mended'. For once she would have been literally correct. So for my father to splash out on a brand-new transistor radio when we already had a radio in the house was a big deal. Now Elsie could listen to the radio in bed; and when she felt shaky and weak, she could go and lie down and listen to the reassuring voices of radio announcers, or the soothing music of the lunchtime programme of requests for people ill and in hospital. When Dr Levy came to attend to Elsie, dapper as always in his dark suit, white shirt and bow-tie, and the antithesis of my father, who worked at the factory in his khaki shirt and shorts, he was given the opportunity to listen to this wonder of contemporary science and entertainment taking up most of the space on my mother's bedside table. Dr Levy sat on the side of Elsie's bed, put his shiny brown leather doctor's bag on the wooden chair next to it, and duly listened. I felt desperately worried, and I also felt proud.

In many ways, Elsie continued outwardly to manage the tasks of life. She did take time off work for a bit, and probably a few days here and there when the blood pressure problems, as they were sometimes called (although Elsie never had any doubt that her nerves were a problem), got too difficult. She would sometimes have fluttery turns in public – even on the bowling green – on which occasions consuming a spoonful or so of salt or smoking a cigarette seemed to help. Elsie managed. She certainly got no respite from the demands of Granny and the Buchenwald Chicken. They were sharing a flat in Rotten Row in the centre of Salisbury, but they would spend all of every weekend with us while Dad schmeitzed (sensibly for him but somewhat inexplicably given his tender concern for his wife in other ways) to the golf course for most of the time. But Elsie's confidence, not that it had ever been that strong, was wavering. I imagine that, if anything, the contrast between how capable she was and how she felt inside made things worse rather than better. Years later I became very close to a brilliant but very depressed woman (no marks for your psychoanalytic formulation of why I chose to become close to her), and she was genuinely anguished by the fact that she was admired for her genius and her competence when inside she felt completely useless. In this way, she reminded me of Elsie and what she went through as a young woman.

Elsie had full-time servants, of course, who kept everything going, but I wonder how many people's undramatic and small breakdowns, but breakdowns nevertheless, are masked by the invisible work of poorly paid domestic workers. Much these days is written about the emotional labour that women perform all the time but studies of this issue in domestic workers (regardless of gender), although they do exist, are far fewer and far between. In our house, as in so many others, our maid and manservant were, as Ena Jansen so perceptively titled her book, 'like family'.[1] We regarded them as much more than employees. Unlike in many of the homes of our peers, Jenny and I were instructed to behave respectfully to these adults whom we called by their first names. Nevertheless, after clearing up after us, singing to us, teaching us how to ride a bicycle, and wiping our tears when we fell, at night after serving our supper and washing up, they returned to their small rooms with high windows in the back yard of the house. In the morning, the maid woke us up early with a tray of tea brought to each of our bedsides. I wonder what Elsie would have done without this help, day in and day out.

She also began to depend more and more on me. I was about nine years old at the time this started, or, to be more accurate, when I started to notice it happening. It was rare for my father to travel away from home, although there was the odd business trip overseas and to South Africa, where there were other cement factories owned by the same British company. The tempo of business trips increased the closer we came to being given the news that my father had received a transfer from Salisbury to Lichtenburg, in South Africa, where he became deputy manager of the cement works there. We moved there in March 1966, a mere five months after the declaration of UDI. This was always presented to Jenny and me as a promotion – which it was, as the Lichtenburg cement works was much bigger than the Salisbury works. It was only years later that we learned that my father had been pushing for a transfer because of his disgust at Ian Smith and his worries about the future of Rhodesia. Although the irony of a liberal young couple and their family moving from Smith's Rhodesia to South Africa at the height of apartheid was not (is not) lost on me, this was also a journey back to their home country, and a better springboard to moving overseas, should the opportunity arise.

When my father went off on his trips, my mother would ask me to sleep in his twin bed next to hers. Elsie said she needed me to sleep next to her because she was afraid to be alone. Given her symptoms, this was completely unsurprising, and I never questioned it. But as far as I recall, neither Jenny nor the maid Mitzi (who would have done what she was told, regardless of her feelings about it) was asked to sleep next to Elsie. I have wondered long and hard about this choice. I think part of it, quite genuinely, was that within Elsie's computations, I was by far the more vulnerable child. I was the child more likely to have distressing nightmares, the child more likely to need extra comfort, all of which I felt myself, though of course it was quite possible that Jenny had, and has, other ideas. As far as I remember, I was the one who would wake up terrified, believing that bad people had got into my bedroom and were standing over my bed; and I was definitely the one who regularly wet the bed intermittently into my teens. Within this logic, the child more likely to be unsettled by a father's not being home in a house in a quite isolated setting was me. So in asking me to help her, Elsie may well have been trying to look after me.

But I also have no doubt in my mind that she needed me. She needed me in a way, in the best of all possible worlds, a mother should not need a child. But who lives in the best of all possible worlds? And, when it comes down to it, who wants to? My mother loved me and cared for me as best she could, but just as we are all broken, she loved me in her broken way. As Leonard Cohen famously put it, 'There is a crack, a crack in everything / That's how the light gets in'. What made her the imperfect mother for me, also made her just right. And nobody who knew this broken, but to my mind brilliant woman, especially late in her life, would ever have doubted that she let the light get in. It's not right that I became her Little Man, and I was neither the first nor the last son, by any means, to be this for his mother. It's not right that it was not clear who was, or should be, looking after whom, when I was just a little boy. I will never know how much my desperate mama's boy need for Elsie was her desperate need for me. I know that she, like all of us, did what she needed to do, and in the best and kindest way she could. It's a tangled mess, still tender to the touch, but it's also a fundamental part of how my life – and it has been a lucky life – has been shaped.

Dr Levy tried his best to help Elsie. My dad definitely tried. Jenny tried, I tried. In some ways my mother's story looks in retrospect like a mundane suburban story, but I have no doubt that she suffered more than she should have. Dr Levy was always on the lookout for the latest thing – hence the changing array of drugs he prescribed.

When I trained as a clinical psychologist in the early 1980s I was amazed to learn that the revolutionary treatment for bedwetting, or enuresis, as we were schooled to call it, of the 1960s was the so-called bell and pad method. This had been invented in Germany in the 1930s, but did not, as far as I can tell, enter mainstream treatment in the USA till the 1960s. I realised that the contraption Dr Levy had prescribed for me in Salisbury, which awoke me with a shrill bell when I wet the bed, and substantially reduced the frequency of my bedwetting, much to my delight and that of my parents, was none other than the bell and pad method. The brown rubber undersheet and the clunky contraption were handed over to Elsie in Dr Levy's consulting room, which was right next to Mr Winterbottom's butchery and down the road from the Greek greengrocer. Here at the edge of the Empire, unbeknown to me, we were using the latest methods. This at a time when I knew other bedwetting kids at school were punished by having to wash their own wet sheets (scandalous in a world where doing laundry was the work of domestic workers, and not suitable for white people to do), being beaten, or being punished in a range of other ways. Granny, in her usual helpful way, insisted that the bedwetting should be beaten out of me, but my parents, thankfully, did not comply. They and Dr Levy (who had his own troubles, I can now see) were not frightened of things labelled psychological. They did their best, but really didn't know what to do.

In moving to Lichtenburg in 1966, we were getting physically closer to the familiarity of Johannesburg, but also entering a world in some ways even further away. There were similarities between our Salisbury lives and how we lived in Lichtenburg – on a housing estate next to a cement factory – but the worlds were different. Lichtenburg was a very right-wing area. In 1992, when white South Africans voted overwhelmingly to support then-President FW de Klerk's decision to enter into the negotiations that ended apartheid, there was one region in the whole country in which whites voted against change, and Lichtenburg was in that region. Most white people there spoke Afrikaans and many of them could not properly understand English. Worst of all for Elsie, in many ways, was the fact that there was no English-medium high school in Lichtenburg, so Jenny was sent off to boarding school. Like all the other children in the school, she was treated strictly and cruelly, and her sad letters home upset us all, and probably Elsie the most. It is testament to Jenny that by the time she matriculated from Potchefstroom Girls' High School, she had integrated well, was a prefect and top scholar at the school.

If Elsie had been a fish out of water in Salisbury, in Lichtenburg the water itself was barely recognisable. It was not done in Lichtenburg for women (and especially the wives of senior factory employees) to work outside the home, and Elsie lost the anchor of work. There was a small Jewish community but aspects of even this felt foreign. Many in the community, though not all, were both wealthy and ostentatious. The first (and only) time I have ever seen a sunken bath was in the en suite bathroom belonging to a Jewish family in that town. In another family's dining room I remember my amazement at seeing a large crystal chandelier hanging from the ceiling, dwarfing everything else in the room.

We were two doors down from the bowling green, which did help, but the overall atmosphere was oppressive. On 6 September 1966, the prime minister and architect of apartheid, Hendrik Verwoerd, was assassinated in Parliament. This led to a feeling of greater oppression amongst the whites in Lichtenburg, greater divisions between Afrikaners and English-speakers, and greater fear of Black people. Everything in Lichtenburg was bleaker and harsher. I was desperately unhappy at Lichtenburg Primary School, and more out of step than I had ever been.

I was about two years younger than my classmates, and having come from the far superior school system in Rhodesia, I was about two years ahead academically. I was a small, weedy ten-year-old, in a class with adolescents, many of whom towered over me. And I was the one arguing with the Afrikaans-speaking language teacher about the spelling of English words (I was always right), and calling him out about his inaccuracies in mental arithmetic. I begged to be sent away to a school that was stronger academically and, in January 1967, I got my wish. This meant that Elsie was at home alone, with both her children away. Like Jenny, I found the adjustment to boarding school very difficult, but having seen Elsie's distress about Jenny's unhappiness, I never complained or told my parents how I felt. This was a matter of pride for me throughout my school years. Of course, with hindsight, I can ask the question of who was looking after whom, who was trying to be the parent to whom, but at the time I just felt in my bones that this was what I had to do.

The giddiness, the shaking, and the vague and distressing array of symptoms continued for Elsie during this time. They abated somewhat when, two years later, my father was appointed manager of Whites Cement Factory in the Orange Free State and we relocated to the eponymous settlement, near to the small town of Hennenman. This place was even more remote and smaller than Lichtenburg, but now my father was the manager, and the general atmosphere in the Free State, despite its reputation for being the back of beyond, was in fact more open and accepting than in Lichtenburg. Elsie was better there.

Eventually, to my parents' delight, in 1970 my father was transferred to head office in Johannesburg. Elsie immediately found a full-time job in the retirement home across the road from our house, and she could see her sisters. By this time Jenny had finished school and was living at home, and I continued at school as a day scholar. The family was together again, albeit with the constant strain of Granny, who was by now living with us. This was not something any of us, least of all Elsie, wanted, but a doctor in Salisbury, who did not know the family context, had suggested she join us in South Africa, so that Granny could be better cared for by us. Granny swept in, as usual, like a battleship in full sail, leaving Lea alone in the Rotten Row flat in Salisbury for some years, though Lea followed later. Despite the burden of having a very difficult mother-in-law ruling the very small house, Elise was, I think, happier back in Johannesburg than she had been in the colonies and the 'country', but she still struggled with all sorts of things. Her new terror was of the road traffic in Johannesburg (which obejctively was really not bad at that time). She would drive circuitous routes to avoid driving on highways, which particularly terrified her. One day when I was in the car with her she was turning right across oncoming traffic on Louis Botha Avenue, a road she greatly feared. She began shaking so violently that she could not get the car to move in the short window of time she had as the lights turned orange and she was allowed to turn. Cars piled up behind her, hooting angrily, quite understandably. She shook and shook, less and less able to move. I have no recollection of how we eventually got across the road, and as a teenager I was too young to drive and unable to help her. When it came to my time to learn to drive at the age of 18, I remember believing with absolute conviction that I would never learn to drive. Luckily, and as with many other things, I was wrong about this. My mother tried to give me a few driving lessons, but her panic during these was so great that we soon agreed that I needed to get a professional driving instructor, which turned out to be a good decision.

Things were better, but there was always the knowledge of how hard they could be.

5 | The archives

Elsie loved language. She read and read, and she and my father discussed books and the news. She was also a prolific writer and, until she was really very ill, she kept in touch with people all over the world with beautifully written letters, usually typed at great speed on her tiny, portable Olivetti typewriter. She taught me many things about writing, not least the art of the well-crafted thank-you note. The story of any life, I suppose, is simultaneously the story of what could have been, the things a person could have done, but did not do. In Elsie's case, I think this is particularly true.

When Elsie was a little girl, because she liked to write stories, she was taken to meet another little girl about 18 months older than her, who was also a story writer. Like Elsie, this little girl was the daughter of Jewish migrants from Zhager (also known as Žagarė) in Lithuania, although her family did much better economically than did the benighted Cohens of Abel Road. The little girl lived in Springs, just under 50 kilometres from Johannesburg, and Elsie was instructed to be nice to her because the little girl, she was told, had a weak heart, as a result of which she spent much of her time at home writing. The little girl's name was Nadine Gordimer.

I wish I knew more about the relationship between Elsie and Nadine, but it was only quite late in her life that Elsie even told me about the Gordimer connection – long after Gordimer was awarded, in 1991, the Nobel Prize for Literature. I don't know how much time these little girls spent together, but Elsie did tell me that she and Nadine would send stories to each other, and that they discussed writing. Elsie also told me two things about the public side of their relationship. In 1936, the year Elsie turned 11, the South African Broadcasting Corporation (SABC) was established, and Elsie and Nadine both sent stories in to the SABC, and had them read over the radio. I have tried and tried to find archival material on this – through the Gordimer archives in Bloomington, Indiana, through the SABC itself, and using various networks – but I have not turned up anything. I have no doubt at all, though, about the authenticity of Elsie's claim, especially because of what came of the second thing Elsie told me.

According to Elsie, both she and Nadine had stories published in the *Johannesburg Sunday Express*. When my mother told me this, she was already quite ill, and I guess there is a story in itself as to why it took her so long to tell me. I had been interested in writing for a long time, had published a number of books and hundreds of academic articles. I suppose there is another story – or is it perhaps the same story? – in the fact that although I recounted my mother's connection with Gordimer in my memoir *Able-Bodied*, it never once occurred to me to try to find the stories in question, or to try to find the SABC stories.

In order to begin serious work on this book, which I was having trouble writing, about eight years after Elsie's death, I decided I needed help. Much of the help came in the form of supervision from Shaun Viljoen and Louise Green of the English Department at Stellenbosch University, where I work. I took Shaun for a coffee at Hazz coffee shop in Stellenbosch in the summer of 2018 with the aim of convincing him that I needed his help and that he was the right person to give this help. We sat on the small veranda of the heritage building, drinking our coffees, and the shadows of the oak leaves played across Shaun's face. We discussed my writing and why I thought I needed help (I knew I needed help!). I didn't know Shaun that well, but I was able to tell him that the reason I couldn't write this book was, in my view, emotional. I generally write quite easily, but this book felt too sore, too personal – and, I worried, potentially too sore for others – for me to work on. I had been avoiding facing it for all the years since Elsie's death. Shaun listened, was understanding and then, completely to my surprise, he mentioned the Gordimer connection, which I had spoken about in passing in *Able-Bodied*. 'Why don't you try and find out about these stories?' Shaun suggested. 'It would be great to know more about the link between your mother and Nadine Gordimer.'

That was it. I was off like a hare released from captivity. Drawing on resources appropriately, I asked my daughter Rebecca, the historian, where I should start. She directed me to Megan Healy-Clancy, who had written a book on women's education in South Africa,[1] and was working on a book on Gordimer. Healy-Clancy kindly directed me to the Gordimer archives at Indiana University and, indeed, there were two stories by Gordimer in the *Johannesburg Sunday Express*. 'The Quest for Sun Gold' was published on 13 June 1937, and 'The Valley Legend' on 18 September 1938. This checked out with what Elsie had told me – she was about 13, then, when Gordimer was publishing the stories. I ordered the Gordimer stories from Bloomington, Indiana, and was delighted when they arrived. Now to try to find Elsie's, if I could.

I am not sure what drove me quite so quickly to look for the Gordimer connection. At school, and long before I had known anything about my small family connection to Nadine Gordimer, we had been given a short story collection to read. One of the stories in it was an early Gordimer one, 'Treasures of the Sea', about perfection, loss and disappointment. I remember feeling at the time (and writing an essay about it) that although I admired the story for the quality of the writing, I found it strangely cold and devoid of emotion. It was well crafted and designed, I thought, to be admired. But it felt a bit bloodless and calculating. With the help of Bev Angus, I tracked down the story and it was, surprisingly perhaps, exactly as I remembered it. It is as beautifully written and has the same sheen as the pearl that forms an important part of the story. It is full of exquisitely turned sentences like the following:

> It was at this beach, or another like it, that she first discovered a hint of the activity of the sea, the strange wet rubbery foliage, the red flowers buttoned along the undersides of rocks, the silent fish and lethargic dabs of mucous living in perfect shells, the hundreds of shells individually fashioned and coloured to a whim. All this delicate craftsmanship, done by the sea.[2]

I read this, and I admire it, but to me now, as I felt 50 years ago, 'all this delicate craftsmanship' refers just as much to the work of the sea as to the work of Gordimer herself. I feel positioned by her to admire from the outside what she has wrought. And a part of me, so positioned, feels resentful, rebellious, but strangely unmoved. Where are the hot feelings in this cool, opalescent (to use a word used by Gordimer herself) beauty?

Over the years, I have tried (and sometimes succeeded) to read Gordimer's books and stories, and some I have really loved, such as the short story 'The Pet', which was published in 1962 and says an astonishing amount in a short space about liberalism in apartheid South Africa. But I have not been able to shake from myself a resentment at being placed as a reader in the role of having to admire the author rather than being left to get into the story. I have always mistrusted self-confident cleverness, books that are heavy with literary allusion and, unless seamlessly executed, the arch knowingness of postmodern writers whose books are about themselves and nothing else. But I don't get as upset about these as I do over the craft of Nadine Gordimer. There is a part of me that wonders whether, despite my having no recollection of this, I knew about the relationship between Elsie and Gordimer much earlier in my life. Maybe I am just competitive with the Nobel Prize recipient on behalf of the little girl who became my mother.

After quite a bit of to-ing and fro-ing, I managed to establish that back copies of the *Johannesburg Sunday Express* were housed in the archives at the Johannesburg Public Library. This in itself felt somehow fitting. In my last two years of high school, after we had moved to Johannesburg, on many Saturdays and other study days, I would sit on the top deck of the double-decker trolley bus and go into the centre of the city for a day of studying. The bus would stop close to Dicks Sweets shop in Loveday Street, where I would buy fudge and a multi-coloured hard-boiled candy in the shape of a large dummy. I slipped the ribbon on the candy dummy over my head and walked down the street sucking the dummy like an adolescent baby. The excitement and novelty value of the dummy candy was inevitably superseded by a disappointment engendered by stickiness all over my fingers and clothes, the dummy eventually falling to bits or being found abandoned weeks later with bits of tissue stuck to it as I had tried to save the treat for later. Despite this, I went back for more (I am convinced that the promise of a sugar rush interferes with memory function). Thus equipped, off I would walk to work in the large, silent reading room of the Johannesburg Public Library. I had learned the habit of working in libraries from Jenny, who by then was at university, and I have enjoyed working in university libraries ever since. I love the feeling that however long I read, however long I live, I will never come close to reading everything in the library – there will always be more to enjoy, and it won't spoil and disappoint like Dicks Sweets.

On the website for Dicks Sweets, you can still order candy suckers in Small, Medium or Large, along with candy walking-sticks, multi-coloured suckers, candy hearts, and even Johannesburg's version of rock candy. You will also find a sad little comment on the page detailing the history of Dicks Sweets. Having opened in 1938, in 1986, 'Due to the deterioration of central Johannesburg, the (Dicks) shops were closed down.' Dicks has more recently reopened online and in suburban Johannesburg, so the story ends on a better note, but the story of its closure in downtown Joburg is a typical lament of loss of white central Johannesburg. When I used to visit Dicks on my way to the library, the shop next door was the Central News Agency, or CNA, where I could buy stationery supplies, and where Elsie had worked as a teenager during the Second World War. From the CNA and Dicks it was a short walk to the library, an imposing building constructed between 1931 and

1935. There I would sit studying and from time to time dipping into the books all around me.

Having established that the archive of the *Sunday Express* was in this same building, I flew up with my wife Louise to discover what, if anything, we could find there. We ubered to the centre of Johannesburg, a place at once completely familiar and totally strange. The Johannesburg Public Library building was, of course, in exactly the same place, but its address was Corner Albertina Sisulu Road and Pixley ka Isaka Seme Street, no longer Corner Harrison and Sauer. There were mesh fences blocking access and what, certainly on the day we were there, felt like a perfunctory parody of heightened security – it was a bit more difficult to get into the building, but nobody seemed much to care who actually did gain access. Once we were in the vaulted library lobby, I rushed to the reading room where I had studied as a schoolboy, and that looked much the same as I remembered it. We asked a security guard at the desk where we could find the old newspapers, and he indicated that these were in the basement.

Unaccompanied, we went down a flight of stairs and in another room we found another guard, who kindly took us down to the room where the newspapers were kept. I don't remember how many floors down we climbed, but it felt completely otherworldly. There was no light at all on the stairs, so in the pitch dark we used our cell phones to light the way. We saw a patch of light and thought we had arrived, but in fact this was a landing, and on it some old posterboard, what looked like a weighing scale of the type that used to be outside chemist shops, and which you could use by putting a penny in the slot, a small metal stool, and a four-plate Kelvinator stove, the pride of many a kitchen in 1960s South Africa. Down we continued in the dark, finally emerging into a large room that smelled of dust, mould and dirt. We were the only people in the room – we did not see a librarian or an archivist at all that day – and part of me felt frightened that we would somehow be abandoned in what looked like a post-apocalyptic scene. We could die here with nobody knowing. I had fantasies of the few souls from the floors above going home at the end of the day, carefully locking up after themselves, and our bodies being discovered only weeks later, human detritus completely in keeping with the detritus of newsprint with which we were confronted.

The room was huge, with blue linoleum flooring and rows and rows of grey metal shelves. There were tables on which precarious piles of bound copies of old newspapers lay, all higgledy-piggledy. There were bound newspapers on the floor, and piles so arranged that pages of newspapers were crumpled and torn. Some of the shelves were empty, others jammed full. There was no way we could know what principles organised how these newspapers – *Cape Argus, Rhodesia Herald, Diamond Fields Advertiser, Die Volksblad, Sowetan* and many others – were arranged. We found no catalogue, and there was certainly nobody here who could help us. Carefully stuck to the metal shelves were newspaper titles. All the labels were made with a larger version of the wonderful Dymo Tape Label Maker we'd had in the late 1960s. I had loved making labels with that Dymo Tape machine, carefully punching out the block letters (you couldn't correct a mistake if you made one), then snipping off the label, removing the backing, and attaching the label to books, cassette tape holders, suitcases. I touched the raised white type of one of the labels and felt my anxiety abate a bit. Now all we had to do was find the *Johannesburg Sunday Express*. Louise started at one end and I at the other, and after some time we found the right label. We looked through all the decaying bound copies of newspapers on the shelf thus labelled. Not one of those huge heavy piles of bound newspaper was from the *Sunday Express*. None was from any Sunday newspaper at all.

For some reason I was reminded of some work we had done in Khayelitsha in the 1980s. In the part of Khayelitsha we worked, as in most of Khayelitsha, people lived in tin shanties. One day, without any warning, we arrived in the area we worked in to find the whole area cleared and completely desolate. The area had been cleared for the construction of more formal housing, and our participants had been moved elsewhere, where they would have to rebuild their shacks. We were informed of the general area to which people had been moved. There was only one problem. People rebuilt their shacks in a new environment in places that suited them, which was not necessarily in the same relationship to neighbouring shacks they had had before. To make matters more complicated, at that time each person's address was a number attached to the shack. So when people moved, they took their addresses with them. Just as those shacks and their locations, and addresses, had been unmoored from the land on which they were precariously settled, in this library basement each bound copy of newspapers, some of them crumbling to dust, had become untethered from the grid according to which they had once, in a different time, been carefully arranged. In my mind's eye, and with all the weight of stereotype, I can see a white librarian/archivist in a grey suit of modest length and sensible shoes brandishing a large red Dymo Tape machine and instructing a Black man to carry heavy bound copies of the colonial past – pages and pages of type – this way and that, the more to order both that past and the solid present housed by these strong walls in the bowels of the Johannesburg earth.

Something profound had happened to this room, deep in the earth in the Johannesburg Library. At one level, this was a scene simply of the entropy of budget cuts, of the need, appropriately, to redirect public funds to the care of the living rather than to the preservation of the past, demarcated not by Albertina Sisulu Road and Pixley ka Isaka Seme Street but by Harrison and Sauer streets. I thought of Mark Gevisser's memoir, which deals in part with his white Jewish boyhood in Johannesburg under apartheid, in which he describes his fascination with the map book his father had.[3] These map books meticulously recorded the geography of Johannesburg, the streets and cross-streets. But suddenly the maps would stop, and there would be nothing. This nothing, where there were no map and no words, was the *terra incognita* of those parts of Johannesburg where Black people lived, places either overlooked or effaced, unknowable, nowhere. Within the solid walls of the Johannesburg Public Library, a building that had stood since the building boom of the New York of Africa in the 1930s, down under dark, unlit layers scurried two old, little, white mice – Louise and I – wanting, for selfish reasons of mine, what had become unmoored in that space, off-kilter and with no axes, to be restored to order, so that I could reconstruct and re-imagine my past and that of my mother. In the Harry Potter films, there are scenes where wizards, at the wave of a wand, cause heavy books to move around in space. I wished I had such a wand, and there was probably a part of me that wished that, like my imaginary librarian in her heavy grey suit and sensible shoes, I would be able to order a Black man with no stake in this particular theatre of a particular past, to shift things around and create for me an order I could easily manage.

There was nothing for it, in this unmoored landscape, but for us to do our best to find what we could, if we could. Louise started at one end of the room and I at the other. It felt hopeless. Though cavernous, the room felt hot and stuffy. There was dust everywhere and true to form I started sneezing. I was intrigued by the old newspapers, was very sad and a bit angry at their state of crumbling disrepair, but I also felt guilty at caring so much about a room full of newspapers written by dead white men. The hoary Churchill quote 'History is written by the victors' floated into my mind. I wondered how I looked to the various security personnel we had seen – yet another foolish, old, white man trying to rebuild a past to which we should all be saying good riddance. But we kept looking. Eventually Louise found some volumes of the *Sunday Express* from the 1930s. We split the huge and heavy pile and each of us started finetuning our search. I quickly found the two Gordimer stories, which I had already been sent from the USA, and I soon found another, which I would later send off to them. We didn't know when or what Elsie had published, if she had at all. We looked earlier and later than the Gordimer stories. Fingers black from newsprint, hot and tired, we were about ready to give up when, perfunctorily, I turned yet another page. And there, in the *Sunday Express* of 8 October 1939, were the words:

"THIS WEEK'S MERIT STORY
What Would You Have Done?"

And a box in the text, which read:

A Problem Story by
ELSIE COHEN,
59 Abel Road
Johannesburg.

Elsie had two first cousins also named Elsie Cohen – people were clearly not as inventive about names as they are now. But only Elsie, my Elsie Cohen, had lived at 59 Abel Road. Only this Elsie Cohen threw her cat repeatedly off the balcony at 59 Abel Road. Only this Elsie Cohen wrote this story. I had never doubted the accuracy of what she had told me, but here was the proof, and I could now read what Elsie had written – her only print publication, as far as I know – when she was 14. Not surprisingly, perhaps, I burst into tears. I was here.

I read through the story quickly and made copies of it and other bits and pieces from the same and other issues from the newspaper. Louise did the same, amassing an archive of advertisements aimed at women and their failed attempts to look more beautiful, suffer from less gas or get relief from gout and dyspepsia.

Here is the story.

LEE ALEXANDER lying in bed, knew that he should not have gone to see that spine-chilling film, yet he did not want to be called a 'softie.' Although he lived in 'Devil's Kitchen,' the slums of New York, he should have really been born in a rich man's mansion, for his favourite pastimes were writing poetry and reading the great classics. Even though he possessed these qualities, he had courage, and, when a kindly millionaire from India offered to treat the poor children of New York to a bioscope show, he was obliged to go with his friends to a blood-curdling film all about corpses and the like. His brother Jimmy had gone away for the evening, he knew not where, therefore he was compelled to spend the night alone in the dark bedroom. Then, suddenly, he heard stealthy footsteps approaching his door. They were soft padding feet, which, Lee was sure, belonged to that awful apparition which had so large a part in the film. He felt his knees turn to water, and his hair stand on end, while his heart thump-thump-thumped in maddening crescendo, as nearer-nearer-nearer came the menacing pad-pad-pad of those feet. He wanted to scream but the sound died in his throat, as cold beads of perspiration broke out of his forehead.

When he felt he could stand the suspense no longer, he heard a sharp rap-tap-tap beat, on the window. He climbed shakily out of bed, and with trembling, nervous fingers opened the window to see the hard outline of his brother's face. He spoke:

'Jimmy, where have you been?'

'Cut the talk an' gimme a hand up. Say, you'd better take this junk first.'

With these words the 16-year-old boy handed his brother a sheet heavily laden with things. Lee gave a heave and pulled Jimmy into the room through the window. Just as the latter was about to speak, his brother looked furtively around, then asked in a hard voice strange to Lee:

'Has anyone been here?'

'No—no one has.'

'Are you sure no one has been here?'

'Yes!' shouted Lee.

His brother gave him a shake, and told him 'to skidaddle into bed, otherwise he'd be sorry for himself soon.'

Naturally, this dramatic gesture frightened the poor boy all the more, so he quickly climbed into bed.

He just made himself comfortable for sleep, with no thought of 'spooks' or 'monsters,' when he was rudely awakened from his reverie by a violent pinch on his shoulder.

'Ouch!' screamed Lee.

'Now listen, buddy,' the soft and silky voice of his brother said, 'help me hide this stuff from Mrs. Colman, I promise I'll give you all the diamonds from the next haul if you do.'

'Diamonds'—'haul'—unfamiliar words to Lee Alexander.

'Jimmy, have-have you been s-stealing?'

'Yes,' answered a crisp, matter-of-fact voice, 'and I tell you it's a jolly good job too.'

'But Jim!'

'C'mon, help me, otherwise I'll plug you.'

'I won't!'

'Oh yes, you will! Look here!' Lee saw a small, silver, menacing instrument pointed at him. 'And, remember, if you speak words to the cops, this'll speak lead into you!'

All Lee could say was, 'A revolver!'

'Yes, so now you'd better shake a leg an' skidaddle out of bed.'

*

AFTER he had helped Jimmy put away the stolen jewellery in a secret alcove in the bedroom, Lee, once he was back in bed, could not, try as he might, fall asleep. The words 'Jimmy's a thief'—'Jimmy's a thief'—'Jimmy's a thief' seared red-hot letters on to his brain. He did not know how his brother could sleep so peacefully when he had stolen the property of another man.

Each evening the same thing happened. Jimmy came home with jewels and beautiful clothes, and made his brother, at the point of a pistol, hide them. Lee was offered some of these things, but he declined to accept them. It never entered his mind to call the police.

Then—one night Jimmy came home with a red, ghastly bullet wound in his shoulder. Just before unconsciousness, he whispered these words, with difficulty, to Lee:

'They—nearly—got—me. Don't tell the c—.'

When Jim came to he smelt the penetrating odour of ether, and saw a kindly man, a doctor, leaning anxiously over him. The youth remained in the hospital for many weeks, with sympathetic men and women in white attending to him, yet the pain of his wound was at times unbearable. Lee visited him regularly and told him all that was happening.

'Listen, Jim, the police have found out about the robbery, and they found fingerprints, but no other clues. You'll have to leave N'York purty quick if you want to escape jail. Jim, please tell me everything, because—well, I want to know whether I should—well—give you up.'

'I'll tell you everythin'.'

'It began this way. Patsy Jones an' his gang was goin' to rob a place in Park Avenue, an' they asked me to join 'em. Well—I did, an' found it was easy to get money quick, so I decided to start a little "business" for myself. You know the rest, except when I got plugged. Well, a watchman was waitin' for me, and he got his .42 an' fired. I got shot, an' just about crawled home.'

'Honest, Lee, I'll never be able to forgive meself. Give me up to the G's if you want to. You'll be right, but, surely I've paid enough in pain?'

Lee went home, none the easier.

After all, Jimmy was a criminal, and he should have paid for his crime by going to jail, yet, he was Lee's brother, and he repented his sin. Although the 'G's' were on Jimmy's track he could escape somehow, but it was not right for Lee to help him got yet, as the boy said, he had paid enough with pain.

Lee did the right thing …

What he did I leave to you, dear reader, to decide.

*

There is so much to say about this story that I hardly know where to begin. The fact of finding it is remarkable to me in itself – the chain of events with Shaun suggesting to me that I look for things written by my mother had led us to this chaotic underworld, and in it we had found something! How many people have the privilege of knowing what their late mother was writing when she was 14 years old, in a quite different world? I was very, very lucky.

The second thing to strike me as I thought about this Merit Story by Elsie Cohen of 59 Abel Road, was that this story, despite all the years in between, the travels abroad and the life in Salisbury and in 'the country', the return to Johannesburg and the trip to Cape Town, where she died – despite all of this – the story was vintage Elsie. It was unmistakable. The title of the story was a question, the last line a challenge to the reader, the whole story a provocation, a demand from the reader that the reader participate. I had heard semioticians talk about open texts – I think the idea comes from Umberto Eco – about writing that demands active engagement from the reader and multiple interpretations.[4] Elsie Cohen, aged 14½, in 1939, could not possibly have had the knowing sensibilities of the postmodern fiction writers who were writing from the 1970s onwards, including Eco himself. But from the title of the story to its last sentence, there she is, calling the reader in and demanding that the reader participate in completing the story. To me, this was a far cry from the Gordimer story I had read at school, and the ones in the newspaper, where stories were presented beautifully whole, complete and there to admire.

Much more astonishing for me, though, than any comparison to Gordimer, is that Elsie's act of setting up an argument for her reader to complete and engage with – something she was doing as a young teenager – is, for anyone who knew her in her last years, quintessentially Elsie. Towards the end of her long and sometimes difficult journey to being old, if Elsie was known for anything, she was known for her love of a good argument. Debate, I often thought, was what kept her alive. She had a mind more nimble and joyful at the sheer pleasure of exercising itself than the minds of many younger people, including academics, whose job it is to engage in and think about arguments. And here she was. 'What would you do?' was, in every sense, the sort of question Elsie would pose.

I feel huge pride in this story, and I read into a brilliance that I have to concede others may well not see – I interpret it in light of my experience of my mother as a fiercely intelligent woman. But the pride I feel in this story is of course mixed with the loss. How I wish I had found the story when Elsie was still alive. How I wish I had discussed more of her writing with her. I don't have an objective way of assessing my mother's literary skills and talents, but I wish she'd had, and had taken for herself, more of a chance. Nadine Gordimer from Springs, as we know, went on to win the Nobel Prize for Literature, and there is no question at all about her place, well deserved, in the literary canon. I don't know what Elsie Cohen might have achieved, if anything, but I wish she had had more of an opportunity.

Within a few months of having her story published, Elsie Cohen was working, from the age of 15, as a shorthand typist. She did not complete high school. She did apply to the *Sunday Express* to train as a journalist, however. Although they liked her writing, the committee turned her down – journalism, they said, was not a job for a woman. For the rest of her life, Elsie was acutely aware of her lack of education, her lack of accomplishments. She would never ever really care about the obvious accomplishments of the other route to greatness, the Goodwill Book route. She might publicly muse about not being able to make stuffed monkeys or perogen, about being terrible at knitting, about not knowing how to crochet (in fact, she could do all those things), but she really didn't care that much about such things. She cared about thinking, and she cared about writing.

The big picture to this story is not a sad one. Elsie went on to have a privileged life. She knew this and was grateful for it. But, indulgent though this may be, I can't help feeling an ache of loss on her behalf, about what she could have said and given to the world. I think I have always had an awareness that Elsie was a writer who in adulthood wrote wonderful letters to family and friends, but who did not otherwise write. No journalism, no novel, no stories, not even a diary. Like so many others, she could not take that position as author. It is this awareness, I think, which animates me to write so much, but the more I write, the bigger the gap between what I am allowed and what Elsie was allowed becomes. I am so much more privileged than she was.

6 | Nadine Gordimer, Anne Frank, Elsie Cohen and me

I have tried and tried to find the stories that Nadine Gordimer and Elsie Cohen read out on the fledgeling SABC. I even imagine in my mind's eye scenes of contented 1930s families listening to the stories, huddled around boxy radios housed in handsome wooden cabinets gleaming with polish. I can see the antimacassars and the aspidistras in brass pots, and the family sitting around listening to the wonders of the wireless, and the stories of two little Jewish girls, daughters of immigrants. This soft-focus image owes a lot to the beautifully staged Woody Allen film of 1987, *Radio Days,* which Elsie loved, telling us that it was just like that – people did sit around the radio as earlier, again within her memory, they had sat around the piano and sung songs. Ada was the musician in the family – Elsie did not have the chance to learn music. And the SABC stories, as far as I can tell, are gone, along with Elsie's own career as a journalist and writer.

Along with many other writers who have similar quotes attributed to them, the novelist PD James is credited with saying, 'All fiction is largely autobiographical and much autobiography is, of course, fiction.' This statement applies as much to this book you are reading now as to anything else, but I was reminded of it so much on reading Elsie's story in the *Sunday Express*. Her hero, Lee Alexander, is a young American man, possibly a teenager like herself, but look what Elsie Cohen of 59 Abel Road had to say about him: 'Although he lived in "Devil's Kitchen," the slums of New York, he should have really been born in a rich man's mansion, for his favourite pastimes were writing poetry and reading the great classics. Even though he possessed these qualities, he had courage.'

I am so touched by this. Like Lee Alexander, Elsie loved writing and she loved the great classics. She had read most of Dickens by the age of 12, encouraged me to do the same, and was disappointed when I did not share this same passion. By the standards of the upwardly mobile migrant Jewish community in Johannesburg, her family struggled financially, and I have no doubt that if she had been 'born in a rich man's mansion', she would have finished high school and gone to university, where, I am sure, she would have done well.

We learn in the very first line of the story that Lee Alexander doesn't want to be thought of as a 'softie'. Well, if loving poetry and reading the great classics means that you are a softie, then there is no question that Elsie was a softie too. She was sensitive, lived close to her feelings, and struggled with them. Even so, as Elsie Cohen the author would have written, Elsie had courage. Here was this young girl, not much wanted by her family, bullied by her sisters, thwarted in terms of pursuing the interests she loved, buffeted about by life, sending off stories to the radio and the newspaper, trying to become something different. On the surface I suppose she failed – she remained uneducated, and for much of her adult life earned a living as a shorthand typist. But she had courage. She had what I would call a breakdown, and struggled for years. But she had courage. Her story, from beginning to end, is not one of rags to riches, of getting past difficult times to learn something from them, but a story that to me feels more honest and familiar – a story in which you feel the feelings, name them when you can, but try your very best to face them. She had the broken bits right to the end, but she let the light in.

And even the story of the brokenness is not as simple as I had once thought. Elsie did well at school, unsurprisingly, and, as was the custom of the day, she skipped standards. At 14 she was in a commercial high school, studying some academic subjects but also shorthand, typing and bookkeeping. She had her Junior Certificate (which meant that she had passed Standard 8 – probably in the same year as her story was published). Instead of doing the last years of high school over two years, she attempted matric, as it was called, in one year. She passed Standard 9 in June and in December, she passed all her final matric subjects except Afrikaans. Passing Afrikaans was compulsory, and so she failed matric and did not get a school-leaving certificate. For a very young girl who had excelled academically, and had skipped standards, this must have been a humiliating blow. There was no question of repeating the year (and hence of attempting to pass her matric in two years, as other children did). She left school at the age of 15 and started working.

For most of my life, I accepted this story as a simple one of the last, unwanted child in a struggling family, trying to rush through school, not quite managing it, and then going out to work to contribute to the family coffers. Only very late in life did Elsie tell me that things were in fact a bit more complicated.

A relative of my grandfather – I don't know who – took an interest in this awkward but obviously very bright and talented young girl. He offered to pay for her to complete her matric over the usual two years, and in an academic high school. This kind of offer, though no doubt generous, was not all that unusual at the time, as it is not today in some communities. Many poorer Jewish children had their education paid for by benefactors in the extended family or the Jewish community. It was not a marked or stigmatised thing to be paid for in this way, and, indeed, I myself, paradoxically enough, was the recipient of just this kind of generosity a generation later. I did my high school at King David, a private Jewish school in Johannesburg, and my fees were paid by a bursary set up by Jack Penn, one of the few plastic and reconstructive surgeons in Johannesburg at the time. And when we were given the opportunity to go on a school tour to Israel in Standard 8, my wealthy Uncle Louis (Ada's husband) approached me about this and insisted that I go at his expense. It never occurred to me to feel humiliated at being a recipient of charity in this way.

So it was not strange for Elsie to be offered help to realise her academic ambitions and, as Elsie told it, her parents were eager for her to accept the offer. But Elsie refused. Instead she went to Commercial High to try to do matric in one year, failed (by one subject), and the rest is history. What was going on? I have wondered and wondered about this decision of hers. I feel the regret everyone feels about questions we wish we had asked people who have since died. So I make guesses. One thing that could have played a part was the fact that by the time Elsie was offered this opportunity, her parents, Jacob and Paulina, were already not on speaking terms. It was Elsie who bore the burden of being a conduit between them, with all her siblings refusing to consider that it was possible that their parents' marriage had broken down. Who could blame her for wanting to become financially independent and to get out as soon as possible? I know that she did not want to be the maiden aunt left caring for her warring parents. But I don't think this was the only story. There is something here about sacrifice, about being the youngest and unwanted, about being bullied by older siblings (much as she loved them and they her), about Elsie's sense of not deserving anything for herself. To some extent, like many women before and after her, she spent much of the rest of her life not allowing herself things, while looking after others. If we look again at her story hero, Lee Alexander, he has an older brother who has seriously, criminally, messed up. Like Elsie, Lee does not want to be seen as a 'softie'. It is Lee who has to show courage. It is Lee, and not the criminal older brother, who is left with the difficult moral choice. Lee bears the burden for the messes of the elders, which was exactly what Elsie was doing, I suspect, holding her badly behaved parents together and making sure that to the outside world all appeared fine. And though I can and do speculate about Elsie's choice to marry a disabled man her family worried would die young (a choice that turned out to be a really good one, I think – they were so happy together), she made another choice that was in keeping with her past. She went into her marriage knowing that this entailed caring for her cruel and endlessly demanding and ungrateful mother-in-law and attendant ghoulish sister. She cared for them for the rest of her married life and beyond (my father died at 63 but the battleaxes battleaxed on), cleaning up after them, putting them ahead of herself and, to some degree, ahead of her own children.

There is a wonderful chapter by Sally French in an influential disability studies reader.[1] French, who has a severe visual impairment, describes going on walks with her caring family, but a family that was, understandably, very anxious about the possible impact of a visual impairment on the life of this loved child. 'Can you see the rainbow?' her parents would ask and, from quite young, little Sally would reply, 'Yes', even though she could not see the rainbow. I love the story because it illustrates so well the role many disabled people play not only in dealing with their own impairments, but also in managing the anxieties of others around them – including their parents – about disability, thereby taking on a double burden, and often from a very young age. Part of my love of this story, I think, is because I see in French's story something so similar to what Elsie did – looking after, and managing, the messes, and messy feelings, of the generation before her, including her much older siblings. And, of course, if I am anything at all, I am my mother's son. I think to some extent I did the same, sealing my parents off from my difficulties at boarding school, not telling them about all sorts of struggles.

All of this resonates with me, and feels true, but it does not fully explain for me my mother's pattern of sacrifice, something she took with her for much of her life. When I was at university in Cape Town I returned home to Johannesburg one vacation to find that she had bought herself a new slacks suit on the Greatermans sale. She took it out to show me, and I can honestly say that I have seldom seen such a piece of clothing in all my life, and I'm not young. It was green and black in colour in a sort of checkerboard design, and though short-sleeved and designed for summer, it was made of a quite heavy crimplene. It gaped, and the buttons looked cheap and tacky. It was really ugly. Before I could say a word, Elsie said, 'It's not very attractive but it's very serviceable and it will wash well – and it was so cheap on the sale.' She wore that bloody slacks suit almost till it fell apart, getting good wear out of the serviceable crimplene. It would probably have gone up in dramatic flames had you put a match to it, but in other respects it seemed completely indestructible.

There are many people who cannot resist a bargain, no matter how useless, and many of us have somewhere something that seemed like a good idea at the time but really wasn't. But I honestly don't think that this was what drove Elsie to buy the slacks suit and wear it for years and years. I don't think she bought it in spite of the fact that she found it ugly (which she did) – she bought it *because* she found it ugly. This was the point, and it was the point for wearing it so often for so long. It's certainly true that, despite the evidence against this, for most of her life Elsie thought of herself as ugly, and I don't have any memory, as many people do, of thinking my mother was beautiful. The belief that she was ugly or, at best, plain, was drummed into me by her from a young age, and I believed it. This was despite the fact that for many years I believed that the print we had on our wall at home of Vermeer's luminously beautiful Girl with a Pearl Earring was a painting of my mother. Looking at the image now, I can still see why I thought it was my mother – the long nose, the light eyes, but, mostly, the vulnerability in that face. Elsie was convinced of her own ugliness, and to that extent the slacks suit was in keeping with what she felt she should wear. But I think that the slacks suit (like many other items of clothing) was part of a broader picture of not allowing herself things, a pattern of self-punishment and self-denial. Story, to some extent, of her life. And therefore, no academic high school for her, no shot at a proper matric, no chance to live in a 'rich man's mansion'.

So off Elsie went at the age of 15 into the world of work, an adult before her time, giving her money to her mother, living as a child at home and a woman in the world. It was wartime and things were difficult, not least for Jews. But Elsie, being honest, unsentimental Elsie, would always say that for her, the war years were wonderful. She received basic nursing training, and for the rest of her life could make a bed with the most expert hospital corners you've ever seen. She volunteered as a waitress at the Jewish Servicemen's League where, according her, she was hopeless, struggling to hold up tin trays and often dropping them. But she loved the interaction with the soldiers, and the dances – the Paul Jones, the cakewalk, the Charleston. She loved the movies, and Yiddish theatre, and spoke often of the Yiddish actress Sarah Sylvia, who later went on to star in English-language plays and even in some films. Until her father died in 1943, Elsie enjoyed life. For her work as a cashier at the CNA, she had to have her nails done every week (so that they would look good for customers), and when she was doing the books at ABC shoe store, working very long hours for a boss she described as a slavedriver, she was sometimes asked to model shoes for customers, as her boss thought she had beautiful feet of perfect size. She was plain, but able to take glamour where she could find it.

The movies were important. Elsie described going to the Empire, to the Colosseum with its twinkly lights that looked like the night sky, and, after the war, to His Majesty's. When the 20th Century cinema opened, she would go and listen to the music of Dean Herrick on his huge Wurlitzer organ, both Herrick and the Wurlitzer being imports from the USA, as were most of the movies. And when Elsie Cohen of 59 Abel Road published her first story, it was written in US gangster patois, which she must have picked up from the movies. She had no connection at all to Hollywood, apart from one tenuous link.

In 1933, the year she turned eight, she helped out a newly arrived migrant family from Lithuania by taking five-year-old Larry Skikne to school on his first day. He could not speak a word of English, and she could manage a little Yiddish. Larry grew up to serve in the entertainment unit of the South African Army during the Second World War, and he later became an Oscar-nominated Hollywood film actor, along with a career on the stage, the obligatory marriages and divorces to beauties and heiresses. His name for most of his life was Laurence Harvey. While doing research for this book, I discovered that Laurence Harvey had had a daughter, Domino, who became a bounty hunter and had died young, apparently of an overdose. A film was made of her life, starring Keira Knightley. You can't get more Hollywood than that. An obituary of Domino Harvey published in *The Telegraph* of 30 June 2005, begins: 'Domino Harvey, who died on Monday aged 35, struggled – ultimately unsuccessfully – to relieve the emptiness and boredom of a life of wealth, glamour and celebrity.'

Elsie would have laughed with me at this clichéd sentence, and then would have felt a bit guilty about laughing about something so sad. From the hand of Elsie Cohen, holding the hand of little Larry Skikne, to a sad and unsuccessful attempt 'to relieve the emptiness and boredom of a life of wealth, glamour and celebrity'. A kind of Hollywood ending for Elsie Cohen, though not of the usual happy type.

When Louise and I were looking through the newspapers in search of Elsie's *Sunday Express* story, we both noticed all the movie advertisements, as well as stories about Sarah Sylvia and her theatre shows. I wondered which ones Elsie had seen, and whether she, like Lee Alexander, 'was obliged to go with … friends to a blood-curdling film all about corpses and the like'. But the thing that struck me most about the film ads and the advertisements for beauty products was that, quite by chance, I had seen very similar images just a few months before our trip to Johannesburg.

Louise and I had been lucky enough to spend a few days in Amsterdam at the tail end of a work trip to Switzerland. I had been to Amsterdam once before for work and I loved it. This time I knew that if we wanted to visit the Anne Frank museum we had to book months in advance, which we had done. Elsie had been honest about the war being the best time of her life, but she was also acutely aware of the horror of the Holocaust, and had given Jenny and me Anne Frank's diary to read when I was about eight. I loved the book, although I think there was quite a lot about adolescence and sexuality that went over my head. I loved, predictably, the ordinary in this story that, by the time I read it, had become a story of tragedy of global significance. The fact that Anne could have such a bad relationship with her mother and be so irritated with her, as would any teenage girl, despite (because of, alongside) the desperate circumstances, really brought home the humanity of the situation to me. As Louise and I were kindly and efficiently shepherded along with hundreds of other people through the Anne Frank House and the annex, the thing that really moved me was the wall of photographs and posters that Anne had had up on her bedroom wall. As a teenager, I myself had ruined my parents' walls by putting up psychedelic posters proclaiming LOVE and similar things, and in this respect, although the aesthetic had changed somewhat in the 1970s from the 1940s, I could identify with Anne.

None of the posters in my bedroom was of South African origin – that was all to come later with the flowering of resistance poster art in South Africa. I am pretty sure that the posters, one of which I bought on a school tour to Israel, were made in the USA. On Anne Frank's wall are pictures, among others, of the Hollywood stars Norma Shearer, Deanna Durbin and Shirley Temple, and of the little English princesses, Elizabeth and Margaret. Victor Kugler (who appears in the diary as Mr Kraler, and in later life received awards for helping hide the Frank family and others), used to bring Anne *Cinema & Theater* magazine, which she reportedly loved. *Cinema & Theater* looks so similar to *Stage and Cinema*, which we would get at the movies when I was a child, and which Elsie loved. Here on the wall of this little German-born Jewish girl, in hiding from the Nazis, was the world of Hollywood and the Royal Family – the same world that fascinated Elsie, growing up Jewish in South Africa. Across unimaginable worlds, there were Anne Frank and Elsie Cohen, both fascinated by the movies. Two ordinary girls who wanted to be writers.

By a stroke of luck, a few months after I found Elsie's story, I was off to Amsterdam again and I decided to go and take another look at the pictures on the wall in the Anne Frank museum. I felt a bit fraudulent making my way along with many tourists through the house till I got to the wall and had a chance to look at it again. So similar to the *Johannesburg Sunday Express* of the 1930s – and completely familiar.

Elsie was a year older than Princess Elizabeth, and in middle age some people used to say that she looked like her. And there was the little princess on Anne Frank's wall. Even before this second visit to the Anne Frank House, knowing as I did that I was now visiting not to learn about Anne Frank but to try to make sense of my relationship with my mother, I felt more than a little queasy. I was worried about my own motives for dragging Anne Frank into my story – she was a real person, with a real life. She lived for many years cooped up and hidden from the world and died a horrible death, of typhus, as far as we know, in a concentration camp. She was four years younger than Elsie. She died while Elsie was enjoying her time at the Jewish Servicemen's League. In 1941, similarly, approximately 3 000 Jews of Zhager were rounded up in Naryshkin Park and shot dead by the Lithuanian militia.[2] By at least one account, of all the Jews of Zhager, only one survived this massacre.[3] Had my grandparents not left Zhager, and had Nadine Gordimer's parents not left Zhager, my generation of descendants of those shtetl dwellers would probably not exist.

On Wednesday, 5 April 1944, Anne Frank wrote in her diary: 'When I write I can shake off all my cares. My sorrow disappears, my spirits are revived! But, and that's a big question, will I ever be able to write something great, will I ever become a journalist or a writer?'[4] In less than a year, in February or March 1945, she was dead. Her diary remains widely recognised as a classic of the twentieth century and a great work of literature, so there is no question that Anne was able to write something great. Though earlier on the same page of her diary she asserts, 'I *know* I can write', she was never to know that her great writing was already almost complete.

What do we make of our memories and how do we justify them? My life as a Jewish boy growing up safely and privileged was inflected by Nazi stories. For many years my parents, like many Jewish people, would not buy German or Japanese cars, because of what happened during the war. Shortly after we moved to Salisbury, my father travelled to Germany to learn more about Humboldt kilns, of the type installed in the new cement works. It was 1957, and everything went well, but both my parents were anxious, and the symbolism of a Jewish person going to Germany to learn about kilns was probably not lost on them. When we would not eat our food, we were asked to think of all the starving children not in Africa but in Europe. Broken people with numbers tattooed on their arms flitted across the African landscape. Elsie would get angry with us for not appreciating how lucky we were to be living in a post-war world. Giving us Anne Frank to read was a way of communicating to us how, whether it felt like it or not, we were part of a collective trauma, always potentially ready to re-emerge. It's contested when the phrase 'never again' came to be used as a rallying cry for Jewish memorialisation, but of course the very idea of 'never again' contains within it the threat that again terrible things will happen if we don't remember properly.

The whole problem of remembering Anne Frank appropriately, if that is possible, is not something that is new. In some ways, the demand is simple – Elsie wanted us to read and learn from Anne Frank's diary in much the same way, I suppose, that those who compiled all those Jewish family books wanted their descendants to model their lives on those who had gone before, and especially on the lives of virtuous patriarchs. Never must we forget our luck in not being on the other end of murderous prejudice. But this comfort comes with a price – the price of memory and the price of conformity. In the early pages of his controversial account of Israel, *My Promised Land*, Ari Shavit raises the question of how it is that early Zionists seemed not to see the obvious – that other people were living in the land that would come to be called Israel, and had done so for generations.[5]

Generations of wandering and trauma seem to have helped Jews to be more sensitised to their own very real plight than to the implications of solving this by displacing others. Similarly, the suffering of Anne Frank could be used to keep us in line – to reproduce where Elsie had come from, however ambivalent she might feel about those origins.

The British artist Simon Fujiwara has something to say about how we remember Anne Frank, and why. He built a life-size model of the

Anne Frank House, based not on the annex itself but on a porcelain replica of the annex that he bought from the gift shop at the Anne Frank Museum. The result is a sculpture you can walk through. It is completely real and embodied but completely surreal. Fujiwara's work, which I have read about but not experienced, fascinates me as a comment on the commodification of memory, and the problem of tragedy tourism. One of the really interesting things Fujiwara has done has been to superimpose over Anne Frank's poster wall images from contemporary pop culture – Beyoncé appears, as do Hillary Clinton and Natalie Portman in her Oscar-winning role in *Black Swan*. People familiar with popular culture will know that Portman is Jewish, has directed a film version of the memoir of the famous Israeli author Amos Oz, and that *Black Swan* deals with self-destructive violence. The images have been carefully chosen to talk to the problem of what Anne Frank has come to mean or not mean today. Pride of place on this new celebrity/memory wall is an image of a bare-chested Justin Bieber with dyed-blond hair. In 2013, famously, Bieber visited the Anne Frank Museum and wrote the following in the guest book: 'Truly inspiring to be able to come here. Anne was a great girl. Hopefully she would have been a belieber.'[6] Like many other people, I am, of course, galled by this statement, but not just by the easy narcissism of a 19-year-old more enamoured of his own cult following than seems polite. The other thing that gets me is the 'Anne was a great girl' comment. First, it feels so trivial to be describing Anne Frank, who is famous because of her suffering and cruel death, as a 'great girl'. Much more problematically, though, I find myself objecting to Bieber's easy claim to know 'Anne', and to know whether or not she was or was not a great girl. What right did this 19-year-old, who himself claimed all sorts of ancestry, but no Jewish ancestry, have to claim to know Anne Frank so well? I am well aware of the irrationality of my response here, and in this I hear Elsie's voice, full of indignation, at who may claim what for their own memories. I just don't know where to put myself in all of this. Part of me wants to be as audacious as Philip Roth. In *The Ghost Writer*, he not only has Judge Wapter recommending to Zuckerman that as a kind of spiritual cleansing he should attend the Broadway play of *The Diary of Anne Frank*.[7] He also has the nerve to create a glamorous character, the mysterious Amy Bellette, who is none other than Anne Frank grown up into an alluring woman and living in the USA. I want to be wild, like Nathan Auslander, who in his novel *Hope: A Tragedy* has a cantankerous, old Anne Frank living in the hero's attic like a nineteenth-century madwoman, smelling, and demanding shipments of matzos, gefilte fish and borscht.[8] Needless to say, the many contemporary reimaginings of Anne Frank and what she represents have been mulled over by scholars, and authors like Roth and Auslander are not without their fierce critics.[9] But, selfishly, I am much more interested in what all of this means for me and my story of my mother.

In another art installation, entitled 'Studio Pietà (King Kong Komplex)', Fujiwara uses his memory of his mother with her then-boyfriend on a beach in Lebanon before Fujiwara was born to explore the process of trying to recreate personal memory. He hires two models to play his mother and her boyfriend, each coming to the shoot with their own histories, their experiences of being represented and misrepresented. He ends up creating an image that both is and is not like the remembered photograph. As in the original (although we never see the original, and we don't know for sure if the original exists), both Fujiwara's mother and her boyfriend are on the beach in their bathing suits, with one holding the other aloft. In the new version it is the woman holding the man aloft (as Mary held Jesus in Michelangelo's Pietà), but with the help of pulleys, because this man, himself a migrant to Berlin where the installation was filmed, is too heavy to carry.

Too heavy for his history. As part of the installation, Fujiwara interviews himself. As an article in *Interview* magazine puts it: 'At the center (of the exhibition) is a video documenting Fujiwara's bid to recreate the photograph, narrated by an interview with himself. "You can say a lot if you only have yourself to answer to," he points out.'[10]

In trying to hold onto my memories of my mother, I suppose I am creating a new person who may be unrecognisable to people who knew her or, worse, partly recognisable. There is something more shocking in creating something (someone) who at times feels true and real but then feels false, a violation of the truth, than in being clear that the character is all made up, bearing no resemblance to reality. Nadine Gordimer, Anne Frank, Elsie Cohen – these were all real people. For very different reasons (a Nobel prize, a cruel death representing millions of other deaths), although I worry about how I am representing Gordimer and Frank, I can console myself with the fact that both of them, by being famous, have come to be something other than just the people they were. But in writing about Elsie, although I can claim all the primacy that comes from being her darling son, unlike Fujiwara, I don't only have myself to answer to. Elsie had two children, four grandchildren, a husband and siblings (am I off the hook with them given that all the siblings are dead now?), nieces and nephews, cousins, friends, acquaintances. She had many people whom she spoke to in what I always called her 'front door voice' – I am almost sure that this expression comes from a William Golding short story but can't for the life of me locate it – a voice designed to indicate to people her own respectability, and to keep people away. I believe in my heart that she would like this book. Like Lee Alexander, her character, she had courage. And in the end she was not one for sentimentality or making nice when nice was not nice.

As I get closer to and further away from her as I write this, I think of Elsie Cohen as many things – but centrally as a writer, along with the more famous Nadine Gordimer and Anne Frank. Like so many women before and after her, she has left the telling to others, and in this case to the old man who was once her son. It's not fair. I don't feel fully equal to the task. But, Mom, I'm trying my best here.

Part II
Losing

7 | Shouting loud

I ran away from home at 17. Sedately, surreptitiously, but I ran away nevertheless. I was happy enough at King David, but I never felt completely at home there. The thought of succumbing to the pressure of going straight from completing school to Wits Medical School with (literally) more than half of my class felt stifling. I opted for a cover story on top of a cover story – I enrolled for law at the University of Cape Town, 2 000 kilometres away and in a town I had never visited. The law cover story can best be explained by the old Jewish joke: 'What is the definition of a lawyer? A nice Jewish boy who can't stand the sight of blood.' I had other, at that stage secret, plans for my life, thank goodness.

Forty years after I left school, the cool kids organised a King David class reunion. Given that by far the majority of the people who had been in my year now lived overseas, and that some (especially, it seemed to me, the naughtiest boys) had become very religious and even rabbis, the reunion was held not in Johannesburg but in Israel. There was absolutely no chance that I would fork out to travel overseas to a school reunion, least of all in Israel, about which I felt deeply and irrevocably conflicted, given the occupation of Palestine. I did not relish the thought of the competitiveness that a reunion would probably engender – by definition, by having chosen to stay in South Africa, I would be regarded as a failure by some of my classmates – and while I did have some good friends at King David, the thought of enforced chumminess with a group of people with whom I now had little in common over some days in a foreign country filled me with horror. As an academic I go to a lot of conferences and meetings and I cannot bear the forced jollity and strained laughs of colleagues forced together for a meeting and having to pretend to be having a great time together. The issue of the chumminess was brought home to me when I bumped into an old classmate, one of the very few living in Cape Town, at the shops one day. She was planning to go to the reunion and was quite excited, but she also said to me, 'Now Heather Feigenbaum is asking me to be her Facebook friend.[i] Why would I want to be her Facebook friend? I hated her 40 years ago!' That's about the size of it.

As it happens, after the class reunion (which by all social media accounts was a great success), one of the more enterprising women of our cohort arranged a small reunion in Johannesburg for those still there. She was now the owner of a spa and beauty centre in California, offering massages, skincare, electrolysis and waxing, and on a visit to Johannesburg she organised this reunion. Completely by chance, I was doing some disability-related training close to Johannesburg, so I was able to drive to the hotel where the get-together was being held. I entered a room in the smart hotel on a freezing Johannesburg night, and the first thing I noticed was the large platters of food covered in clingwrap. Some of my former classmates kept kosher, so kosher food was necessary. There is a certain look to these kosher food platters, which will be known to anyone who has seen them, but suffice it to say that both herrings and salmon were harmed in the production of the food. The sight of the platters took me back to the few Jewish weddings, barmitzvahs and funerals I had attended. The mere fact that I noticed the food in this way reminded me of my outsider status – I was the one who had run away, married out. There must have been about 25 people at the reunion out of a school-leaving class of about 180, all of us not teenagers anymore, all close to 60. Many of the people had kept in touch, and chatted companionably. I recognised almost nobody and, worse, when

i Not her real name.

people said their names to me, this was no help. I could not remember ever having known people by these names. They all seemed to know who I was but I had no memory of them at all. Repression is a wonderful thing. Many of them looked like the sort of people that I felt Elsie had wanted me to turn into – amiable, satisfied, successful, and part of the Jewish community. Many were grandparents, and their genealogical lines stretched forward into the future, in an uninterrupted line. I am of course not so naive (and, thank goodness, no longer so young) to imagine that they did not have all their own private and, possibly, public struggles. For those who asked, I tried to explain what I was doing training disability activists from southern Africa in basic research skills, but this work seemed ephemeral, and, I thought, incomprehensible to those living in the real world of property development and small business. I was pleased to reconnect with an old friend I had not seen for the 40 intervening years and to discover that our professional lives were not dissimilar. Apart from the pleasure of talking with her, the conversation forced me to acknowledge, once again, how the gulf between what I thought was expected from me before I ran away, and what I had become, might not be as big as I had made it in my mind.

As I was about to leave the gathering as soon as it felt polite to do so ('Long drive back to Benoni – I don't know the Joburg roads very well and must factor in time to get lost' – 'Early start tomorrow with my trainees'), one of the women there, now a well-padded matron, made a comment. 'Leslie,' she said, 'you haven't changed a bit. You were always the quiet one, at the edge of the group, not saying much. And look how well you have done in life.' I have no doubt that she meant this comment kindly, and I am aware that the 'You haven't changed a bit' line is one that is generally viewed as a compliment. But the comment struck me in two, intertwined, ways. I was amazed to realise that at this gathering of late-middle-aged people on a freezing cold night in Johannesburg in 2012, I had behaved exactly as I had at school. I had been pulled back, or had pulled myself back (did I fall or was I pushed?) into a version of what I had been at high school; I had gone so far, but my 17-year-old self was still in there somewhere. So what this woman saw of me that night was indeed exactly as I had been at school – peripheral, hesitant, quiet, thinking that I should be somewhere else. Her comment, based on what she saw, was absolutely accurate. The other side of this, though, was that anyone who knows me now, and especially people who have not known me for many years, will not recognise me as 'the quiet one on the edge of the group, not saying much'. In fact, I have a deserved reputation of being something of a loudmouth, the person who says the difficult things, the one who won't shut up.

I want to explain just how far I have travelled from being the quiet one, not saying much, because this says something about me, I think, but also about Elsie. Many years ago, when I was still working at the University of Cape Town (UCT), I was asked, as academics are routinely asked, to conduct an external review of a department at another university. The details of the review are not important. What is important, though, was that in contrast to every other review I have ever been part of, I felt quite strongly that there was a cover-up of sorts going on, a refusal on the part of the internal members to listen openly to negative feedback.

I was not altogether surprised, given my estimation of the process, that when the internal review chair drafted the first version of our report, there was no mention at all of what I viewed as a crucial part of the widespread dissatisfaction we had found. I thought it was important for the committee to note the issues in our report, to which I, like all other committee members, would be a signatory.

Predictably, these recommendations were not welcomed by the review chair, and there ensued a long slew of round robin emails with the chair and me arguing about whether to include mention of the discrepancy in views. The chair said that commenting on the issues I thought central was beyond the terms of reference of the committee. I countered strongly. And so we went, round and round, copying each response to all the other committee members. Eventually I suggested that those people on the committee who agreed with me could offer a minority report in addition to the main report, and alongside the minority report the chair could provide a document outlining why she thought the minority report was effectively ultra vires. I was not giving up. I drummed up support for my approach from other committee members, but there is no question that I was the ringleader of the insurrection. Then transpired one of those moments that are really not thought about enough in this postmodern, interconnected world. This is a variation on the terror of the mistaken 'Reply All' when one is saying rude things about some of the All (it is not for nothing that Reply All is a popular meme travelling, I am sure, at this very minute, somewhere on the internet). My rebellious behaviour (and my clear refusal to back down over it) was causing some consternation in the institution I was corresponding with, and, by accident, I was copied into an email string that clearly was not meant for my eyes. In this email string, there was a discussion about what to do about my irksome intervention. I cannot express strongly enough the extent of my pride when I read a comment about what to do about me. This read, 'We cannot be seen to be giving in to the one who is shouting loud.' All my life, I had waited to be seen as 'the one who is shouting loud'. I had my moment, but I had more. I have long held the deeply scientific and evidence-based view that there is a link (could it be fibre-optic?) between the unconscious and the World Wide Web. Given this undisputed fact, I had no doubt that this person who was so angry with me for shouting loud, at some deep level wanted me to know about all the trouble I was causing, and why that person was not standing for it. Goody. I think I won what was an essentially pyrrhic victory after all this mess, because I got my way, but I very much doubt whether very many people ever saw the report. That's not important here, however. What is important is that although I had been absolutely correctly identified as very quiet and on the sidelines, I am now probably known much more for shouting loud – getting in there, boots and all.

The truth is (and I honestly don't think many people know this – and especially many who get on the wrong side of my self-righteous indignation) that, despite the admitted thrill of the chase, I commonly find shouting loud really difficult to do. I worry for hours about having upset and hurt people, and I anticipate terrible retributions that, generally speaking, do not come. I lose sleep. But I grit my teeth and (usually) do it all the same. I realise as I say this that, unfortunately, the book I should have written instead of the one you're reading has already been written – it's called *Feel the Fear and Do It Anyway: How to Turn Your Fear and Indecision into Confidence and Action.*[1] Like the author of this 8 million copies sold work, I believe that though on the surface it may be a million miles between the quiet one on the edge, never saying a word, to being the one who is always shouting loud, it's actually not that far. And you know who knew this in 1939? None other than Lee Alexander – Elsie's hero. Lee did not want to be seen as a 'softie', and his heart 'thump-thump-thumped in maddening crescendo'. But, as she puts it so simply, 'he had courage'. Well, so did Elsie, and, being my mother's son, so, I hope, do I. To be honest, I don't think life has thrown as much at me as it did at Elsie – I often say that I think I have had a better life than my parents had because I had better parents than they did. But I did learn from Elsie, very young, that mixed in with all the brokenness and the difficulties (and she really suffered with her 'nerves') is a kind of strength and determination to make life better. And because I knew this, because I saw her courage and tried it on for myself, I broke her heart, and more than once.

My cover story for leaving home at 17 was watertight. My ghastly grandmother was very much around, living with us, bullying everyone, and interfering in my life, going through my desk drawers, and shouting, shouting, shouting. Combine this with the charms of the Buchenwald Chicken, who had recently moved to Johannesburg, and you have the best reason to argue that it's time to get as far away as possible. I don't remember much about broaching the subject of my going away to university rather than staying in Johannesburg as was the custom, but I do know that my wish to do this was devastating for my mother. When we moved to South Africa, Jenny had gone off to boarding school for the rest of her school life, and from the next year I was gone too, only to live at home again over three years later, when my parents moved to

Johannesburg. Now, just after Elsie had her children back, here I was, planning to go away again. To add insult to injury, I had gone to boarding school not from my first year of high school, as was the custom for English-speaking children in Lichtenburg on account of there being no English-medium high school in the town, but a whole year earlier. I had suggested this myself (and my parents had sadly but readily agreed) because of the very bad fit between me and Lichtenburg Primary School. So in the big reckoning of things, which Elsie made, and made publicly, not only was I suggesting that she lose me, but she had already had an unfair burden of having lost me before. For the rest of her life, she would tell people that I 'more or less' left home at the age of 10 and, apart from a brief respite, never returned home. This was more or less – more more than less – true.

From my point of view, in all this painful conflict my father was magnificent. He supported my wish to go to Cape Town, and helped make sure that it happened. We all stuck to the cover story that I was getting away from Arsenic and Old Lace, but I suspect that my father, at some level, knew that another reason, and possibly even a more fundamental one, was that I felt I had to get away from my mother. The problem was not that I did not get on with her. Quite the contrary. I knew a mama's boy when I saw one, and I saw one in the mirror. It is completely true that I needed to get away from Granny and Auntie Lea, and away from the cliques of King David in which I never felt at home. But, most of all, I had to force myself to grow up away from the mother I loved so desperately. I had to make my own life, and I felt in my bones that if I stayed in Johannesburg I would never grow up. I knew that leaving would hurt my mother deeply, and it did, but the only way I could think of getting away was with this difficult, traumatic and, for me, wonderfully exciting breach. Years before I had been sent to big school without the cushion of the nursery school experience I still believe I really needed. Now here I was, launching myself off into the unknown of a university and a town I had never seen, as far away as it was possible to get and still stay in the same country. At the time I had no sense of how, in breaking with my mother at this age, I was at the same time reproducing a decision she had made about my education all those years ago, in pre-petrol rationing Rhodesia.

I was far too young for university. I had just turned 17, and I was a young and in many ways very naive 17-year-old, not that I would have described myself as naive in those days. My parents did not have a great deal of money, and I was desperate to get good bursaries so as to lessen any burden on them. While still in my last year of school, I applied for a generous and prestigious bursary to study law. The bursary was given by a huge corporation based in downtown Johannesburg. As a short-listed candidate I went to the imposing offices of the company for an interview. Despite the fact that my father worked in an office block not far from this company's, and that office politics was discussed every evening at home, I went in completely unprepared. I had not researched the organisation at all, and I had not made the obvious link that if they wanted to train young lawyers, they probably wanted these lawyers, or some of them, to work for the company. When asked about what kind of law I was interested in, I didn't have a clue. I mumbled something about going into my own law practice.

I was a child. But I was a child who hurled himself out of the nest, ripped off the band-aid joining him to his mother and his family, and threw himself out into the world.

Luckily for me, it was, I think, the best decision of my life. I struggled in my first year at university, passing all courses but none of them well (much to the delight of an envious cousin, who cheerily informed me that it was a known fact that people who did very well in high school academically all struggled at university), but I adjusted slowly and really came into my own, or what I thought was my own. I was off into the world. To be honest I did not think that much about what a loss this was for my mother. I had given up being her little man, and she would have to get over it.

To add insult to injury, I suspect, I travelled not only from Johannesburg to Cape Town when I went to university, but also from one social class to another. I don't know quite how it happened, but I fell in with a group of people at university all of whom were interested in classical music. I had wanted a piano and to study music as a child, but my parents said we could not afford this, and petrol rationing did make things tricky. Now my friends were people who had studied classical music all their lives and played instruments proficiently. Many of them lived in draughty old houses with shabby furniture and smelly, overindulged dogs – the epitome of old money. When I read Curtis Sittenfeld's novelisation of the life of Laura Bush,[2] I identified with the main character's introduction to the fictionalised Bush family, who were clearly old money but seemed to take a patrician delight in the lack of comfort of their summer home. I learned from my new friends that really rich people act poor and that hopeless arrivistes, like my family, were the only people who would sink to the comfort of fitted carpeting. Friends in this group would in time flit off to Oxford and Cambridge in time-honoured upper-class or colonial service Church of England tradition.

I did not choose my friends on the basis of class or religion, and I had my share of Jewish and Afrikaans friends (there were almost no people at UCT in those days who were not white), but I was dazzled by this new world, which seemed to accept me more than King David had done. Not that all of this was without its edges. One day, with two of my friends, I was making a joke in a broad Yiddish accent and one of them interrupted me, saying, 'Just stop that, Leslie. Stop it. Stop it.' I honestly don't think that this cruel intervention was anti-Semitic or had anything to do with social class, new money or old. The friend in question was depressed and irritable, and not known in general for tact. But, I am ashamed to say, the comment really cut me – why else would I remember it today? It said to me that although I was clever and interesting enough to be part of the group, I would never really belong and be accepted. I had escaped the 'there' of King David, but I would never fully be 'here'. Story, in some ways, of my life. And story of Elsie's life too.

After the war, Elsie took the outrageous step of going overseas for a few years. Off she went on her own, a single woman, to live and work in bombed-out London. This was many years before gap years and ramblings around the world to find oneself. She went off to a foreign country where she knew nobody, unimaginably far from Johannesburg and the shtetl of just a generation earlier. Brave, foolhardy, risky, probably hurtful to her mother, but it all sounds remarkably familiar. Like son, like mother.

Elsie had a number of clerical jobs in England, the longest being with the Jewish Board of Deputies, which she really enjoyed. Her boss was a senior figure in the organisation, a scion of Anglo Jewry, and he was kind to Elsie, inviting her for weekends to his country house with his family. He was also, Elsie told me, inclined to 'tapn' her.[ii] She didn't like this 'tap-tap-tapning', as she described it, but she had to put up with it. There was no question at the time of her making any complaint about this.

London after the war was cold, wet and dirty, with legendary pea-souper fogs, which Elsie used to speak about often. She was often cold and did not always have enough money to put in the gas heater. Bathing was allowed once, and occasionally twice, per week at the grubby boarding house where she stayed. But she loved it. She described being taken on dates by a South African artist and photographer. He took her to look at bombed-out buildings and pointed out the beautiful colours and patterns in the rubble. 'The man was mad,' Elsie would say. 'These were ruins of houses where real people used to stay.' But she was thrilled by a different way of seeing the world.

She loved sitting drinking tea and eating something at the Lyons Corner Houses, with their waitresses known as 'Nippies', then really in their heyday, serving good quality food and drink at low prices. When, as children, Jenny and I had enjoyed Lyons Maid ice creams, including the two-in-wonderful Mivvi, in Rhodesia, Elsie would sometimes talk about the link to the Corner Houses, which were owned by the same J Lyons and Co. Recently I read and enjoyed a popular history of the company entitled *Legacy* by Thomas Harding.[3] The descriptions helped me

ii 'Tapn' is Yiddish for grope or feel.

visualise a young, pale, Elsie Cohen, sitting drinking tea alone in a bustling cafe on a grey London day. I had one of those moments of wanting to phone her to tell her that I had found this book and its related website so that she could read the book, enjoy it and reminisce. It made me think of other books she and I had enjoyed together and especially Jung Chang's *Wild Swans* which, like *Legacy,* was a non-fiction family saga spanning generations.[4] Elsie would have loved reading about the Gluckstein family and their journey from poverty and oppression in Germany through a long route to being so influential in shaping the outlines of the post-war London she had revelled in.

London was certainly not all excitement and minor setbacks. A young woman travelling on her own at that time (and probably today) was seen as vulnerable and fair game. There were unwanted advances to fight off, as I have mentioned, and a reputation to try to maintain. There was the cold, the wet, the fog. Elsie had run away, but she still had herself to maintain and keep together. But she could (and did) do it. And when I think of this act of bravery, this breaking of convention, I can't help remembering that a generation later, irony of ironies, I also ran away, as far and fast as I could. The running has been a lot of fun, and I have such a good life, but here's the thing: just like my mother, I ran and I ran and I ran. The pace at which I work and live my life is testament to how I am still running. But of course, the further you run away from home, the further you run from yourself. I'm working on trying to find my way back. Paradox of paradoxes, though many have helped me with this, Elsie is one of them.

8 | Coming home

My father died suddenly in 1983, and my mother was a widow at the age of 58. He lived longer by far than Elsie's brother Hymie and her brother-in-law Alec, who both died in their 40s, and my cousin Stanley, who died in his early 30s. The family's anxiety about Elsie's being a very young widow was therefore misplaced to an extent, but 58 is still young. My father lived to see both his grandsons, Jenny's children, but died before I had children.

The fact that my parents had such a happy marriage, despite many difficulties along the way, is something I treasure and am grateful for. Partly because I was so close to my mother, I was much further away from my father when he died, and this is something I still regret, but there is so much I have from him that is not to regret. Elsie was devastated by her loss, as was my grandmother – it is no easy task to bury your only son. Almost immediately, though, Elsie had a battle on her hands, as Granny and the Buchenwald Chicken decided that as my father was now dead, the best plan was that they move permanently into my mother's flat with her. It was a large flat and they could each have their own room. Their plan was that they would all settle into a kind of toxic but comfortable intergenerational mourning, tended to by Anna Mothupi, Elsie's long-suffering domestic worker, and one of the few people who knew how to handle the vicious old women.

How did Elsie handle the demand for creating an intergenerational commune, akin to a Johannesburg suburban equivalent of a Lorca play?

I worried that she might just succumb to the pressure, as she had done to varying degrees (to her cost and ours) throughout her long marriage. She proved herself made of sterner stuff, but went to some rather extreme lengths to get done what needed to be done. She was absolutely clear that she would not have Granny and the Chicken come and live with her. She would visit them, take them out on weekends, and tend to their needs, but she was not going to have them live with her. Elsie's sister Hannah, herself a widow now, and to whom Elsie felt close, came to stay, but there were still two free bedrooms in the flat. Saying no to the old ladies felt impossible, so there was only one thing to do: move to a smaller flat.

Not long after my father died, I went to Johannesburg for a few days to visit Elsie, and she took me along to see a flat she was interested in. In my view, everything was wrong with this flat, including the fact that a huge shopping centre was about to be built just a few metres away from it. The estate agent was, like Elsie, a Johannesburg widow, but a good bit older than Elsie. She was also a distant relative. Using all the rhetoric of concern for the welfare of a distant relative in need, the estate agent put on a virtuoso performance of how urgent it was that Elsie sign immediately to secure this highly desirable property. This story is like many others about estate agents, and there was indeed something of a cliché about the whole situation, but what shocked me, and made me realise how deeply Elsie had been affected by her bereavement, was how completely docile she was in this woman's hands. Had I not been there, I have no doubt (and Elsie herself had no doubt) that she would have signed there and then. Needless to say, I was not the estate agent's favourite for shouting loud just as she was moving in for the kill. But who gets killed? The ones who are weakened and separated from the pack. Elsie was alone. She had her children and grandchildren, Anna Mothupi, and her sisters and other relatives, but she was so alone in her grief. She may have been in the process of manoeuvring her way out of being invaded by the toxic old ladies, but before my eyes she almost succumbed to the pushing and shoving of another unscrupulous older woman. Old habits, alas, run deep.

In the event, Elsie solved the problem by moving into a smaller flat in the same block where she lived. Now there were only two bedrooms – one for her, one for Hannah, and none for you know who. She continued caring for those old women and dealing with their attacks, and arranged for them to move into a comfortable aged home. The Chicken developed Alzheimer's and in a radical reversal of character, all the sweetness and kindness that she had been repressing for years now emerged as her brain's frontal lobe withered away. She became compliant and sweet, and a favourite of the care staff at the home. Granny, for her part, softened too, and even began thanking Elsie for what she did for her.

Jenny and her family were in the process of emigrating to Australia, and Elsie wanted to move to Cape Town to be closer to me and my family once they were gone, but she dutifully delayed her move until Granny died. Elsie cared for this woman to the end, fulfilling to the letter the injunction her own mother had given her all those years ago. She did leave Auntie Lea behind, but by that stage, she felt that Lea's capacity to recognise her was completely diminished. Nevertheless, she felt a bit guilty about putting her own needs above those of a woman who had tormented her for over 30 years.

I wish I could say that I felt ambivalent about my mother's move to Cape Town in 1994, but that would not be true. I was dreading it. I had run away and run away, and until her dying day, Elsie never forgave me for having married out of the faith, and for having two children who, technically, were not Jewish, because in Judaism, religious status is inherited from the mother. My father had been amazingly supportive about my decision to marry 'out', and given Elsie's own marginal status in the Jewish community, I had not anticipated quite how hurt she would be by this or quite how badly she would behave. She railed at me, shouting, 'The blood of Eli is in your veins.' I had no idea who Eli was and what his blood was doing in my veins, and for some inexplicable reason I was reminded of the title of a film I had never seen, *Who is Harry Kellerman and Why is He Saying Those Terrible Things about Me?* Luckily,

I managed to restrain myself from informing Elsie of this facetious connection, but it does speak to my adolescent reaction to her upset.

Elsie behaved badly about my decision to marry out, both before and after the event, but she tried her best to be reasonable and forgiving. In some ways this made things much worse. I found myself at times wishing that she had done what many lesser people in her position did – cut me off, refused to speak to me, even sat shiva for me as though I was dead. Instead, mixed in with all the kindness was the drip-drip-drip of disappointment and disavowal, with what felt to me awful and cruel things popping up almost by themselves into what otherwise felt like ordinary conversations.

On the wedding day itself Elsie was magnificent, as were her sisters, who came all the way to Cape Town for the wedding, were kind, and behaved themselves. It really helped that by the time I got married (and, later, divorced) our extended family was inured to scandals, marryings out and the like – it helped to be the youngest cousin. I was unable to top the marrying out of one of my cousins, though, who not only married out but had the distinction of having a Catholic nun for a mother-in-law – her mother-in-law had taken orders after being widowed. By comparison my marriage to Sally, a non-observant Anglican, was small potatoes.

If my mother never forgave me, there is much, I realise, that I am still deeply angry with her for. Although this changed later, and dramatically so, she really struggled to accept my children, and I found it hard to feel that they were being rejected through no fault of their own. In the Jewish tradition, Alison was named for my late father, and I remain pleased and proud about this decision to this day, but it did not seem to mollify Elsie, not that that was ever the primary aim with naming.

When Alison was about three months old, Sally and I went on a trip first to Johannesburg and then on to Zimbabwe to introduce the new grandchild to our mothers and siblings. There is no question that Sally and I were anxious and probably over-attentive parents to our precious new child, and when the three-month-old baby burst into very loud tears after being handled roughly and spoken to very loudly by a visitor who was never known for her softness, subtlety and tact, we did rush in to comfort our fragile child. 'Poor thing,' proclaimed Elsie to all the assembled tea guests, all of them Jewish women of a certain age, 'she doesn't like Jewish people.' I cannot begin to count the ways in which this stung me. It seemed hopeless to point out, although I did, that Alison's godmother, and still one of my dearest friends, was not only Jewish but very serious about her Judaism, as she remains to this day, or that we had many friends who were Jewish. This would get us straight into the 'Some of my best friends are Jews' rabbit-hole, and there's really no decent way out of that one. Elsie was right, of course, that I struggled with my Jewishness, as did she, but she had pushed me somewhere rather awful and I felt deeply misread. It is not for nothing that I have, in my atheist way, celebrated every Passover and New Year (eating a lot but observing the occasion nevertheless) since I left home at 17.

The disapproval waxed and waned, but it was always there, and it seemed to me that the story was more about betrayal than about religion itself. One Thursday evening, Elsie phoned me and said, rather aggressively, 'What do you say?' 'I don't know what you mean?' I replied. 'What do you say? What do you say?' I knew I was expected to say something, and that I was being tested (and failing) but for the life of me I didn't know what the thing was that I had to say. Eventually, after multiple, and increasingly exasperated 'What do you say?', Elsie shouted, 'You say, "Good shabbos".' Now, we had never been a family ritually to say 'Good shabbos' as a Sabbath greeting to one another every Friday evening over the phone, although there are plenty of families that do. But there was another, technical problem, as I took some relish in pointing out to my mother on this occasion. It was Thursday evening. Nobody says 'Good shabbos' when it is not shabbos. I tell this, of course, partly as a funny story against Elsie, but there is also a part of me, with the benefit, and the cost, of distance, time and her death, which feels desperately sad for her. I had done it – I had run away, cut her off, married out, broken her heart. Try though she might to forgive and to accept, and she did try, I was lost, lost, lost to her.

Elsie certainly did not have the copyright on bad behaviour. For much of my life, though I was an adult, I behaved towards her with the casual cruelty of an adolescent. Anybody who knows my younger daughter, Rebecca, knows that from a very young age and until this day, she has been very sceptical of received wisdoms, and is especially wise to the shenanigans of manufactured piety. We sent our daughters to a state school, but there was a strong and, in my view, stickily coercive and saccharine ethos of Christianity in this notionally non-sectarian institution. Alison was once advised to be the little light of Jesus in her father's dark home, which did not sit well with this heathen father. Many of the proponents of Christianity at the school – teachers, other pupils, and parents – went in for what I saw as a kind of commercialised, New Age-y born again-ism, very different from what I saw as the demanding and substantial Christianity practised by religious friends I greatly admired and still do. Accepting Jesus as your personal saviour, in this context, felt to me like a kind of religious Get Out of Jail Free card (many of the most pious girls were also bullies in their spare time), and a guaranteed entrée into what I nastily called The Christian Girls' Dance Club. At every school event, the Christian girls, the most pious ones, would club together and do a dance to the latest pop song, complete with suggestive hip movements, but tastefully done. Don't put your daughter on the stage, Mrs Worthington.

But I digress. Well, not really. I guess what I have been trying to say is that I did not and do not accept this Uriah Heap-style coercion dressed up as piety, not that there may not have been some genuine religious conviction in some of the girls thus practising piety. And in terms of scepticism of all of this, fair or unfair, Rebecca was with me – she was having none of it. So when I casually said to Elsie that Rebecca had accepted Jesus as her personal saviour, in my conscious mind I was making a very funny joke about my respect for Rebecca's astonishing ability to see through cant and humbuggery from a very young age. To my horror Elsie took my comment literally. She said she had always known that Rebecca had been very keen on Christianity and why shouldn't she be, after all? Elsie was deeply hurt, her worst fears realised. And I can now, of course, see the aggression towards her in my ill-judged joke. I still think the idea of Rebecca accepting Jesus as her personal saviour, at that age and under social pressure she would never buckle under, is nothing short of hilarious. My cruelty towards my mother, however, was far from funny. Worst of all, although I tried my best to explain the joke and to make things better, I think that for a time it put extra strain on the relationship between Elsie and her non-Jewish grandchild. I hurt them both.

My marriage broke up not long after Elsie moved to Cape Town and for a long time I was broken. I was terrified of telling Elsie about the failure of a marriage she had not approved of in the first place, and I waited for the 'I told you so', but it never came. I was worried that, in a macabre and ironic re-enactment of what Granny and the Chicken had planned after my father died, my mother might try to move in on me, take me back as her little man. I knew for sure that I would never have another adult relationship, and I feared slipping back into everything I had run away from – mama's boy.

In the event, Elsie was wonderful. She was supportive but did not intrude, listened to me but never bad-mouthed Sally (I could not have borne that). Best of all, I started to see a change in how she was with the children, who had a lot to bear at this difficult time inflicted on them by their parents. Elsie rose to the occasion. Although things were often difficult (no miracle here), she started, it seemed to me, really to see Alison and Rebecca for the remarkable people they were – far more than as evidence of my betrayal, but living, breathing beings in their own right. Strangely enough, it was in this time that I began to allow myself to see fully what I had been subliminally aware of for some time. There had been major changes in Elsie over the past ten years.

For a long time after my father died, it felt to me that Elsie would never recover. Slowly, however, she began to change. I arrived in Johannesburg once to discover that she had dyed her hair, something she had never done in her life. She looked much younger now that her hair was not grey. Her clothing changed too. I never saw the green and black slacks suit again, indestructible though it was. She told me, and others, that she was in the market for a new husband, that she didn't want to remain alone for the rest of her life. This shocked some people as inappropriate and disloyal to my late father, but I saw it differently. My parents had had a marriage beset with difficulties and constantly in danger of being overshadowed by the bile of the older generation. But it was not for nothing that, to my embarrassment, I used what has become a Shakespearean cliché to describe their marriage as one of 'true minds'. Whatever else (and there was a lot of else), my parents respected each other, each with a real interest in the mind and feelings of the other. The fact that after 32 years of marriage, my widowed mother could step out into the world and say she wanted more from life was a tribute to her marriage and not a disavowal of it. She did not have to prove anything, to remain stuck in a show of mourning to know in her heart just how much she had had, and how much she had lost. Her good marriage allowed her, encouraged her, to move on.

For a while, she went out with a widowed relative of a relative – a man both she and my father had known and liked for many years. Jenny and I hoped that this might lead to something more, but it ended. There were one or two other hopeful-looking possibilities, but nothing developed very far.

More fundamental than Elsie's wish to find a husband, though, was how different she became in the world. The change in physical appearance was dramatic. Here was a woman who had convinced herself and others (including me) that she was ugly, and now she was a stylish dresser and always beautifully turned out. Elsie had astonishingly bright blue eyes ('Royal blue, like Elizabeth Taylor,' people would say) and now these eyes seemed more prominent and noticeable. Her adventures with hair dye were short-lived, but the well-coiffed grey hair seemed to set off her eyes very well indeed.

Of course Elsie, being Elsie, did keep up old habits. Determined never to do what her mother-in-law had done – she would never want to live with us and interfere with our lives – she took up residence in Sea Point Place, an old-age home in Sea Point. This suburb, apart from being the natural habitat of elderly Jewish women, is also the playground of the young and glamorous, and has no shortage of shops offering to beautify you, including hair salons. Trust Elsie to find a really excellent hairdresser, great at cutting hair, but clearly with a serious drug habit and a salon that was dirty and depressing. On one occasion, she insisted that I go to this man to have a hair and beard trim. It was not a good day at the office for him and he cut my neck, not too badly, but enough to draw blood and to hurt. When I told Elsie that I would not be returning for further butchery, her response was, 'Shame, if we don't go to him, who will? The poor man is trying to make a living.' For some reason, this reminded me of an exchange between the hero's parents in the film *Annie Hall*. The father berates the mother for firing the 'cleaning woman'. The mother says she fired her because she stole. The father's furious response is that the cleaner, being what he called 'colored', had a right to steal, because 'colored' people, being persecuted, had enough trouble in their lives. And, after all, who was she going to steal from if not from her employers?

In a word: if this hairdresser didn't have my throat to cut, whose throat, after all, would he have to cut? Elsie stayed loyal to this man until it was absolutely clear that the injectables had won, but in keeping with the changes happening in her and in our relationship, we laughed and laughed about the situation, and told anyone willing to hear about Elsie's support for this man and his drug habit. Enabling addiction has never been more hilarious.

Another side to this, though, was that after the grief following my father's death, and that of her mother-in-law, Elsie's courage, although there was no question that it was always there, came much more clearly to the fore. If she wanted to have her hair done by a drug addict, so be it. In fact she relished shocking some of her straight-laced friends with stories of what she termed 'the drug abdict', explaining her using one of Granny's many malapropisms. She had always held very strong, and sometimes surprising, opinions. For example, for as long as I can remember she was vocally in favour of women's rights to abortion on demand, being pro-choice before pro-choice became a thing in the 1970s in South Africa. But now she shouted loud, and a lot. She told anyone who would listen what she thought and why she thought it. My particular favourite related to Elsie's decision, after she decided she did not want to drive any more, to use minibus taxis at times. In Cape Town, it is very rare indeed to see white people in these crammed and fast-moving vehicles, vehicles which definitely do have higher accident rates than others, given their common state of disrepair and legendary dangerous drivers. So it was not surprising that other women at Sea Point Place would ask her how she could possibly use these taxis. Elsie's proud response was: 'Why not? Are you scared the black skin will rub off on you?' Trust Elsie to get to what was probably the heart of the matter: the racism and classism of her contemporaries.

She revelled in her stories of how kind everyone was to her, and I am sure they were – it was important to her to treat people respectfully. When I became worried that she was giving money to street addicts with which they would probably buy drugs, she had two responses. The first was that if she chose to give someone a gift, as her own mother had said, the minute the gift leaves your hand, it is no longer your property; it becomes the property of the person who has received the gift. In one fell swoop she had firmly addressed my multi-layered paternalism towards the drug users of Sea Point. What they did with their money, Elsie was saying, was none of my business. The second solution to my worry about her giving money to addicts was that she should rather give them food or other things they needed, but her interpretation deviated somewhat from how I envisioned things. From then on, Elsie made sure that she always had an assortment of delicious sweets in her handbag, and she delighted in telling anyone who would listen that she became known as 'the lollipop lady' to all the addicts, and would be hailed as such: 'Hey, lollipop lady, you got a sweet for me?' Given that many of the addicts were shooting what was colloquially known as 'hard candy',

I doubt that the joke of calling Elsie the lollipop lady (as opposed to the candy man, I suppose) was lost on them.

I think with such pride of this small, elderly, well-turned-out Jewish lady with a handbag riding the Sea Point minibus taxis, and more. But of course there is more to it, and Elsie was not 'cured' of her troubles. Her car was not the most reliable, but the main reason she gave it up was that she remained terrified of driving and hated it. She sternly instructed her granddaughters never to drive on highways because they were too dangerous (an almost impossible injunction to obey in Cape Town). She had got herself into a number of dodgy situations in Cape Town's impossibly narrow streets while trying to take her own advice. We were lucky we never had to face the situation many of my friends have faced, of trying to convince an elderly parent, who has become a hazard on the roads, to give up on driving and all that this means.

Similarly, I was initially shocked at Elsie's decision about where she would live when she came to Cape Town as a healthy and competent 69-year-old (not much older than I am now). She secured a very small sea-facing room in the old-age home. She was absolutely determined not to repeat what Granny had done to her in moving in on her in various ways. Having worked in an office in an aged home earlier in life, she said that the time to go there is when you are well. This gives you a chance to build relationships with people (other residents and staff), and when you become frail, as is inevitable, it will be easier for people to care for you because they know you. Although she was not much of a joiner – she eschewed most social things at the home apart from playing bridge ferociously several times a week – she worked at her relationships with people whose help she might need later. In this she was not being cynical or insincere. She made friendships with people she really liked, but she was also strategic, and why not? And the fact is that much of this was designed as a long-term gift to me and my family. She was all too aware that I was her only child in South Africa, and she did not want to become a burden.

Things got better and better with Elsie – in terms of how she felt about herself, her adjustment to living in Cape Town, and her relationships with all of us – including her grandchildren. She had her bridge and her friends, and she was healthy and active, walking the roughly five-kilometre round trip to the Waterfront a few times a week. Her confidence in her bridge playing improved, and she became sought after not only as a player but as somebody who was a good and patient teacher.

Much to my surprise, not that long after my first marriage broke up, I met and fell in love with Louise, who lived in Johannesburg. When it became time for me to introduce Louise to Elsie, Elsie was thrilled, though she did pull me aside and say, 'She's very nice, dear, but isn't she a bit young for you?' Louise is 18 months younger than me, so we could laugh about this. Elsie adored Louise and the feeling was mutual, and after Louise came to live with us in 1997, things got better.

Elsie turned 80 in 2005. Jenny and Ian came all the way from Australia, and we had a magical time, including a few days away in the country with friends for the birthday celebration. Elsie had the capacity to enjoy absolutely everything. She never tired of eating ice cream and was always up for trying out new varieties. She enthusiastically enjoyed the theatre and the movies, and it was a pleasure to take her there. There was a showing of *Capturing the Friedmans* at the brutally uncomfortable Labia cinema, and from the early moments of this brilliant and upsetting documentary, I felt worried that this film about child sexual abuse allegations might upset her. She loved it, and talked about it afterwards. I was (and am) so proud of this bright, witty woman, afraid of nothing, and so much part of the world, arguing about politics and loving every minute of the argument. She was a brave woman who had found her stride, taking on the world.

It wasn't all so simple, of course, and the wounds were still there. Before she had moved to Cape Town, I was promoted to senior lecturer. I told her the good news while driving her in my car up Adderley Street. She looked at me sideways on, with my long hair and scruffy beard (I have been an academic cliché my whole life), and she said, 'You know,

Leslie, if you look so messy, people won't take you seriously, and you won't get far in life.' When I was promoted to full professor the year after she moved to Cape Town, I took her to a restaurant to tell her the news. 'Look,' she said, 'you can even get chips with your pita here.' I won't pretend that these things did not hurt me – would I ever be good enough? – but the real sadness I feel is for her. Here she was, this intelligent woman (brighter, by my own, admittedly biased, reckoning than most academics I know) who somehow had participated in never finishing high school, and felt she had never been taken seriously as a woman of substantial and serious opinions. And I had had it so easy. Which I had – I had gone to the university of my choice, studied what I felt like, fell into a job quite quickly, and was promoted fast. In no small part, to add insult to injury, because of her. She was no Goodwill Book matron sacrificing herself for the next generation, but in some ways this was exactly what happened. I was visibly successful, and it hurt. Thinking about my mother's envy towards me, my own envy towards my children, or the envy any parent may feel towards their child is not an easy thing to do, but there it was.

This did not stop Elsie for one second when it came to beaming genuinely proudly and delightedly at my inaugural lecture, complete with the pomp of academic robes – a world she would have felt so at home in if she had had, or had given herself, a chance. And at the core of it, I came to think, was her having to reckon with the consequences of the sacrifice she had made all those years ago. We don't know, and won't ever know, whether she fell or was pushed, but the loss was real.

All of this makes her enthusiasm for life, her pleasure in everything, all the more remarkable. She had lost and was losing, but she was also fully aware of her privilege. In some ways her joy was also an enactment of responsibility – she would not take all she had for granted. This was the Elsie that many of my friends knew, this woman who would tell people that she loved being old. She was sad to have lost my father, and she always acknowledged it, but when you are old, she said, you can do just as you please, nobody can tell you what to do, and you can get away with everything. She did sometimes take things much too far with her new-found confidence. Although she was much more accepting of me than she had been, and the fact that Louise is half-Jewish and identifies culturally as Jewish (though technically she isn't) really helped Elsie get away from the idea that I was what is nastily termed a 'self-hating Jew'. But Elsie did love a good argument; she would attack an argument with the same pleasure she attacked a chocolate ice-cream cone. And issues Middle Eastern and Muslim were a great place to start. I honestly don't think that she was Islamophobic (and I have many relatives who are), and she really liked some of my Muslim friends, but discussing the injustices or otherwise of the occupation of Palestine was always a guaranteed way to get me going, and I fell for it every time. After 9/11 and the Iraq war, the issue of women wearing the hijab became a hot topic, with a huge amount of scaremongering about people – especially dangerous men – covering themselves to avoid being recognised as they committed violent acts. Elsie firmly declared, looking me straight in the face, and just waiting, waiting for me to explode, that she didn't think the 'kebab' was a good form of dress. You could never know who or what was under there and besides – and here she looked at me even more intently – didn't I think that forcing women to cover themselves like this was a form of oppression and interfered with their liberty? I could have strangled her. Sometimes I rose to the bait, and sometimes I did not, but she had great fun seeing me squirm. Those twinkling Elizabeth Taylor eyes, and recognising that we were really fighting – this was such fun.

She did, I am embarrassed to recount, take her fights to the streets as well. One day, she was sitting on a bench at the Waterfront where we were doing her shopping. A woman who was completely covered from head to foot, with dark lace covering even her eyes, came to sit down next to Elsie. 'Do you like wearing that thing?' Elsie asked in the tone of a schoolmarm. 'I get frightened when I can't see people's faces. Don't you think you should at least show your face?' The woman was silent. Elsie tried again, and again got no reply. She turned to me and said, gesturing to the woman sitting absolutely motionless next to her, 'Poor thing. I suppose she doesn't understand.' I did my best to get Elsie out of there, and fast. Once we had all calmed down, Elsie was well able to laugh at what she had done. I didn't think this exonerated her in any way, but it did show that even though she was a woman of very strong opinions, she could also think about and reflect on what she may have done wrong.

It was often sheer fun to be with Elsie for these years, and her capacity for gratitude and enjoyment made everything so much easier. It could have felt burdensome to see her every week and take her out – and it was – but mixed in with the exercise of responsibility was much real joy. I've thought long and hard about the irony that Elsie only really came into her own after the man she loved so much died. And I am well aware that many people would welcome a story about this, which would be compelling but, as far as I can judge it, untrue. This is the story of the dutiful woman, oppressed by her husband and his mother and aunt, but really only finding herself once they were dead and buried, and good riddance to them. This story fits neatly with so many others, but I honestly think that it would amount to an 'honest trifle', to use the phrase from *Macbeth*. Of course it was true that Elsie was now free from the burden of having to look after my father, Granny and the Chicken, and I think her relief at having served her time in thrall to the old women was unambivalent. My father had not been an easy man and had taken setbacks later in his life hard – he could be cantankerous and angry. I don't think she missed that. But she also mourned and mourned what they had had together and she never had again – and, to me, this is what made the joy stronger. She knew, this clever, sensitive, insightful woman, what loss was. She had faced it and was still facing it. And it was precisely that constant connection with loss that made the many good and bright things better and brighter.

9 | Avoiding surgery

Getting old is difficult, my mother used to say, but the alternative is worse. She repeated this often, and now, so do I. Of course, she had to deal with both the getting old part and the alternative. She was so well at 80 that it's hard to think that she didn't live for another 20 years. Her sister Babe lived until she was 103, outliving Elsie by a number of years although she was 10 years older than Elsie. But life happens, and so does death.

Elsie started developing stomach pains. We began the rounds of consulting health professionals. My mother had always had a stated predilection for Jewish doctors, and in fact had expressed to me her upset that the family doctor I had chosen to go to was not Jewish. But when it came to it, she started going to a white, Afrikaans, rugby-playing doctor, an outlier in her area. This man was gruff and distant, and though I have no doubt about his competence, he was a far cry from sweet, understanding Dr Levy of Salisbury days. I had gone to him once at Elsie's recommendation when my own doctor was ill, and very shortly after my first marriage had broken up. I was feeling weak and vulnerable. I had a palmar wart, which was growing fast and was quite painful, and I wanted advice about what to do about it. Without discussing options and without preparing me for the brief but intense pain I was about to undergo, the doctor applied liquid nitrogen to the wart. I flinched. 'Bite the bullet,' he said. He did not tell me what would happen next, and through the ensuing weeks I dealt with a sore palm with a blackened spot, and eventually, finally, when the wart was loose enough, I was able to pull it off at its root. I did not understand why Elsie was going to this doctor when there were other choices, but I was reminded of the issue of the hairdresser with the bad haircut. What was there still lingering about her not allowing herself to get proper care?

The doctor did various investigations, but it was soon obvious that he had Elsie down for a neurotic old lady (which she was), and as a result did not take her complaints seriously (which was unprofessional but not uncommon). After much goading on my part, Elsie came round to getting a second opinion, and off we went to consult with the doctor recommended by Elsie's friends. The waiting room was large, peopled by old women and men, most of them clearly Jewish, and there was a lot of loud conversation. The reception staff were also chatty, and the whole place had the atmosphere of a market. The subject matter of the talk was often somewhat depressing: 'Well, my dear, my lungs are just finished.' 'The next thing I knew I was lying there on the street – on the street!' 'It's in the family so what can I do?' Despite the subject matter, the atmosphere seemed to me to be quite jolly – everyone seemed to be part of a shared community of suffering, but doctor would help as best he could.

Elsie insisted that I accompany her into her consultation with the doctor. He spoke to her as though she was about five years old and not too bright with it; a patronising man who seemed so self-satisfied that I wanted to punch him. Still, he was better than the rugby player. Suspecting diverticulitis, he referred Elsie to a consultation with a dietician he worked with.

It was the height of Sea Point summer when we went to the dietician. From most of those occupying the waiting room it looked like the practice focused on helping people lose weight. The door opened and there was a young woman, very tanned, in the shortest possible minidress with a low-cut halter-neck and a full, tanned back showing. Elsie shot me a look. I could hear my father's voice in my head, saying, 'Look at the dress she's almost wearing.' In the event, the young woman was competent and professional, and she gave Elsie good advice about eating a high-fibre diet and good dietary hygiene, advice I knew there and then

Elsie would not take. Elsie had been told by somebody that you treat diverticulitis with low-fibre food, white bread, and none of the fruit and vegetables that she loved. In short, nursery food of the kind given to Victorian children was to become the order of the day.

The stomach pains got worse and worse. Elsie began to tell everyone who would listen, and those who wouldn't, that she was hanging on and avoiding surgery for her deteriorating health. I had been present at every medical consultation she had been at, and there had never been any discussion of surgery. There was no surgery to avoid. When I pointed this out to her, she was adamant. I had many jokes at her expense about this, much to my shame as I write this.

Things got worse and she was losing weight. There was a crisis around inflammation of the intestines, and there was a worry that she would have a rupture in the intestines. She was admitted to hospital for a few days where she was fully examined, X-rayed, prodded and poked, and sampled for blood to within an inch of her life. The hospital stay was not designed to be therapeutic in itself, but Elsie felt much better for having been taken seriously. I was hoping that we had reached a turning point.

We had not. Elsie continued having pains. We went back to her GP and consulted a few others, taking our portfolio of X-rays and pathology reports with us, but no explanation for her feelings of pain and general malaise, accompanied by some weight loss, were forthcoming. The doctor who had referred her to hospital helpfully informed me that my mother was a 'neurotic old woman'. Well, that came as a revelation. When I suggested to him that it was quite possible that a person could be simultaneously 'a neurotic old woman', and have a painful health condition that could benefit from treatment, he was not impressed.

We went on like this for about 18 months. I lurched between being sympathetic with Elsie and berating her for 'avoiding surgery', between support and overt aggression. I don't know why it took me, a psychologist, so long to come to this decision (though I have my suspicions), but eventually I suggested to Elsie that we consult a psychiatrist who also had a strong interest in medical conditions. It was obvious that Elsie was anxious about her health, and she had struggled with anxiety her whole life, but perhaps she was masking a serious depression, given that there seemed to be no obvious medical reason for her ongoing pain and weight loss. Wonderful Elsie, unlike so many of her generation and others, had no qualms at all about going to a psychiatrist.

It was one of those beautiful, late summer days in Cape Town when I took Elsie to see Michele Rogers, a psychiatrist whom I knew slightly, and who was known to be a good diagnostician, as at home with 'physical' conditions as with brain disorders and emotional difficulties. We entered her office, which was furnished like a slightly old-fashioned comfortable sitting room, putting our large sheaf of X-rays and medical reports on the floor beside us. Michele is warm and attractive, and she unobtrusively asked us why we were there. I offered to leave so Elsie could speak privately but she was having none of it. In fact she asked me to start. I told Michele about the history of vague complaints that a number of doctors had said had no cause, about a history of anxiety (in Elsie and in our family), and about my worry that Elsie might be depressed.

Michele turned her open face to Elsie and started to take a history. The more Elsie talked, the more happy and animated she became. Michele was a skilled listener and seemed genuinely interested, and here was my notionally depressed mother becoming more and more animated, witty, funny and utterly charming. There could be nothing that looked less like the behaviour of a person with depression. I felt a bit embarrassed at my completely obvious misdiagnosis – no seriously depressed person could fake the engaged animation that Elsie was showing. She just needed the right listener. And for months, if not forever, that right listener had not been me. Eventually, Michele looked through all the bits of paper we had brought along, one by one, and then she turned to the X-rays. She didn't have a light box (she was a psychiatrist) but just to get an idea, one by one she held the X-rays up to the light. They had been taken 18 months previously in the hospital, and we had been toting them around to various health personnel ever since. She turned to us, and said with quiet but direct clarity, for which I will always be grateful, that there was evidence of a lesion on the lung, and that we would have to have a repeat X-ray now to confirm her suspicions. We knew that she was pretty sure Elsie had lung cancer, which was later confirmed. She showed us the lung X-ray (which I had never looked at myself) and there, absolutely clearly, was a well-defined spot on the lung. And it had been there for over a year. The X-rays had been available to every clinician in the hospital and every person Elsie had consulted since. It had taken a psychiatrist to diagnose my mother with lung cancer.

It's hard to catalogue the range of feelings I had in that moment. I felt embarrassed about my worry about depression, about my not having diagnosed lung cancer myself, even though I have no training at all qualifying me to do so. I felt enormous relief, as the pieces of a puzzle going on for years suddenly fit seamlessly into place. I felt (still feel) rage at the arrogant health-care professionals who had judged my mother and her neuroses without doing the basics of looking at the medical evidence (why bother, after all? This was just another neurotic old biddy in a long line of neurotic old biddies). I felt terrible, crippling regret because Michele thought, though she could not be sure, it was likely that the cancer that could have been dealt with by surgery 18 months ago had mestastasised and spread. Michele estimated that Elsie was probably in Stage 4 cancer by now – way beyond any chance of operability and cure. She referred us to her brother Sean, a pulmonologist, for a full diagnosis and follow-up. In everything she did for us that day, Michele was a good doctor and a good person.

Elsie and I walked out of the clinic into the warm summer day. I took her for lunch at a nearby cafe/pub and we sat outside. I can still see the shadows of the oak trees dappling Elsie's face. 'What do you expect?' Elsie said. 'I'm old. I've had a good life and this isn't the end of the world.' I couldn't stop myself, true to form, from blaming her for having cancer because she had smoked for so many years and I had warned her of this very outcome. But mostly I was comforted by her. She was so well in herself, as though the weight of what she, and she alone, had known all along was there had been taken off her, and she could face the truth. She said there and then, before she had the diagnosis confirmed, that she did not want treatment. She didn't want to suffer to prolong her life, and she would take what was coming to her. Well, here we were. The woman who had spent her life jumping at shadows, beset by worries about things that nobody – even she herself – believed to be real, was now facing down the reality confronting her with composure, and, yes, relief. She could do this.

There followed a quick round of consulting doctors before we settled into a pattern. Sean, whom Elsie found delightful, had a gung-ho, hail-fellow-well-met persona, which belied a soft and caring interior. He confirmed Stage 4 cancer, and referred Elsie for ongoing care to an oncologist. To my relief, there were no heroics here. The oncologist respected Elsie's wish to have palliative care only – no chemotherapy, no radiotherapy. She worked closely with St Luke's Hospice, she told us, and would contact them when the time came. In the meantime, she suggested, we should get on with life.

There was a part of me that wanted to round up every person who had disavowed Elsie. I toyed for five minutes with finding a lawyer so we could begin to sue for malpractice all those practitioners who had not bothered to do the basics of their job. But Elsie did not want this, and neither did I. It was time to get on with the next phase of our lives.

10 | Closing in

> Illness is the night-side of life, a more onerous citizenship. Everyone who is born holds dual citizenship, in the kingdom of the well and in the kingdom of the sick. Although we all prefer to use only the good passport, sooner or later each of us is obliged, at least for a spell, to identify ourselves as citizens of that other place.
>
> Susan Sontag, *Illness as Metaphor*

I have lived my whole life as a healthy person. I had my tonsils and adenoids out when I was five, and I had an operation to repair an inguinal hernia. That's it. Especially because of my work in disability, I know this could change tomorrow. It may already have begun to change – there may already be something lurking inside me that will later manifest as illness or debility.

Over 30 years ago, in my work as a psychologist, I was fortunate to be consulted by an exceptionally articulate and intelligent middle-aged man. Amongst other concerns he had, he worried that he had early onset dementia. Something, he felt, was not quite right. To me, there was absolutely nothing to support his fear. I had seldom met someone so articulate, and whose thinking seemed to be so well organised and controlled. But in order to respect his experience, and to get a more expert view, I decided to refer him for a second opinion. Neuropsychology was not very developed as a field in Cape Town in those days, and I referred my patient for an assessment to a neurologist, writing in my referral letter that I could find no evidence of dementia, but wanted to be absolutely sure. Not unexpectedly, I got a rather exasperated response from the neurologist, who also found not a shred of evidence of dementia, and seemed irritated that I had wasted his time. I worked with the patient for a number of years, and never once in those years did I revise my view that he did not have dementia, but we did discuss in some detail his fear of dementia and of what it might have been about in terms of how he felt about himself and his future.

Many years later, and long after we had stopped seeing each other, I read a newspaper article about a freak accident that had befallen this patient's brother, to whom he was very close. It is always tricky as a psychologist to make contact with a former patient, especially after many years, but on balance it felt like the humane thing to do and I sent a brief letter of condolence. A few weeks later I got a letter from my former patient's wife, who was also a health professional. She thanked me for my concern, and informed me that my patient could not himself reply as he had dementia, now quite advanced. She had been going through his things, my patient's wife wrote, and she had seen a copy of my correspondence with the neurologist all those years ago. She commented that perhaps I had known something about the dementia all along.

I had not known this, and it is of course completely possible that my patient had an irrational fear of dementia when he was well, but then did indeed develop dementia later. But to my mind, though the rational part of me says this may just be magical thinking, something fell seamlessly into place. This man, with his exceptional insight, intelligence and self-knowledge, had known all along, I thought, that there was indeed something going wrong. Early dementia is more difficult to diagnose in highly intelligent and articulate people than in others, as the intellect and all it has built over the years can mask and compensate for the decline – this was superbly portrayed in John Bayley's now-controversial memoir of his wife, the novelist Iris Murdoch.[1] Although I was very sad to hear about my former patient's dementia, part of me felt vindicated for taking him seriously. But I had also worked with him on the assumption that he was not dementing, and I wonder now to what extent I disavowed something that was not only real to him but was also empirically true, but not yet measurable and noticeable to others. I don't think I behaved badly or unethically in this case, but it has forced me to think about what I might have been doing completely unintentionally (and with, in fact, the best of intentions). Along with everyone else, I may have been saying that I knew better than he did. He thought he was in the kingdom of the sick, and he may well have been right, but we would not countenance this. We revoked his passport and insisted he was really in the kingdom of the well, rendering him, to all intents and purposes, stateless and in limbo.

For Elsie, receiving the cancer diagnosis was many things, including a relief and a vindication. She had for years known, or felt, that she was ill when others thought she was well; she had known that she was dying as she struggled with the panic attacks for which at that time neither she nor anyone else had a name. She had decided to live after my father died and had taken on life with gusto, but had been avoiding surgery for years. Although the concept of 'avoiding surgery' had given us some cruel laughs at Elsie's expense, there was a part of her that always knew in which kingdom she had rightful citizenship, and that was the kingdom of the sick. She was frightened to a degree, she would rather not have cancer but, as she said, 'What do you expect?' She was sick, but she was home. All the nameless flutterings and giddiness of the past, all the feelings of stumbling at the edge of the kingdom of the well, technically in that country but not feeling completely of it, could now be replaced by a calmer foothold of a different place.

The problem was, though, that this migration required of all of us around her to move with her. And I didn't want to. Elsie was wonderfully calm and philosophical about being so ill – a model of mature acceptance. But with her illness came a time of neediness and clinginess, which pulled me back to somewhere I would rather not revisit. One day, we were taking her to the shops, and I wanted to dash in somewhere for a few minutes while Elsie sat safely in the car with Louise, whom she adored. My mother did not want me to leave her to do a simple errand. As much as both Louise and Elsie, I was surprised and frightened at the rage I felt, and expressed, towards Elsie in that moment. 'Just let me go,' I thundered. 'You will be fine.'

Just let me go. You will be fine. There must be a thousand ways of saying these two sentences, and the best of them must be in a calming but reassuring tone, 'friendly but firm', as Dr Spock would have it. But Elsie was not my child and I was not her father – but what was I? The way I said those words calmed nobody, and spoke not to reassurance but to my desire to abandon my mother, to get out of the small banged-up Toyota outside the Silwood Kwikspar and to run as fast as I could, not looking back, not collecting $200 as I passed Go. I had been doing so well looking after her, was doing so well, but here was something I wasn't in control of, as elemental as the rage every parent must feel (and I have felt it) when an infant will not stop crying. I often say that the strange thing about child abuse in some ways is not that there is so much of it but that there is so little. Show me a parent who has not felt rage towards their howling and inconsolable infant and you will be showing me a liar, but somehow most of us overcome the urge to hit out at that tiny roiling vessel of rage. And this is how, unbidden, unheralded and shamefully, I felt towards my mother. I wanted her to shut up, let me go. And I didn't really care whether she would be 'fine' or not. I wanted out. Out of the car, out of her grip, out of a story of caring for her, which I had been trapped in my whole life. You can run (and I had run and run) but you can't hide.

The problem was that I was not nine years old anymore. I was a respectable man in his 50s, invested in shouting loud for all the right reasons but desperate, always desperate to be seen as the nice guy, fair and reasonable. What was I doing turning on a frail woman in her 80s, recently diagnosed with cancer? Surely I had more compassion than that? The problem, of course, was that I feared not that I did not have enough compassion, but that I had too much, that I would be dragged back back back into the eddies of what it meant now and had meant then to care for my mother. Next to me in the car was a feisty and admirable woman – and I did admire her so much – a woman of opinions and character, a woman who had courage. She was facing cancer in the best way possible, a model to others. Yet at the first sign of her vulnerability I worried that she would drown me, that I would lose my footing and be washed back with her somewhere deep and long ago – to a subterranean kingdom I thought I had left behind, but where I remained trapped, it felt, forever. My true story, a version of the boy trapped with his finger in the dike, the story of a life repeating my mother's own history of resentful but complicit self-sacrifice, would re-emerge. It would wash away the carefully crafted but (it felt to me at that moment) false narrative of being a man who stood on his own two feet, a good man, a father, a husband, a professional. Gone, gone, gone. Engulfed by the tidal reality of who and what I 'really' was – a small broken boy not sure where he ended and where his small broken mother began.

In academic circles, we often speak of 'impostor syndrome' – the feeling that many academics have, however competent and even brilliant they might be, that they are not really clever enough and will be found out for the fools they really are. They are not really impostors, of course, and I often say that the only academics, in my experience, who are completely confident of their abilities are not very good academics. But the feeling of being an impostor is powerful and corrosive, and I was feeling like an impostor not in terms of my academic abilities (I have that in spades, but that's another story), but in terms of who I was. A long time ago, the poet Robert Frost said, 'Home is the place where, when you have to go there, they have to take you in.'[2] In that moment (and for many moments before and after) I felt that home is the place where, when you leave there, they don't really let you go.

When we first moved to South Africa in 1966, I had to learn a slew of robust and generally nationalist Afrikaans poems. One I particularly hated was by Jan FE Celliers, ironically a professor at Stellenbosch University, just as I have become. It was called 'Trou' (which means, roughly, loyalty) and it begins:

Trou

Ek hou van 'n man wat sy man kan staan;
Ek hou van 'n arm wat 'n slag kan slaan;

And continues:

Ek hou van 'n man wat sy moeder eer
In die taal uit haar vrome mond geleer,
En die bastergeslag
In sy siel verag.

This is a translation of these parts of the poem:

Loyalty

I like a man who can stand his ground;
I like an arm that can fiercely pound;

I like a man who reveres his mother
in tongue from devout lips mastered,
detesting the bastard breed
to his soul indeed.[i]

Let me count the ways in which I found, and find, this poem offensive. I don't like the nationalism, I don't like the gender politics, I don't like the racism. I can give you a thousand or more academically argued reasons why I don't like this poem. But when I had to learn it as a 10-year-old, it spoke directly to me and my sense of shame. The first few words – 'Ek hou van 'n man wat sy man kan staan' – say it all. 'I like a man who can stand his ground against another man' is how I understood it. This was a poem telling me all the ways a (white, Afrikaans) man should be – and mother's boy that I was, I felt my failure in all of the ways. I felt that I was the last person to stand my ground. I was fearful and weak, and would

i I thank Eduan Naudé for this translation and Ilse Feinauer for approaching Eduan on my behalf.

avoid conflict, despite some evidence to the contrary, even at that young age. I had an autograph book when I was a teenager (we all did), and an Israeli adult I knew wrote in it in Hebrew 'Chazek v'amtez' (this is my transliteration) which is roughly equivalent to 'Be strong and powerful'.[ii] I hated this as much as I hated the Celliers poem, as it also seemed to require from me a manly toughness that I didn't have. I could not be the person who stood up like a man – I was a boy tied to his mother.

As I bolted out of the car that day outside the Kwikspar, with the words 'Just let me go, you will be fine', I felt I was being a different kind of man, the kind of man who is cruel, ignores the feelings of vulnerable people, is inured to the needs of old sick women. Celliers' poem, as it continues, though, has a lesson for me: 'Ek hou van 'n man wat sy moeder eer / In die taal uit haar vrome mond geleer'. 'I like a man who honours his mother / In the language learned from her pious mouth.' I find this exhortation to mother love mawkish, and it makes my flesh creep. Every part of me rails against the cliché of the pious mother as custodian of culture and language, and it doesn't help that the word 'vrome' (pious) is so close to the Yiddish word 'frum', also meaning pious. We were not frum people, and had never been. But a good man, the poet tells me, looks after his weak old mother, with all her softness and frailty.

The problem, of course, was that I was not nine years old, but a grown man of nearly 60. With all my conscious heart I wanted to help my old, sick mother as best I could (and on balance, I believe I did), but I felt almost undone by the strength with which I was resisting doing the right thing. It was, of course, the rage of a nine-year-old boy who had been done an injustice – the injustice of having to care for his mother as a father would a child, or as a good man would care for his wife. I was not a good man at the age of nine – I was not a man at all. I should have been furious and in a rage at the age of nine, but what nine-year-old

---

ii A Hebrew-speaking friend tells me that the term is metaphorical for something like 'Go forth and prosper.' I think it is equivalent to 'May you go from strength to strength.'

can allow himself this fury? What could this fury do to his weak and fragile mother? I had learned about what in the trade we call parentified children in my training as a clinical psychologist, and had certainly seen families with such children (it's not that uncommon in clinical practice), but somehow I had not made the links to myself as I felt them so viscerally now, and in such an out of control way.

In *Able-Bodied* I spoke of how all children feel that things that go wrong with their parents is their fault. To learn that you are not the centre of the universe and the source of all good and bad is a developmental achievement. I also mentioned that, in my case, I think this issue was complicated because my father, being disabled and having chronic pain, clearly had been damaged in some way, and, as any child would, I believed not only that I could cause this damage (look at the evidence!) but also that I could do it again. So how could I possibly allow myself to be angry with my mother's demands when I was just a child, and still dependent on her? I am not a great fan of the 'pressure cooker' model of human emotions – the view, much peddled by mental health professionals and advocates that if you do not express your feelings, they will build inside you until you eventually explode. The metaphor feels just too mechanistic to me, and sometimes an excuse for people to behave cruelly ('I was just expressing my feelings'; 'I was just being honest'). But here I was, having just the kind of explosion of feelings that the pressure cooker metaphor predicts, and it scared me. I also, at this time, remembered something that I used to do to my mother when I was little, but only at times when she was feeling strong, never when she was in her most nervous state. I can see myself now, lying on the parquet flooring in the passage of our Salisbury house, completely still and my eyes open and staring. Elsie would find me like this, and I would not move until she was genuinely distressed, convinced that I was dead or had fainted. I managed to do this a few times before she got wise to me. What can I say? Funny joke. I had it in me to punish her, although I had no words for it then.

My whole life, then, up till my rage outside the Kwikspar (and since), had not been lived as clearly in the kingdom of the well as it might have appeared to have been. I did have that easy way of taking my physical health for granted, as is common with children. As I experience very minor but real symptoms of ageing, like arthritis and hearing loss, I smile ruefully at the 'youth is wasted on the young' adage, because I took so much for granted, as was appropriate then. But I also felt weak, unable, small, and of a different species from the bulked-up men at the gym Elsie took me to. Other boys could speak of wanting to grow big and strong like their dads or other men, but this did not seem like an option for me. And now, with my career established and my children grown, and in a good relationship with a good woman, it was time to man up and look after my dying mother. Part of me, and probably the larger part of me, knew that I could and would do it. But another part felt undone by what was being asked of me.

Years before, I had read Michael Ignatieff's *Scar Tissue*, a remarkable fictional account of a man who falls apart as he cares for his mother with dementia; the trajectory of his life mirrors the insistent decline of the increasingly chaotic brain of his mother.[3] It's hardly surprising that this novel, whatever else its considerable merits were, would appeal to me, with its theme of sacrifice to caring for the older generation. And here I was at the precipice – the edge of the end, the void that caring for Elsie might mean for me.

One of the things that Ignatieff describes so well is how incomprehensible the book's protagonist's life, consumed with care for his mother, becomes to others around him. As his mother becomes more mysterious and difficult to read, so does his life to others. Imperceptibly, he has crossed over a threshold, if not to the kingdom of the sick, because he himself is not ill, but to a fundamentally different, in-between world, a world very real to him but not possible to see from the world of the healthy.

When we talk of youth being wasted on the young, where exactly is the 'waste' we speak of? I think it lies in the unconsciousness that many young people have that their health and physical strength, their vitality and acuity, are all in fact qualities that they are lucky to have and will not stay the same throughout their lives. The waste we speak of has nothing to do with waste, but with the taking for granted of what is, and should be, taken for granted by young, healthy people. There is plenty of time to learn about frailty, about our bodies not effortlessly doing what we want them to do. But the gift that is the effortlessness is not experienced by many young people as a gift – it is simply the way the world is. And given what we as a society do with illness, ageing and disability – we do many things, but here I'm talking about our hiding them away – the world of caring for those affected by illness, disability and ageing is also hidden away.

I did not know it at the time, but some of my Kwikspar rage was not just at my mother (although she bore the brunt of it) but also at all the other people who went about their own lives and could not see or imagine what my family and I had been going through. I had felt this sense of disconnect with others and the world in general, more powerful than a general sense of being out of step with others, once before in my life. This was around the time of my divorce, which came as a shock to me. Not only did I have to grieve for the end of my marriage, it also felt as though everything I had ever known about the world and my place in it was wrong. When I saw others going through their ordinary, predictable lives, there was part of me that could not understand how they could just carry on. Elsie had liked the old Skeeter Davis song called 'The End of the World', with lyrics asking how the world could go on after the end of a love affair. 'Don't they know it's the end of the world?' the song went, 'It ended when I lost your love.' I had always found these lyrics silly and sentimental (and I can see why I did!), but there was indeed part of me that wanted to know how life could go on around me while I stood teetering at the edge of the happy, grown-up world I had created, when everything, it felt, could fall apart.

I am absolutely clear that these strong feelings came from me and from the pull of my own particular past on my particular present. I also got to learn, though, about the otherworldliness that was caused, not by me, but by taken for granted social arrangements about what it means to be a successful, functional adult in the world. Well, not everybody's world, perhaps, but the dominant world I lived and worked in. Part of the problem of care, I came to see, was not the care itself, but the wholesale failure of imagination about what care is. There is probably no parent caring for young children who has not at some time had the experience of the weight of this care being misunderstood – or, more accurately, not seen at all – by others. Women (and it's usually women) know what it means when co-workers (of both genders) become exasperated when the child is sick again, or the childminder is late again, when the reality of care disrupts the rhythms of work. Childless friends (and even some who have older children) complain of feeling abandoned by those who have recently become parents and whose lives are wholly absorbed in the complexities of caring, trying to get enough sleep, and trying to keep a life and household going. These acts of disavowal of care, of its invisibilisation, and of reading the real burden of care into a character flaw of the person doing their best to care, are well known. We have feminist scholarship to thank for showing us how this disavowal of childcare as a reality has had, and continues to have, profound consequences for the life trajectories of many women – millions probably. Though we have come a long way in trying to give childcare its rightful place, with some societies doing better than others, my own experience has been that other kinds of care – like my trying my best to care for Elsie – are far less socially acceptable than women caring for young children, and, indeed, far less imaginable.

During one of the many crises with Elsie's health, I had to make a difficult decision. I was due to attend a meeting in another African country on a mental health project I was lucky enough to be part of. I really liked the principal investigator on this project, an interesting and unconventional psychiatrist from Europe whose work focused on getting much-needed mental health services to low-income communities, and I knew how lucky I was to work on projects like this one. As I was due to leave for the meeting, Elsie became very unwell and very distressed. My first impulse, I am ashamed to say, was to go to the meeting, knowing, as I did, that Louise would, if she had to, step in for me and do whatever was necessary to help Elsie. Louise is not only an exceptionally caring person, but in the politics of all of this, she is a woman. Like my father before me, I could, and did, contemplate running away and leaving the problem of caring for the older generation to my wife. Nothing to see here.

In the event, after discussing things with Louise, I decided not to go to the meeting. These meetings are largely performative, I truthfully told myself; I would show the project team how committed I was to the project by working very hard remotely on it for the next few years, and in fact I did do this. I was sure that the project leader, an unconventional and very caring man, would understand. But it was very hard not to go, and I felt ashamed at not meeting my responsibility by being at the meeting. I told myself sternly not to be silly – this was life. Not long afterwards, I heard from another European friend of mine, who was also working on the project, that the project leader had been angry with me for not being at the meeting; in fact he had said that he did not want to work with me again if this was my attitude. It is a measure of my own sense of shame about my non-participation in the meeting that I have not in the 10 years since the meeting ever raised the issue of my non-attendance with the project leader. I just can't face the idea of a dispute about this. So I have no idea what the project leader did in fact say or feel, or of the extent to which the difficulty was just an interpretation on the part of my friend. I have also not discussed the issue with my friend. What's going on here? I think that between the project leader and my friend, there was something in all of this about Leslie's allowing the needs of his sick mother to overtake the more important needs of the role he must play as a professional man in the world, doing his work as part of an international project that has its own demands and deadlines.

As for me, a big part of the reason for my writing the book I am writing now is that I want to talk about the problems we have in our invisibilisation of, disavowal of, the realities of care. But you know what? I may be writing this book, but I have not had the courage to deal with this issue directly with the people concerned because, try as I may to tell myself otherwise, there is an important part of me that agrees with them. What kind of a man, what kind of successful professional, backs out of an important meeting to look after his mother? Only a weak mother's boy would do this. Only somebody who is an impostor and not a real man at all. I hate writing that and part of me really wants to erase it, because it feels much too totalising. But it is there, a part of me, inside me.

So much has been written about the internalisation of oppression by people in oppressed groups – the ways, for example, that women come to believe that they are weak, that disabled people believe they are disgusting, that Black people believe that they are unintelligent. But part of all of our problem with all of this is that powerful people like me do this too – we keep the cop in our own head alive. As we do this dance of keeping us looking independent and strong, a dance we are often not aware of doing, we make life worse for ourselves and, indeed, get others lower down the pecking order to do the caring on our behalf. If I sound angry about this, it is because I am. I cannot bear the honey-coated nonsense of Celliers' man honouring his pious mother. Honour is easy. It makes you look bigger. Trying your best to do the work of care is much more difficult. I'm by no means clear that I've succeeded at it, but at least I have given it a try.

11 | Scar tissue

Elsie was relieved, as were we, that she had taken the decision all those years ago to move into Sea Point Place. She would get care in a place where she was known and liked – it had been a smart move. She did not seem or feel very ill, and in fact with the diagnosis of cancer she seemed much less troubled by physical aches and pains. She had been recognised, her worries validated, and the pains in her body now had a story. The oncologist was kind and promised Elsie that she would never lie to her, and Elsie (and we) felt that she was in good hands.

Not long after the diagnosis, Elsie had a fall in her room, which upset her but did not seem to hurt her that much. As a precaution, she was moved into the hospital section of the home for a bit, so she could be properly monitored. My heart sank at the bleak atmosphere and the shiny yellow paint on the walls, but Elsie did not seem to mind this. She took on the role of being frail and sick without complaint, and indeed with some gusto. A few nights after she moved into the hospital section, where she was being monitored, she fell hard on the back of the head, and sustained a nasty gash. We took her to the hospital where she was cleaned up, and discharged back to the hospital section of the home.

I was due to do some training in Zimbabwe, and felt anguish about whether to go or not. I decided eventually to go – I would not be that far away, and the home had realised the mistake they had made in not looking after her carefully before. When I was in Harare I got a call from Louise. Elsie had fallen again, this time onto her face, and she needed stitches. She was at the casualty department at the hospital with her. I felt awful. This had happened while I was away. Now I was in Harare having to make the decision to leave the training and run home to mother. There was no real problem, as I simply handed over the training to my more than competent research assistant, and I knew he would do an excellent job. It helped that Alexander Phiri, secretary-general of the organisation I was assisting, said to me, 'Leslie, of course you must go. This is the African way. You are a true African to look after your mother.' This, coming from a Black Zimbabwean to a white ex-Rhodesian, meant a great deal to me. Of all the things that happened and were said to me over the time of Elsie's dying, this stands out as a significant interaction. Here was somebody saying not only that it was all right that I was putting care for my mother first, but also that this made me more of an African. I have thought about this so often since, and the interaction has a particular poignancy for me because Alexander himself died not long after Elsie. He was about my age but succumbed to complications of diabetes; his death was a huge loss for many people.

Recently I was doing yet another training in another African country (work I really love) and I referred to myself as an African. At this, the group erupted in laughter, arguing that as a white person I could not possibly be an African, despite the fact that I was born in Africa and have spent my whole life here. I won't go into the complicated identity politics of this, but this kind of discussion is not atypical. In this ongoing context, I was so grateful to Alexander for making me feel part of something because of my commitment to caring for my mother.

I flew home to Cape Town relieved, but also apprehensive about what I would find.

In some ways, I needn't have worried. Elsie had made herself at home in the hospital where she was stitched up, and although she looked awful – a tiny wizened woman often without her false teeth, yellowish skin and a spectacularly purple forehead – she endeared herself to the staff. She flirted with the handsome young plastic surgeon and established quickly that most of his work was making beautiful young women even more beautiful. Lots more joshing and teasing. She chatted away with nurses and aides, sometimes with a front door voice. She seemed to revel in all of this – she had spent her whole life feeling frail and not properly cared for, and here she had a group of people who took her seriously, and liked her. Some of the staff called her 'brave'. While I do think Elsie was a brave person, this did not look like bravery to me. Elsie was enjoying herself.

Louise and I faced a difficult decision. Elsie had been in the highest care section of the aged home where she lived, and she had had two serious falls in quick succession. She was willing (and she expected) to go back to the home after her hospitalisation, but Louise and I couldn't do it. We arranged that she come and stay with us in our home. We would employ 24-hour carers so she would never be alone – there would always be someone there watching her and making sure she didn't fall again. We didn't plan for how long she would stay, and for a bit I think we thought that in a while she would be better and return to the home. The oncologist had estimated, with all the caveats that such estimations go with, that Elsie would probably live for another six months, if that.

Louise is very good at making places cosy, and she made our spare room, which had once been Alison's bedroom, comfortable and bright. Beautiful French doors led out onto the garden, and we foresaw Elsie sitting cosily looking out at the purple plectranthus and other shrubs. It was a scramble to arrange for the carers, but we used an agency recommended by the oncologist, and we got into a routine of people coming and going. Susan Filtane, who did char work for us after being a carer for the children, knew and liked Elsie, and on the days she was there, she was an important help. The children were in town, as was my lovely cousin Pamie and our close friends Bev and Tony. We could do this.

Jenny, being in Australia, was in the difficult position of caring deeply but being far away. We were on the phone constantly (this was before WhatsApp, so it was a big, expensive deal) and she did her best to help. She was worried about our taking Elsie into our home – 'You are making a rod for your back' – and it was true that we were taking a big step, which might not be reversible. Jenny wanted to protect us, but also respected our decision. I will always be grateful to Louise for making it clear that to her mind, we had to do this. We wanted to do it. We wanted Elsie to get the best care and we thought that would be with us. In reality, though, I honestly can't remember when it began to hit home fully what it meant that we would never send Elsie back to the home.

This was exactly what Elsie had not wanted. After her own experiences with Granny and the Chicken, she had sworn that she would never live with her children. But we didn't feel we had a choice; we did not believe that she would be safe at the home. We did consider letting her go back to Sea Point Place and organising full-time carers for her there, but it was already becoming clear to us that there was a lot of administration regarding carers. They usually depended on public transport, for example, and would sometimes arrive late and harried for their shifts. Louise and I knew that if this happened in Sea Point, we would be fielding frantic phone calls from Elsie at all hours, and with both of us working full time (and me in Stellenbosch to boot), we did not relish the thought of having to drop everything and drive across town to try to sort things out. Elsie was such a mixture of emotions and attitudes at this stage. She was so positive and grateful, so accepting of her situation, but she was also very anxious (who wouldn't be, I guess). She would suddenly demand that we stop whatever we were doing – including work – to attend to something she needed.

Once she was in our house, Elsie's world shrank to the bed she spent most of the time in, and to her little room. She would get up and move around the house and watch TV, all of which she was fully able to do, but she felt safer, I think, in the cocoon of her little room. Like a matron at a British public school, I would march into her room, open the curtains and throw open the French doors to get some air in, and to link the room to the outside. Five minutes later I would return to find that Elsie had told the carer to close everything up, including the security gate, which made the room feel to me like a prison. Exactly whose prison it was, of course, and for whose needs I was so insistent that we needed fresh air and a bracing environment I am not sure.

What I was sure of was that Elsie needed to be with us. It felt much easier having her in our home than anywhere else – no more dramatic call-outs – but, especially in those early days, I would lose myself and become very irritable with her. Just as in the Kwikspar incident, I would suddenly find myself shouting. I was often cruelly sarcastic. I don't know where the words came from but I know that they came from me. Elsie would then say that it was clearly time for her to leave us and to return to Sea Point – she didn't want to be in the way, this was what she had been afraid of, nobody should have this burden. This would enrage me further as Sea Point did not seem to me to be an option, for reasons we had repeatedly discussed. I raged against her suggesting that she leave, when this felt impossible.

I remember a row we had had once in Johannesburg when I was a student and on a visit home from university. I was trying to say to her, as rationally as I could, that I wished she had protected Jenny and me more from the poisonous old ladies who had blighted her life and ours. I remember trying very hard to be rational and grown up, and with my newly found psychological skills (skills I rapidly and repeatedly came to realise are of no value whatsoever when you are trying to argue with your family), I was trying to share (perish the word) with her that I understood that she herself had been in a difficult position, but also that I wished she had done things differently. All those years ago, and I still flinch at the memory of her response, which was, 'Well, I suppose I have just been a bad mother.'

When I try to think rationally about it, I guess this was an honest response, spoken with a kind of resignation. But I was damned if I was going to be caught either agreeing with her – 'Yes, you have been a bad mother' – or disagreeing with her and reassuring her – 'No you haven't, you're wonderful, it's just this one small thing ...'

My parents' joint failure to protect their children from the nasty old women is no small thing, and however difficult it was for them, they should have done better. But they were also wonderful parents in other ways. I did not want to be trapped by Elsie's response and I fought (unsuccessfully) to get out of the trap.

And here I was, in her little prison room with the security gate and curtains closed, feeling trapped again. I could throw her out and abandon her to falling and the ignominy of the impossibly bleak sick-bay, or I must be a good boy. I wanted her to see me as more complicated than either of those things. I wanted to be as good a son as I could be, warts and all, but spare me from being all good or all warts. It's so easy to chalk up what Elsie was doing as 'manipulation' but, as I tell my students when they describe patients as 'manipulative', life must be pretty hard for you if the only way you feel you can get things is by manipulating other people, by being devious, and then never knowing if what you get has been freely given. I think it's more accurate to say that at that stage Elsie and I were both trapped. She was my jailer as I was hers. A big part of each of us wanted out, just as we were searching for a way to be properly in. So this felt like a replay of everything, everything that had ever happened between us, but it was also something new, and terrifying for both of us. Elsie could not stop being ill – the only way out of this for her was death – so I held more power, I suppose. At the time, however, it didn't feel like that. Her illness was what the anthropologist James Scott, in another context, calls a 'weapon of the weak', and I felt she was using it.[1]

As I write this, I worry about giving too one-sided a picture. I want to be clear about how hard this all was for all of us, but that's not the whole story. Earlier, I mentioned Ignatieff's novel *Scar Tissue,* which deals so unflinchingly with scars and with the hurts that cause them. Elsie and I had spent a lifetime of scarring, and being scarred, each by the other, in the dance of mother and son bumping up against each other because we were much too close. But there was (is) a lot more to both of us than the scars.

When my first daughter was a very tiny baby, a friend summed up early parenthood in a way that I quote to every new parent I know: 'It's better and worse than you can possibly imagine.' There is no way to be prepared for the assault that new parenthood is, for the sheer physical schlep of it all. But there are also no words for the wonder of life with a new baby, a life at the edge. I am glad the ordeal of caring for my mother is over, and with hindsight I don't know how we I did it, but it was also one of the best things I have done in my life. I would sign up for it again, despite how hard it was, and in fact, Louise and I did sign up for this kind of experience again, which is something I'll get to later in this book.

We settled into a sort of routine, much of which was full of pleasure and fun, but with an admixture of really awful bits in between. It was important to me to get Elsie out of the house as much as possible, and this involved endless cups of tea at the garden centre nearby (they got to know us well and were always kind), and various treats. Although Elsie could walk, she was weakening, and I got to know which places had wheelchairs available. Trips to see the flowers at Kirstenbosch were hard on my back as I pushed the wheelchair, but always pleasurable. The Waterfront was also a good place to trundle around.

We would try to keep Elsie as involved as possible in managing her own life. I had power of attorney and dealt with her business affairs, such as they were, but if she wanted something from the shops we would try to get her, where possible, to go with us to buy just what she wanted. One day in Pick n Pay she complained of feeling weak and nauseous. I got her to the front of the shop and she sat down. Her whole body seemed to convulse, and she vomited on the floor. I will never forget the look of revulsion and rage of the first shop assistant who saw what had happened. 'What have you done?' she said, looking at Elsie. (Wasn't it obvious?) But the message was clear – Elsie had been a Naughty Girl. I was embarrassed, seriously concerned about Elsie and what this might mean for her ever-deteriorating condition, and also absolutely furious. The mess was mopped away more quickly than were the feelings, but after this it became more difficult to persuade Elsie to get out of the house, much as we felt she needed it.

One day I got a frantic phone call to come home. There was a crisis. Elsie's false teeth were missing. She looked at me with that tiny, sunken face, like a little goblin adrift in the world. We tried to think where the teeth could be. I crawled around and looked under the bed to no avail. Eventually, the hugely embarrassed carer of the day told me that Elsie had vomited (yet again) and that, as usual, the carer had managed to catch the vomit in a bucket and had flushed the vomit down the toilet. Could the teeth have fallen out and been in the vomit? We all inspected the now pristine toilet as if our looking at the clear contents would suddenly magic the teeth into appearing. No such luck. I phoned the emergency plumber. 'You're not going to believe this…' my communication with him began. Two young men in denim overalls and with a variety of tools arrived at the house. After what felt like a very long time, one of them, working in the drain outside, held in his gloved hand a set of dentures, none the worse for wear except for a layer of vomit and shit. This was a first for him too. I feel such a pang of longing and tenderness when I think about how Elsie and I laughed and laughed over those teeth, which, once I had carefully cleaned and disinfected them, were as good as new and continued to provide sterling service. Elsie never lost her sense of humour, and the absurdity of all of this really tickled her. A great story for all our friends.

Eating was a problem. As Elsie lost weight, her teeth, which had never been a great fit anyway, became looser and looser (hence, I guess, the plumbing incident); eating soft foods became the order of the day. But her appetite was gone. I tried cooking this, buying that. Begging, cajoling, shouting. The less she ate, the less she wanted to eat, and I became worried that she would starve to death. This is not without irony – she was, after all, a woman who had a terminal illness, and we all knew what terminal meant. But I couldn't bear the not eating. I have always felt lucky that my children, when they were young, ate well; I have known parents beside themselves with anxiety that their children would starve. There is something elemental about being able to provide nutrition for someone you love. I have many regrets about my care for my mother at the end, and one of them is about the many fights we had over eating – I just could not let it go. Was my food not good enough? Was my care not good enough? Where was her gratitude?

I have spoken with many people who have cared for a loved one with a terminal illness, and not one of them has not identified with my experience of having felt murderous towards the people they cared for. I first became aware of this feeling, not with Elsie's illness but when Louise's brother, Peter, was dying of cancer in his early 40s. It was clear to both Louise and me that Peter was dying, but until the day before he died, Louise's parents in particular spoke about the necessity for hope and for a wish for a cure. Louise wanted a chance to say goodbye to Peter, to have a chance to talk about what was happening between them as he was dying. This is typical of Louise, who is not scared of difficult things, or who, more accurately, I guess, feels the fear and does it anyway. But it was completely foreign to her family (she is something of an emotional changeling, and I admire her greatly for this). As Louise and I spoke between us about Peter's impending death and what it would mean for his young sons in particular, Louise was told by her family, explicitly or otherwise, 'Don't talk like that.' As though it would be our words that would kill Peter rather than the cancer which was eating him away. Even speaking or thinking of death in that context was tantamount to killing someone.

But this murderousness has another side. Elsie was fading away, but she just would not die. She passed the outer limit of time the oncologist thought she would live, and on she went. When would this end? I did not want my mother to die but I did not want her to be dying forever. My life was so upside down, so consumed by what the illness meant, that I wanted an end date, a date by which this would all be over. And with those murderous thoughts, I felt guilty. The only way the suffering could be over – Elsie's and ours – would be when she died. I never doubted that I wanted to care for her and that we were there for as long as it would take, but it would be a lie to say that I did not wish, often, for it to be over. Like teenagers sneaking off to the movies, Louise and I would sometimes meet surreptitiously after work for a quiet cup of coffee before returning home to the demands, the vomit and the shit (both of which, understandably, preoccupied Elsie), and, worst of all, to the presence of the carers, on whom we were completely dependent, but who also felt like intruders in our home. Looking at this from a distance, now, I can see nothing at all wrong with our taking these cups of coffee, and I have no doubt we needed them, but the trysts felt like acts of abandonment, and even murderous in themselves. We wanted this to be over, and for me, though I hate to think about this, that meant I wanted my mother dead.

This said, and my talk of murder is true (I did feel that way), there was also something astonishing about how Elsie was dying. Until the last six weeks of her life, and through the wasting of her body, Elsie was one hundred per cent alive. She was herself, alert, out there. As her world became smaller and smaller, her mind continued to soar. She couldn't concentrate enough to read books anymore, and barely looked at the newspaper. I would get very upset about this – reading had been so much part of her that in not reading she was telling me that I was losing her. But she listened to the radio constantly (that bloody 567 Cape Talk, which I hated), and watched television, and still loved to argue about politics and what was going on in the world. We didn't always agree and would have arguments about things, but she loved the fight – her blue eyes in that shrunken face blazing with life. Once, a carer, who meant well, stood behind Elsie as I shouted at her about how wrong she was to differ with me on a political issue, and rubbed her eyes, indicating, as far as I could read the gesture, that in my wrath I would make my mother cry. Quite apart from my feelings about being put in my place by this woman, something I'll get to later, I knew she was wrong. If Elsie could no longer eat what I cooked for her, she could sustain herself, in part, by the fact that I still thought of her as a worthwhile sparring partner, a powerful adversary. Our arguments were only partly about the content of what we were talking about – they were also acts of love. We were two people, mother and son, and for now, as we argued, we knew that we were both alive. I treasure many things about that last year with her, and our fights are part of that. Shouting loud, shouting loud. Is there anything else?

One evening, when I was especially exhausted and Elsie was lying on the bed we had in the lounge so she could watch television with us, I was sitting on the edge of her bed and chatting about nothing in particular. Suddenly, and unbidden, a sob erupted from somewhere inside me, literally shaking me. I put my head down next to Elsie's. 'How will I live without you?' I found myself asking, a question I had not known was inside me. She put her hand on my back and patted me as a mother does a small child. 'You will manage, you will manage,' she said. With her comforting words, my tears flowed. Whatever else was happening and had happened, whatever the many, many imperfections of our lives then and before, I had a mother. And she had me.

I was completely absorbed by my mother's illness and by the sheer grind of managing, together with Louise, what felt to me quite a complex household. Even things we appreciated and really felt we needed, like the visits from friends and family, at times felt like a burden, yet another thing to arrange for. All these practical things were superimposed on the drip-drip-drip of worry and grief, fear and uncertainty. We were lucky to have things so easy, but we were exhausted. I decided to be sensible about my work life. I have always worked at a ridiculous pace, and I am an unusually productive academic, publishing more than most of my colleagues do. With my mother's illness, I knew that my productivity would decline, so I went to see my departmental chair, Tony Naidoo, about this. Kind and caring man that he is, he told me not to worry, that everyone would understand, that everyone knew how productive I was in general. I was immensely grateful to Tony. When it came to it, though, in the year of caring for my mother until she died, I completed more articles than I had done in any year before that. Cop in the head, cop in the head. Consciously, I was giving myself permission, and had received formal permission, to slack off a bit, so what did I do? I over-compensated, and did more, pushed myself harder. And part of this came from my inserting myself into an argument I really despised.

In Oscar Wilde's *The Importance of Being Earnest*, Lady Bracknell famously says, 'To lose one parent, Mr Worthing, may be regarded as a misfortune; to lose both looks like carelessness.' When people heard that my mother was dying and that she was living in our house, they were invariably sympathetic, and many continued to be. But as the months dragged on, and my distraction and grief continued, their tolerance of my misfortune morphed into exasperation at my carelessness. Just as I longed, murderously, for my mother to die, people wanted me to be over my difficulties and back to my old self. I had had my time out, but this was going on for months. Why couldn't I just man up and get on with life and work? At the time, as it happens, I was managing part of a difficult and complex international research project, and I'm the first to admit that at times I was not as on top of things as I usually am. Though I always feel that my life is in a state of chaos (and, believe me, it is), I was also the person that a secretary had once nicknamed 'Hawkeye', because of my attention to detail (I am quite proud of this!). She said I could pick up a problem at 50 paces. Well, while Elsie was dying, Hawkeye's eye was not always on the work, and I lost some of the control I usually have over things. I tried to deal with this responsibly, informing all my local and international partners of the situation, and putting in procedures for others to take over. And, my goodness, people did step in to help. Imperceptibly but powerfully, they just did what needed to be done. But this was not an easy project, and there were tensions with one of the area partners in particular. They did not work easily with the rest of us, and their approach to the work, it seemed to me, was a dangerous cocktail of incompetence coupled with an unshakeable belief not only that they were indeed competent, but much more competent than the rest of us. They performed the reasonableness of listening to outside views but did what they liked, did really shoddy work, and then, effectively, it felt, blamed me for their mistakes when they had not listened to a thing my team and I had suggested. Had I been less distracted, I might have handled this better and seen the problems earlier, but I did not. The overall team leader's solution to this, I felt, was to collude in my being blamed for not managing an unmanageable group properly. Then I was deeply humiliated by a further step that was taken – I would no longer be managing that portion of the project. This portion was handed over, without any consultation with me, to the very area partner who had not delivered, and had blamed me for this.

Not without *Schadenfreude*, I am able to report that in the event, the team I was managing continued to produce good quality work at a reasonable clip, and the area team that was now to manage what I was mismanaging have, to date, 10 years later, produced nothing. This is a fairly typical story of how things can go awry in big projects – these things happen all the time – but there is another part to it. Although I have worked happily with the project partners since, and I have been, as usual, exceptionally productive, I have never quite got over the humiliation of this whole farrago. This goes beyond the usual recurrent flashes of anguish I often feel years later about silly things I have done, or ways in which I have embarrassed myself. I have no evidence for this apart from my own feelings, but I think that a key reason I got into trouble in this project was not that I was not producing. I have performed worse before and since then in other projects.

The key problem was that, responsibly, I thought, I told other people that I thought that my caring for Elsie as she died could impede my work functioning. I irritated other people by making this admission that caring for Elsie was a central and defining part of my life. Both men and women, but men in particular, I felt, were irritated that my short-term misfortune, which could be tolerated, had become long-term carelessness, which was unforgivable. Didn't I have a wife who would look after things, I could hear them saying. Couldn't I organise my life properly and put this issue of my dying mother in its rightful (and private) place? In experiencing the disavowal and, at times, the retaliation from others, I was not, of course, in much of a different situation from millions of women who get into trouble at work because of their need to care for their children (and, not infrequently, the father of their children).

But I think I got an extra knock from some of my colleagues precisely because I was a man. What I was doing in caring for my mother, and allowing the whole process to affect me, was unmanly. I deserved the knocks I was getting because, as the poem says, 'Ek hou van 'n man wat 'n man kan staan'. My soppy girlishness – the ongoing preoccupation, anxiety and grief – was reprehensible and it must stop. Men get over things, men get on with things. I feel an enormous amount of pride that I refused to give in to this, and I can even see my continued caring for my mother, and my continued talking about it, telling others that it mattered and affected my life, as an example of shouting loud. But with all of this, of course, was my tacit agreement with everything that was said and not said. What kind of man was I, after all? The soppy fellow who looks after his mother, who can't manage his wife to do this for him – somewhere inside I felt that was me. It's important for me to point out that throughout Elsie's illness, Louise was there doing everything she could and, it often felt, even more – she could not have been better. The problem was not that I could not manage my wife (who has never needed managing from me, in any case), but that I chose not to offload my feelings onto her, for her to look after. My father dealt, in part, with the burden of emotion he felt about his own impossible mother by offloading her onto my mother (and onto us). I did not and would not do that. Consciously, I know I did the right thing, and I am proud of it. But the reason I still feel so bruised by how some colleagues behaved is that there is a part of me that agreed with them that I needed to be brought into line. If it is anything, this book is a rebellion against them, and against the part of myself that knows them to be right.

12 | Care

For 11 and a half months, for 24 hours a day, every day, we had a paid carer in our home. I travelled a bit for work, and Louise and I went away for a weekend when our friend Sharon Kleintjes, who herself has cared for many people in her family, insisted that she move in for the two days so we could have a break. Apart from that, we had carers in the house. The first thing that needs to be said about this, and it's really important that it is said, is that we were enormously privileged to have these carers. The vast majority of families in the world who care for sick and dying people do not have any help at all in the home. A not insubstantial number of women in these families will work as carers for wealthier families, and after a full day's work will return home to start caring for their own relatives.

In a huge and growing international industry, some women will travel across the world to wealthier countries to look after sick, disabled and dying people, leaving their own sick, disabled and dying families at home. Tied up with their care of rich people is their abandonment of their families; tied up with their abandonment of their families is often the best way they can care for those families – by earning in a strong currency and sending remittances home. The layers of this are obvious, and why, with all the international concern about human rights, we are not more concerned about this is something that troubles me.

While I was writing this book, the popular and well-regarded author Deborah Moggach published a novel titled *The Carer*. I have not seen a bad review of this book, and I have seen many very favourable ones in good publications. I must be the only reader who found it brittle, formulaic and, though funny and well written, ever so slightly sanctimonious. But then, I have skin (and a lot of it) in the game. The third paragraph of the book reads, in its entirety:

> Phoebe liked her, truly she did. She'd come to the rescue after her father had his fall. Two carers had come and gone. Rejoice, from Zimbabwe, who talked all through his beloved Radio 4 and fed him some sort of maize-meal that clogged up his bowels. Then there was Teresa from County Donegal who was having a love-affair with a baggage-handler from Luton Airport and who sat texting him, in a fug of cigarette smoke, and reading out the replies while the kettle boiled dry and Dad dehydrated.[1]

The famous *Jerry Maguire* line 'You had me at hello' held a negative echo for me in *The Carer*: Deborah Moggach lost me at Rejoice. Part of me feels that, if I were more charitable, I would, like Phil Baker, writing in *The Sunday Times*, be able to see that the book is a 'masterpiece' by an author 'at the height of her powers'.[2] But I am not about to offer charity to a book, the third paragraph of which, to me, smacks of racism, classism and a middle-class Englishness content to reduce working-class women, one of whom is a Black African, to comic bit parts, like Oompa Loompas providing a hilarious background to the magic that is Willy Wonka. To be fair, the paragraph that I quote here is written in the voice of one of the characters, and is not an authorial comment. I am not accusing Moggach of racism and classism. It is true that the book is a kind of moral fable through which snobby middle-class people come to see the value, contribution, decency and fundamental honesty of their working-class counterparts. But the carefully named Rejoice (there are indeed Zimbabweans with this name and names like this, but the choice of this name does not seem to me to be by chance) and (Saint) Teresa are relegated to the flotsam of plot devices. Rejoice is mentioned once again in the book, again with reference to her constipating cultural food choice (the words 'some sort of maize-meal' really give the game away), and as I quickly made my way through the book I did not see Teresa and her cigarettes again, but I may have missed them. The Zimbabwe reference is the one that really gets me, as there is nobody in southern Africa who has not been affected by the tragic reality of the Zimbabwean meltdown, with Zimbabweans themselves, of course, bearing the brunt. The Zimbabwean diaspora is not a matter of choice, and women like Rejoice are keeping people in Zimbabwe from starving. Moggach, accurately, I think, describes *The Carer* as 'a comedy about class, and death, and family secrets'.[3] But I suspect there may be a mote in Moggach's own eye while she so entertainingly demonstrates the motes in the eyes of others.

Why am I so worked up about a piece of light fiction by the author of *The Best Exotic Marigold Hotel* (I'm holding myself back, I promise you, from commenting about that title as well)? Let's get some obvious contenders out of the way. I would love to be a bestselling novelist. I would love to reach a wide audience with a discussion about the dilemmas people face when employing carers. In a nutshell, I'm jealous and mean-spirited. I can agree with all of this, but I also believe that the complexity of intimacy and exploitation, the layers of dependency, the gentleness and the violence that are intertwined with the employment of paid carers really have not been thought about enough. In researching for this book I have read many books about death, and death as a topic is very in these days. Even a writer as brilliant and insightful as Atul Gawande slides past the question of paid care in his deservedly highly praised *Being Mortal*.[4] For me, one of the most magnificent and useful recent books about ageing and death, and about a lot of other things, is Nicci Gerrard's *What Dementia Teaches Us about Love*.[5] In this book, Gerrard does mention paid carers but doesn't really deal with the issue in any depth. I'm not saying that there aren't any accessible books about paid carers, because there are: some of the most interesting and accessible (non-academic) discussions of care are by South African or ex-South African writers. I think here particularly of Marlene van Niekerk's *Agaat*; Ena Jansen's *Like Family: Domestic Workers in South African History and Literature* and, to my mind, the vastly underrated *Slow Man* by JM Coetzee.[6] However, I think it's true to say that paid carers often play bit parts in other stories – they are often portrayed briefly as 'wonderful' as the story moves on to focus on the more interesting, wealthier characters. The book you are reading now – my book – is of course reproducing this tradition, because my book focuses on my mother and on me. Nevertheless, I hope I can do the issue of paid carers, and of paid care, some justice here.

I grew up with domestic workers, and, as I've mentioned earlier, accepted it as natural that a grown woman would wake me in the morning with my tea, and would finish her day washing up my dinner plates. Like most middle-class people in Africa (and the vast majority of these people are not white), I depend on the labour of domestic workers. Susan Filtane looked after my children when they were small and still works part-time for Louise and me today, over 30 years later. I hope I am less exploitative than most, and Susan is certainly much better paid than the established recommended rates for domestic work suggest. I don't know, and given the power relationship, will never know, how Susan feels about our relationship – she is paid, has a pension scheme and benefits. She is in my home a few times a week, and has played a key role in the upbringing of my children and the care of my mother and my father-in-law after her. I have always paid a multiple of the recommended wage, but I feel in my bones like an exploiter. Money is not the only issue here. I also know that if we had chosen not to employ Susan after we no longer needed childcare, her chances of finding employment, especially at a living wage, would have been slim. There are a million ways of justifying anything. I was at a conference on care ethics a few years ago and there was excited discussion about the potential of robots to do domestic work. Joan Tronto, one of the people I admire most in the field, and a friend, provided an alternative to this brave new world of automated helpers: 'Let him pick up his own damn socks.' Care work is so inflected with gender, class, race and the intimacy of both genuine affection and concern and genuine exploitation that we don't like to think about it or talk about it.

From the first day of our employing carers in our home for 24-hour care for Elsie, I made some decisions that suited me but deeply affected our relationships with them. I was in such a vulnerable psychological state that I did not want to be the formal employer of carers. I wanted somebody else to be the boss, and somebody else to have the worry of making sure that we would get full coverage of people to see that Elsie did not fall, regardless of the circumstances of a particular carer on a particular day, the weather, taxi strikes and so on. I did not want any of these things to be my problem. So, we enlisted the help of an agency recommended highly by the oncologist. I was shocked at how much all of this would cost, but this felt to me preferable to having to deal with carers as direct employees. We had to pay for it, but everything would be at one remove. Business was business, or so I hoped and thought.

It was quite a few months into this arrangement when I found out what I had known in my heart for a very long time. These women, who came into our home with the huge responsibility of looking after a dying woman, making sure that she did not fall, keeping her clean, preventing bedsores, spending hours sitting around bored stiff but on hand in case something went wrong – these women, who had a job that to me would be worse than my worst nightmare, were earning almost nothing. We were paying a huge amount to the agency, but the carers were earning, for 48 hours per week, a fraction of what Susan got for 16 hours a week. They were at the bare edge of what is considered a living wage in South Africa. I could cluck at how exploited they were (and I did), but I was paying – and paying a lot – for the privilege of not having to deal directly with this exploitation. If I had taken the money we were paying monthly to the agency and paid it directly to carers, the income we paid to each of the carers would have almost quadrupled. Believe me, I've done the maths more times than you have had hot breakfasts. But I couldn't face the work and emotional toil this would take. If I was concerned about exploitation, I also took a decision (although, if I am accurate, it felt as though the decision took me) to collude in it. I felt I would fall into some sort of abyss if I became a private employer to carers, and I just couldn't bear it – so I made others bear it.

But in all of this, I am nothing if I am not my mother's son. We wanted the carers to be comfortable and we wanted them to feel cared for themselves, however much we were involved in a web of exploitation. We started offering them food, and soon I was cooking regularly for the carers. Once, my father-in-law David was visiting from Johannesburg. He watched me rushing about in the kitchen, feeling overwrought but needing to get all the cooking done. 'I thought it was the job of the servants to cook for you, not the other way round,' he commented. Well, yes, I guess.

I tried to become more efficient. With the aid of the wonders of the slow cooker, I was able to cook with very little effort. One day I had just finished cooking a batch and I had to go out to the chemist to get something for Elsie. I will never forget what I saw when I got back. The kitchen door was closed but it has glass in it, and sideways-on I could see Sarah, one of the carers we really liked, with a plate of food in front of her. She was eating the food I had prepared for the household. It was less than an hour since I had turned off the slow cooker and ventured out to the chemist in relief at a cooking job done. Needless to say, I said nothing to Sarah (I didn't even enter the kitchen), but I did run to Elsie to ask what was happening.'Sarah was feeling hungry, poor thing, and she was too shy to ask. I told her that you had cooked a meal for her and it was important to me that she eat all of it – every last bit.' When she saw that I was ready to scream, Elsie asked, in her virtuoso victim voice, 'Did I do something wrong, darling?' No, of course not. I knew all too well when I was being told, in clear terms, that I was 'a hundred per cent right', and this was one of those occasions. For the second time that day, I started cooking.

Early on in their relationship with us, many of the carers told us that we were different from others in whose homes they worked. We spoke to them and we always invited them to eat with us when we had meals. It was important to us and to our sense of ourselves to treat these women with respect and dignity. As we were not home for large parts of the day, and not with Elsie during the night, furthermore, there was self-interest in the way we treated the carers. We believed that if we treated them well, they would be kind to Elsie. The carers told us that they fought among themselves to come and work in our house because we were nice people, because the food was good and because that whenever Elsie was well enough we took them on outings with us to nice places.

One of the carers, Flora, became very friendly towards us, but after some time her demeanour changed and she began to seem resentful and angry.[i] We were not sure why. One issue was that she began dropping large hints about her need for money. We 'lent' her some money, which we did not expect would be repaid. One day when Louise's father was due to come and stay with us for a few weeks, we were unable to find his radio. We thought that we might have put it in Elsie's room and we started searching for it there, looking through her cupboard. We did not usually go through Elsie's things. Flora did not say anything, but clearly became very angry indeed. We stopped looking for the radio (which in fact was in the cupboard, as we discovered after Elsie had died) and asked her what was wrong. Flora said she did not like being accused of stealing. She would not listen to our protests that we did not think she had stolen the radio (which we did not). Very ostentatiously, she began writing notes in Elsie's file.[7]

When she had left in the morning and another carer had taken over, I read the file for the first time. We had been told about the file when the agency had started working with us, and had been given access to it, but it had never occurred to me to look at it. I was shocked to read lengthy

---

i In the stories of Flora and Sarie and others, which follow, I have changed details and amalgamated some stories. I am not in touch with the people who collectively make up the characters I mention, and I am convinced that nobody can be identified here. I have used the stories of Flora and Sarie, in slightly different form, in two journal articles, and some of the text is reproduced directly.

notes by Flora, going back weeks, about how nasty and disrespectful we were to her. Other carers agreed in their notes that we were rude and difficult and that I was particularly rude. On one occasion, apparently, I had failed to greet one of the carers when I came home and she was angry about this. I am sure it is true that on one day I may well not have greeted her, but nowhere in any of the notes were recorded the long conversations we had with carers, the food, the outings, the ('illegal') 'loans' we gave them not expecting to be repaid, the printing out of pages from the internet for homework exercises for their children, and so on.

I was surprised by how very hurt I was by this, and also by the fact that these notes were read every week by the care agency but nothing had been said to me about my allegedly abusive behaviour. In the event, the discovery of the notes was a positive turning point, from our point of view. We asked that Flora be transferred to another patient, and we had some painful but I believe very helpful discussions with the other carers, who all stayed on and, to our knowledge, did not complain about us again.

I felt humiliated and wronged by how I had been portrayed, and by the fact that I had been given no opportunity to get feedback and to change. The agency's response to my query as to why they had not informed us and taken us to task about our allegedly rude and exploitative behaviour was that we had allowed the carers to get too close to us. We must stop giving them food and we must stop including them in discussions in the way we'd been doing. We chose not to take this advice.

When I try to make sense of this very painful incident in the long story of Elsie's illness, a number of things come to mind. There are echoes here of generations of stories about domestic workers who are accused of stealing. I can hear other echoes of the way people talk casually about domestic workers in South Africa – 'Don't pay them too much or they will get ideas'; 'Don't let them get too close.' The agency's solution to the difficulties we had, it seemed to me (and I was enraged by this), was to put us back into the comfortable ascribed roles of white oppressors of Black women. I refused to do what the agency said, but of course we were employing through the agency women who were appallingly paid with dreadful working conditions. Who were we fooling? It's really not surprising in some ways that our being 'kind', although initially clearly attractive to the carers, seemed to come to some of them to feel worse than our not being kind. We behaved as though we were their equals and friends when in reality we were not offering friendship. Indeed, when Flora upset us, we made sure we never had to see her again.

Another person who made a huge impact on me was Sarie. When she came to work with us, Sarie was living with her husband and her two youngest children in a council house in the greater Cape Town area. Her elder two children, aged 18 and 17, were living with relatives in Wellington, about 50 kilometres away. Some time into Sarie's stay with us, her neighbour's house burned down and two of her neighbour's children came to live with her temporarily. This was Sarie's third job as a care worker. She had been employed previously by two other agencies but she was much happier working for her current employer who, she said, treated the care workers more fairly than her previous employers had done. Unlike some of the care workers we met, she expressed a keen interest in care work and she told us that, had she not had to leave school at 17 when she was pregnant, she would have liked to have got her matric and become a registered nurse. Her husband worked on a casual basis as a security guard; her very low salary was the only marginally steady income coming into the house. She was employed on the basis that she was paid only for the days that she worked. If the agency did not have clients for her to care for, she did not earn. Two weeks prior to her coming to work for us, the young woman for whom she had been working as a care worker for six months had died as a result of a brain tumour; Sarie had not worked in the intervening two weeks.

We immediately took to Sarie and she to us. She especially liked the fact that while Elsie was well enough we would take her out whenever we could – usually for tea and as much cake as we could get Elsie to eat. The first time Sarie came with us to a shopping centre (one that caters mainly for the middle class), she commented, 'Jesus must have sent me to you – you are taking me to such a wonderful place.' Born and bred in Cape Town, Sarie had never been to this shopping centre or to any shopping centre like it. Her first visit to the Waterfront was also with us; she enjoyed pushing Elsie in her wheelchair near the water's edge. When she wanted to go to the toilet, I pointed out the public toilet. 'No, Mr Leslie (I could not convince her to call me Leslie),' she said, 'that is not for people like me.' After much remonstration on my part, she agreed to use the public toilet.

One day when Elsie was not well enough to stop for tea, I took her and Sarie for a short drive near our house. I drove up to Rhodes Memorial above the University of Cape Town (UCT) and explained to her how the wealthy colonialist Cecil John Rhodes had given a large estate to the South African nation. I pointed out UCT and Groote Schuur Hospital and explained how the National Botanical Garden, Kirstenbosch (where we had also taken Sarie for the first time in her life) was also part of a gift to the nation from Rhodes (all such highly contested 'gifts' from a man representing a colonial power that stole land, but this I did not discuss). A few days later, Sarie said to me, 'You know, Mr Leslie, Mr Leslie is a very generous man.' I laughed and asked her why. 'Well,' she said, 'Mr Leslie gave all that land to the nation.' In my telling of the story of Rhodes' 'gift' to the nation, Sarie had thought that I was the benefactor. To this woman, a fellow citizen of Cape Town, whose home is 20 minutes' drive from my own, I was unimaginably wealthy. Feeling the considerable financial strain of caring for Elsie, and running a house in which by choice we shared our table and our food with the care workers, and looking at the damp and the cracks of my crumbling house, I felt the irony of being seen in a league of wealth on a scale enjoyed by Rhodes. To readers of this book, I am sure, and certainly to me, there is an obvious difference between my wealth accumulated as a middle-class psychologist and an academic and that enjoyed by Cecil John Rhodes, arch-imperialist, magnate and entrepreneur. But not to Sarie.

Somewhat to my dismay, I returned from work one day to find that Elsie had agreed that Sarie would bring her eight-year-old daughter,

Jolene, to meet the family the following Saturday, when Sarie was on duty. Sarie said that Jolene would be no trouble, that she was very well behaved. This was true, and we had a happy few hours with Sarie and Jolene at the Waterfront. Elsie had not been in contact with children for a long time and she said that being with Jolene did her good. She insisted that I buy Jolene a colouring book and crayons; this I did happily. For some time after this Jolene telephoned Elsie; Elsie did not feel well enough to take the calls, and we heard from Sarie that Jolene was disappointed, that she wanted to visit us again. But Elsie's health and her tolerance for distractions beyond her own immediate needs was deteriorating rapidly, and we put Jolene out of our minds.

We were now about six months into our relationship with Sarie. Something had shifted subtly since Jolene's visit. Elsie was very ill at this stage and in need of more focused attention, both physical and emotional. But Sarie would now speak quite often of her financial difficulties and for the first time she asked to borrow money from us (a practice not allowed by the agency). We 'lent' her small amounts of money without expectation of repayment, nor were we repaid. She told us about her abuse at the hands of her alcoholic husband, and showed us her scars. We suggested she get help at the local clinic on her day off. Sarie became more withdrawn and moody.

The following week, with no explanation and no goodbye, Sarie no longer came to us as a care worker and we never saw her again. We thought that this must be because she was no longer happy with us (and this might have been a factor), but later in the week we received a tearful phone call from Jolene who asked us where her mother was. Worried, we contacted the nursing agency. It turned out that during her time with us Sarie had decided to leave her abusive husband. She gave the appearance of leaving for work as usual one day, but went to live with a friend in a town about 50 kilometres from Cape Town. As it happened, there was a patient there whom she could care for through the agency. She walked out on her abusive husband in the only way she knew how – by walking out on her own two children and the neighbour's two children, leaving them in the care of her abusive and substance-abusing husband, and by walking out on us. We never heard from Sarie again.

After Elsie died, through other care workers at the agency, we invited Sarie to a memorial tea for Elsie, which we held at our home. She did not come to this, and we don't know if she ever received the gift we sent her via the other care workers to thank her for the kindness she had shown Elsie over a period of months.

There are so many other stories about the carers, and I am not convinced that they are mine to tell. After Elsie died, I worked with a graduate student to capture and tell some of the carers' stories, and I am glad I did this, but I am not sure this really helped anyone.[8] I have what feels like a thousand stories to tell. Some are telling, and funny, like my own reaction to Josephine, the carer who was clearly actively psychotic and experiencing delusions. In my professional work and teaching, I make it clear that the stigma and discrimination many people with mental illnesses face is unacceptable, and that even when people are actively psychotic, they may be able to function quite well, and that they should be supported in this. Now that Josephine, who had been called by the Lord (and not in a low-key way that could be explained away by evangelical religion – we had a lot of those and this was different), was in my home, and caring for the tiny, broken bird that was my mother, I could feel every prejudice I thought I did not have against people with serious mental illness well up inside me. I immediately worried that Josephine was dangerous, not to be trusted, you name it. Luckily for us both, I managed to contain myself, and Josephine managed to do both her and the Lord's work rather well. But there is no question that I had been caught out.

The carer I liked least was an older woman I will call Hetta. Hetta was exceptionally competent and experienced, unlike some of the terrified young women who turned up on our doorstep to work. She had home nursing qualifications, and her understanding of human anatomy and physiology seemed to me far superior to the sometimes alarming understandings held by some of the carers. She was not going to suggest, for example, that regular vomiting would help Elsie purge herself of the cancer, and that the vomiting should be encouraged rather than avoided. But Hetta, some 20 years younger than Elsie, would address Elsie as follows, 'Now little Mommy. Is little Mommy going to put on Mommy's shoesies for Auntie Hetta? Mommy must eat up nice and good so Mommy can get better. Mommy's little beddie needs a good good cleaning so Hetta will put Mommy in the little chair so long.' An added problem was that Hetta would not shut up – there was a constant jingle of 'Mommy – little – shoesies – beddie – poo-poo – wee' which just went on and on and on. The mixture of Elsie being called 'Mommy' and treated like a rather stupid baby, and all in a sing-song nursery voice, nearly drove me bats. Part of the fun of Hetta, though, was that while Elsie never complained to her face, the eye-rolling and knowing exasperation, blue eyes flashing, the minute Hetta's backie was turned were a tonic to us. I loved to be a co-conspirator with Elsie, who could not have been further from the second childhood Hetta ('Shame, you know, sir, they just go back to their second childhood') ascribed to her. Of course, Elsie's first childhood was probably nothing like this second one she was claimed to have returned to, but I wasn't about to argue this with Hetta. It worked for Hetta, if not for us (and certainly not for Elsie), and I understood from the care agency that Hetta's services were much valued by others. Give me the crazy light of the Lord any day.

Most of the stories the carers told us, or that we came to learn in bits, were not funny at all, however. They were stories of poverty and abuse, of families torn apart, children and parents lost to one another. We knew (and this was true) that when Elsie died, this difficult chapter of our lives would be over, whatever its long-term effects for us. We would resume what for us was normal (read: privileged and predictable) life. For the carers, when Elsie died, if they were lucky, they would move straight on to care for another dying person. If they were unlucky, they would wait, unpaid and unemployed, for the next call; or they would look for other jobs. I lost count of the number of them who asked if they could come to work for us as domestic workers – anything, anything.

Not that long after Elsie died, I was asked to give a keynote address at a conference focusing on trauma. At that conference, I told, in slightly different form, the story of our relationship with Sarie. I used this story to point out how the concept of 'trauma', so much part of the currency of contemporary psychology, and contemporary society more broadly, still depends on the view of a functioning, predictable world. The concept of post-traumatic stress disorder (PTSD), which entered the lexicon as recently as 1980, depends on life going on as 'normal', something terrible happening, then people having to react to it, and to live with the aftermath. I am oversimplifying quite a bit here, but I think the general point about PTSD and similar formulations depending on the idea that 'trauma' is something that disrupts 'normal life' for a fixed amount of time is about right. These questions have been more fully addressed in a number of academic publications.[9]

For the carers, life was hard, and the work they did to make our relatively easy lives easier was simply part of the ongoing difficulty of life as they experinced theirs. Was it any wonder, given this context, that our kindness to the carers, though well meant from our side, would sometimes be experienced as yet another assault? Our largesse, it seemed to me, was sometimes experienced by them as a way of our rubbing their noses in how little they had. From on high, we could give out food, money, homework help for children. Kind indeed. But they had to live their lives, with all their difficulty and pain, lives that would not be improved by cooking, outings and short-term charity.

There were two reactions to my talk from people at the conference. A number of them who, like me, had been through caring for dying relatives, thanked me for the talk. One said, 'This is the first time my experience has been spoken about. And we are psychologists, but there's no space to talk about these things.' The more common reaction, though, I thought, was of disappointment and even, possibly, some anger, though this was not expressed. Psychology colleagues, all wanting to do good work, had paid good money to come to this conference on trauma, and they had expected me, a senior professor in the profession, to give them tips on how to do their professional work better. How could my maundering on about these women who had looked after my mother help them with their patients? The women I chose to talk about would almost definitely never see the inside of a psychologist's consulting room, and especially not a consulting room of a practitioner in the private sector, as most of these psychologists were. I can see why people were disappointed – this wasn't what they had signed up for. In my defence, I had told the organiser in advance that what I wanted to talk about did not, I thought, fit with what her conference participants wanted, and I recommended a really excellent colleague who I thought would do a far better job. The organiser insisted (I think she wanted to grace the conference with a senior academic name). I was flattered, I guess, and in this case, flattery gets you everywhere and nowhere.

In so many ways, having the carers in our house and our multiple mistakes in dealing with them was the most difficult part of that last year with Elsie. We couldn't manage without them, and I remain grateful to all the women who looked after Elsie so kindly and respectfully, especially at the end, when things were really difficult. But what a mess it all was. Part of my problem in thinking about this is that I am not sure if, or how, I would do things differently if I had to have the time over. I was beside myself, distracted, vulnerable, angry. Unlike so many people all over the world, I didn't have to deal directly with my dying mother's body – I didn't have to clean her up, apply creams to her skin, see her naked. I don't think she would have minded this all that much, to be honest, but I had the carers to protect me from something I would have minded a lot. Of course I was exploiting them – I live with this knowledge – but if I am honest, I can't see myself being able to play the role of traditional master to their traditional servant role. This was the solution suggested by an experienced and reputable agency, smacking as it did of comments from other middle-class people that you should not pay domestic workers too much as they will get 'spoilt' and 'get ideas'. Maybe the agency was right – let the police be the police – and perhaps if we had been clearer, we would have had fewer problems. But we also had many good experiences with most of the carers – and I am good at hanging on to my privilege, as I did and do, but less good at the police stuff. That's me, softie that I am.

Elsie's story about Lee Alexander was a story, in part, of jewellery theft, and for some reason I am reminded as I write this about what a friend and colleague once said to me about a very famous academic. This academic has built a considerable international reputation by writing beautifully about the lives of oppressed and excluded people. My friend said about this academic, 'She wears other people's pain like jewellery.' Regardless of how fair this comment was about the particular academic concerned, there is no doubt at all that many academic careers are built on well-written stories of other people's miseries. These people as portrayed in the stories, furthermore, elicit an emotional reaction from readers, and I do think there is sometimes a conflation between an academic's describing misery and abjection well, and the academic's being seen as a good academic. Even worse, we often assume that simply collecting information about people in difficult situations must be good for them and makes their lives better. As I write this, my friend and colleague Jason Bantjes and I have been taken to task by colleagues studying suicide for suggesting that there is no necessary link between telling the stories of people who are suicidal and contributing to efforts to prevent suicide.[10] Our colleagues may have a point, but I am not convinced that telling another person's story, however kindly, and with whatever good intentions, necessarily is good for the person whose story is being told.

Am I, then, wearing the pain of the carers, of these women who did so much for me, like jewellery? Of course I am – I can't deny that I am enjoying writing this book, that I want it to be well received, that I want to be well thought of. I can get into lots of arguments about whose story this book is but ultimately it is mine, and every other person I mention, including Elsie (including myself!) is, in the end, a character in a book I am writing. All this is true. But it is also true, and I've looked and looked, that the story of carers, though mentioned, is submerged or trivialised in the bigger stories commonly told about death and dying. This is wrong, and I want to redress the balance, to shout loud, as Elsie did. I recognise that I'm doing this for me, but somehow, somewhere, I hope, I am also doing this for Rejoice and her 'some sort of maize-meal'. In colonial Rhodesia, and in Zimbabwe today, we call it sadza.

13 | What ends?

Elsie moved in with us at the beginning of February 2010, and died in our home on 15 January 2011, a day after what would have been her 60th wedding anniversary, had my father still been alive. Every week for those 11 and a half months, and much more often towards the end, when it became every day, Elsie was visited by Yvonne Jackman, a nursing sister working for St Luke's Hospice.

The first time Yvonne visited, she sat down at the edge of the bed, and said to Elsie, 'I will never lie to you.' She kept her word. She was honest, caring, fearless. I don't know of course how Yvonne got on with other patients (and I suspect she got on brilliantly with them), but from very early on I got the feeling that Elsie was special to Yvonne. Elsie was so alive, so witty, so willing to discuss and engage with anything. She didn't complain to Yvonne – she was clear that there were things she would rather not endure, but in the midst of dying she could experience pleasure. We all loved the visits from Yvonne. She was very different from us in many ways, and a committed Christian, but she was, above all, respectful of us all. It was not just that she offered help, but also that Elsie could accept and appreciate what Yvonne had to offer. Louise often says that there is a generosity in being able to receive from others, and we could see this in Elsie.

Another source of support was the practice where our GP, Alan Wood, works. For a time, we were at Colinton Surgery practically every week. There was always a physical concern that Elsie had about this or that symptom or sore place – a lot was going wrong with her body. But as Elsie got to know almost all the doctors and other staff, and they got to know her, there was much more to these visits. They were pleasant outings to a place where Elsie would feel safe and be heard. Just as my gratitude to Yvonne and St Luke's Hospice endures, so does my gratitude to Alan and Colinton Surgery. They really helped us.

Elsie was not much for spirituality but as she got closer to death, she asked to see a rabbi. Greg Alexander is an exceptional person – a very good rabbi, and exceptionally tolerant, especially, in our case, of my heathen family. He visited a few times though we were not congregants, and was really kind to Elsie. He didn't mind that Elsie immediately, with that flash in her eyes, turned him into a sparring partner. 'This is all very well, Rabbi,' she said with obsequious politeness, as I waited for what was bound to come next, 'but nobody knows where I am going, because nobody comes back.' She was willing him to argue with her, but he knew better, and took the joshing in good part. Then, with a sweet spiritual earnestness, he tried to explain to Elsie that this might be a good time for her to write an 'ethical (or spiritual) will'. He explained that this was a document for the children and grandchildren explaining Elsie's values, and what she wanted them to value as their lives went on. 'Very nice, Rabbi' (a theological version of 'You're a hundred per cent right'), a bit of exaggerated bright blue eye-rolling, and my generation and those that follow remain burdened with having to chart our own spiritual courses without a roadmap from Elsie. There are worse ways of having to navigate our future.

On three or four occasions during that last year of Elsie's life, Jenny and her husband Ian came to see her and to stay with us. Both Jenny's sons visited as well, at different times. I think this is a big part of what made that last year bearable for Elsie, and I will always be grateful for it, but it was not completely simple. I was the younger sibling, the one who had run away at 17, married out, chosen an odd career. I had always felt that Jenny had been the one to do the right thing – she stayed in Johannesburg, married a nice Jewish boy, provided two Jewish grandsons, and even when she emigrated it was as part of the great Jewish diaspora to Australia. She had remained one of the flock. I am not of course so naive as to think that Jenny, being as savvy and as sensitive as she is, may not have her own issues with being inside or outside, that she may not feel comfortable at being stereotyped in the way I stereotype her here. But in my narrative, she was the older sister who did well, remained understandable to my parents, whereas I had (by choice) flown the coop and condemned myself to a life incomprehensible to Elsie, a life which in some ways was a slap in my mother's face. In this calculus, I think we shared an assumption that of the two of us, it would be Jenny who would be the main carer for Elsie. In addition, Jenny was the older sibling and, although I rail against the gender stereotypes, also the daughter. Jenny would have done, and did, everything she could to help care for Elsie, and she was grateful, admiring and supportive of Louise and me. I knew I could turn to her at any time, and I did. But our long stories of growing up together, of the choices we both had made, of the worlds we now inhabited, affected everything.

When Jenny and I were children we had a miniature dachshund called Winky, whom we both adored. We would fight about who Winky loved more. Just like our mother before us with her cat experiments, we decided to test this question empirically. In my studies in psychology in later life, I was to learn how difficult it is to study emotion, especially in animals, but with the rare insight of youth, Jenny and I had an excellent, and valid, operational method. We would clear all furniture off the threadbare red lounge carpet, one of us would plonk Winky as close as possible to the centre of it, and then Jenny and I would sit at opposite ends of the carpet calling Winky to come to us. In terms of our research protocol, whichever of us Winky came to as we thus called, was the person who was more loved. As any scientist will understand, there were numerous confounding factors to consider, including:

1. Which of us plonked Winky down in the middle of the carpet;
2. The orientation of Winky relative to the two potential love objects when so plonked;

3. The tenderness of the plonking;
4. How loudly each of us called Winky;
5. How imploringly each of us called Winky;
5. Wind conditions;
6. Barometric pressure.

And so on (believe me, this is not an exhaustive list). This required multiple experimental trials under a range of carefully adjudicated conditions. After all that work, and after all these years, I honestly don't know what the experimental outcome was (but I know deep in my treacherous heart exactly where Winky's affections truly lay, and science be damned). If you think, though, that this intense wrangle in the 1960s for love from an animal weighing five kilograms has no bearing on issues of care for my dying mother, you don't know me. The fight for love, the fight all siblings have, and the fight Jenny and I had in spades, had a lot of influence on how two late-middle-aged people dealt (on balance, very well, I think) with our mother's illness and death.

If this seems trivial and a stretch, just you wait. The year I turned 13, along with millions of Jewish boys before and after me, involved my having my barmitzvah, which in turn involved having to buy a new suit. As the older sister, Jenny would also be on show, and she would need a new dress. Elsie drove us all the way from Whites, where we were living at the time, to Welkom, the nearest town of any size. I remember nothing of buying my suit, blue shirt and polka-dot tie. What I do remember, over 50 years on, is how long it took to find a dress for Jenny. It's completely understandable that as a teenaged girl she felt self-conscious and wanted to look her best, but I felt resentful that somehow this day of looking for my suit for my barmitzvah was overshadowed by her worries about not finding the right dress. I completely overlooked, of course, the fact that there had never been any discussion of Jenny having a batmitzvah and that in many ways she had every reason to be jealous of me, rather than the other way around. I don't think I complained about the day, but inwardly I filed this slight away, a slight I think I felt all the more acutely as it was further testimony to Jenny's ability to ask from her parents what any teenaged girl in her situation should be able to ask. I, on the other hand, never spoke about what I was feeling. So – pack it away, put it aside, and what better place to have the feeling pop out than 50 years later at your mother's deathbed?

Jenny got married in fairly traditional Johannesburg Jewish style of the period – she wore white, had a shul service and a reception at a nice hotel with a live band (a really modest affair by today's reality show-mediated standards). As the only brother of the bride, I had the honour of being a pole-holder, and I was expected to wear a hired dress suit to fit in with the rest of the retinue. When I think now of the fuss I made about this – I disapproved of the expense and thought the money could be better spent in such an unequal society, etcetera, etcetera. I may have had a point, but I was not 12 years old – I was an adult, a university graduate. The sub-text (which was not so sub, I don't think) was that Jenny had chosen to make it in mainstream terms, much to the delight of everyone, including my parents, and I felt both proudly and angrily marginal. I could not shake the sense of my having been a disappointment to both my parents, something I lived with until they died, and still live with today. I am well aware of the other side – the pride they felt, the joy I gave them – but if there were a good, honest book written about my family, I still feel (perhaps wrongly) that I would not get pride of place or, worse, that my choices would have to be explained away.

So in that last year of Elsie's life there was, from my side anyway, the weight of a long rivalrous history. It was very difficult for Jenny to be away, and she always thanked us profusely for what we were doing (and I have no doubt she meant it). I don't know how we could have managed without her help in all sorts of ways, not the least of which was her and Ian's clearing out Elsie's room at Sea Point Place. I could absolutely not face this, and Jenny took on this task lovingly and without complaint, difficult though it was for her. Jenny and Ian also looked after Elsie and the house one night so that Louise and I could go away. They, and their children, who also visited, could not have been kinder. But the minute

Jenny made even the slightest claim to knowing something about Elsie's needs that I didn't, my hackles would be up. After Elsie died (surprise, surprise), I started to do some research with colleagues about adult siblings, emigration and care for ageing parents.[1] I learned, to my relief, that my sibling issues are far from unique, and I was comforted by that. And my story is my story.

About six weeks before Elsie died, Jenny and Ian came to see us on what was to be the last visit. Elsie was deteriorating, hardly leaving her bed, thinner than I thought a person could be, with cancerous growths causing lumps and bumps to the skin. The sheer schlep of managing all of this was really getting to me. I think I had two conflicting wishes in my head regarding Jenny's visit (alongside a whole lot of others). The first was that I really needed a break and for Jenny to take over for a bit; and the other was that I wanted Jenny to see what I was going through and to let me get on with it and not interfere. I had been through the late nights, the vomit, the scariness of it all and, through no fault of hers, Jenny had not.

On the second day Jenny and Ian were here, Jenny told me that I couldn't see it, but our mother was actually much better than the last time they had been here. I have no doubt that this was well meant and kind, but I felt blind rage. First, from where I stood, it was glaringly obvious that Elsie was close to death and much, much worse. Could Jenny not see this? And therein, of course, was the second source of my rage: Jenny had said to me that there was something I could not see about our mother, something she could see. She was the big sister, the authority, the one who knew things I didn't. All a grown-up and macabre replay of testing for Winky's love. I was proud that I managed to contain my anger (although Jenny would probably have preferred me to express it), and I just changed the subject. It would soon become clear if Elsie was better, I thought, not without guilt, as I was almost willing our mother's decline as a way of proving my sibling point.

By the time Jenny and Ian (and their lovely son Dean) got here, we were hardly taking Elsie out at all as she was so ill. Against my advice, they took her out a few times, and I thought this exhausted her. After Elsie came back really tired after one of these outings, I was sitting quietly with her for a few minutes when Jenny came into her room. Jenny called me aside. 'I think you're exhausting her, Les. I know it's hard, but you must give her time to rest.' Imprinted on my mind is my marching to another room in the house, where I was changing the sheets. The sheets were a particularly strong shade of light green, and Louise and I had just bought them, and loved them. I see the sheets billowing over the bed as if handled by some sort of demon or dervish. I tried to keep quiet, but when Jenny, who could read banner headlines when she saw them, wanted to know what was wrong, out it all spilled in a messy rush. 'You come here and you tell me she's better, when she's really much worse. She's dying, she's dying, Jenny! Then you take her out and exhaust her when I warned you not to do this, bring her back in pieces, and then have the gall to tell me, who has had a year of this, who has been here every day, taken her to every appointment, dealt with everything, you tell me, of all people, to get out of the way …' And so on (I regret), and so on. And then, of course the floods of tears and the apologies, with Jenny being really good about hearing everything and really, really trying her best to listen. We were trapped in the cul-de-sac of our mother's death, our shared grief, our divisive rivalry, every good thing and every bad thing that had happened in our family brought to bear on that moment. I thank goodness that Jenny has such a capacity to listen, that she is so kind and cares so much. It has enabled us to go on as loving sister and brother. But my rage was my rage.

Part of the problem with all of this was that the reality was that we were not doing at all badly as a family. But this fact brought with it its own pressures. I loved it that our GP Alan, and all the doctors at Colinton, commented on how well we were doing, keeping Elsie at home and caring for her in an extended family in which our children, my cousin Pamie, and our friends played no small part. I loved it that people praised us as an extended family to spend the little money Elsie had left in her savings not on wills and memorials, but on contributing to some of the considerable costs Jenny and Ian incurred flying out to see her three or four times in that last year. The approval and good wishes, in sharp contrast to the hostility I experienced with some work colleagues, really helped keep me going. But they added to the pressure to get everything right, and I didn't know if I could.

Yvonne had spent many years working with families going through the process of someone dying, and it meant a great deal to me that she valued the care and attention we were giving to Elsie. She strongly supported our choice for Jenny and Ian to visit so often. When Louise and I were close to the end of our tether, some months before Elsie died, we spoke to Yvonne, asking her if she knew anyone who could look after Elsie for a few days so that we could have some respite. Her first reaction was that we had the carers, but she did not argue when we said we didn't feel that we could leave them alone with Elsie with nobody else here. She promised to think a bit and to see if she could find someone else, but in the event our friend Sharon Kleintjes stepped in and we did go away. But while we had been talking with Yvonne, she had mentioned her admiration for our family, how close we were, how well we got on, and so on. I really don't want to deny Yvonne's perceptions and I knew, as she had said at the start, that she would not lie to us. And, as I have mentioned before, Louise says that there is a generosity in receiving, and it's important to accept compliments with grace. But part of me felt really uncomfortable, not only because I was so overwrought and feeling that I was doing nothing at all right, but also because I worried that the happy families exterior we were managing to show to everyone was not really true, and that eventually the disappointing cracks would show. The last thing I needed was for people I was so dependent on to find out all that was wrong with me and then to remove their care. It never happened, and there was something a bit mad in my anxiety about this, but I guess I had earned the right to be a bit mad.

There was something else going on at the time, though, and this has stayed with me. It has to do with the economy of care. I am hugely admiring of Yvonne and of St Luke's Hospice and all they did for us. I was amazed that although we had resources, they would not charge for their services, preferring instead to allow us to make contributions as we would see fit. St Luke's is an organisation doing work that others often don't like to think about – the work of death. They often get very little in return. I have come to see that part of what they wanted from us was not a big thing, not a bad thing to ask or to want – they wanted us to be the family (or one of them) that gave someone what they would call a Good Death. They wanted us to be in concert with them, to give them a rare chance to see their work and their philosophy reflected back to them through a good experience for Elsie, and for us. And, you know what, for all the tensions, the difficulties in the family that felt so impossible at the time, the exploitation of others in the service of what we needed, my vacillations between good care and raging at my dying mother, despite all of this, and perhaps because of it, I think we did do quite well. But the idea of our being a poster family for how to help someone die scared me then, and it scares me now. I can't do it, and I don't want to. But in all the roiling emotions from everyone, I think this is what Yvonne and the other St Luke's people wanted or needed from us, a small and really harmless payback for all they did. In some ways, I prefer this idea of there being an implicit payback to the idea of the work of Yvonne and others being 'thankless'. To me, people who want no thanks are not quite human. They may be better than human, but not quite human nevertheless.

For most of the (almost) year that she spent with us, Elsie was dying very well indeed. She was so alive. Although the cancer spread all over the place, it didn't go to, or seemed not to affect, her brain. I kick against the patronising belief that old, sick people who are not demented and have 'all their marbles' are 'wonderful', somehow better morally than those who succumb to the often cruel ravages of brain disease. Elsie was lucky, and so were we – she had lived her whole life by her wits and her keen intellect, and as she died this did not change. When a kind friend commented, 'There are no flies on your mother!' I suppose I should have been flattered and taken this in good part, but I was irritated. We were lucky, that's true, and while Elsie could indeed be praised for being realistic and cheerful about her own death, the fact that she could still think and behave like the adult she was, with an intact brain, was a matter of luck.

If most of the year was, on balance, good, the last six weeks were awful. I'm well aware that compared to what many families go through, Elsie's experiences and ours were small potatoes. In addition, things that would really upset others didn't bother Elsie at all. I was bemused and not a little angry at her enthusiastic embrace of incontinence pads and nappies, for example. I found it almost unbearable to think of her not being continent. Elsie, who had waited her whole life to be cared for in some ways, had no problem being dressed and undressed by others, wiped clean by gentle hands, powdered, disinfected and perfumed. I would hear her through the door chattering away to the carers as they ministered to her, no doubt making their embarrassing and distasteful work easier for them.

Within a week of Jenny and Ian arriving that last time, the deterioration which had been there all along seemed to me to get faster and more dramatic. More lumps and bumps on that yellow old body, even more weight loss (she was already so thin that it had seemed to me impossible that she could lose another gram and continue to live), and much, much more pain. Worse than all of this for us, and probably partly as a result of the morphine and other drugs, she was not always fully conscious or fully aware of herself in the way we had almost come to take for granted.

One day, when Louise and I were sitting with her, she opened her eyes and looked at me with a terrified expression, and said, 'Leslie, I'm dying here.' These were the last words she said to me, and they were filled with such fear, such bewilderment, such desperation, and so different from how she had been throughout her illness. She was pleading with me, and I could not, or would not, help her. I can rationalise everything. I can say that she didn't really know what she was saying. I could say a million things, but that naked fear was as real as I have ever seen, and I wish she hadn't said those words.

A big part of the problem was that she just wouldn't die. She had outlived the oncologist's reluctant prognostications by a good number of months, and her heart was strong. I kept thinking about Babe, who had not been a smoker like Elsie, and who was doing well and living a very long life. With all the anguish of these last weeks, my mind kept returning, rebelliously, to the issue of Elsie's smoking. I had never blamed Elsie for starting smoking at the age of 17, but from a young age I had really hated her smoking and had argued with her about it, largely because the smoke made my eyes itch and my nose run. I have no way of knowing, of course, whether it was the smoking which had definitively led to the cancer (living for years in cement dust, for example, couldn't have helped either), but I was focused on this habit I had hated for so long. Elsie hadn't smoked for some years – a very clever gynaecologist had told her she had to give up smoking before having a hysterectomy and while she always threatened to start smoking again, she never did. But round and round in my head went the thought that if only Elsie had not smoked, she would not now be on her deathbed. Her heart was so strong that perhaps without the smoking she would have lived forever, or at least outlived me so I wouldn't have to go through this. I was so angry. Of course it does not take a psychoanalytic training to see that my anger was about the loss, and the horrible, senseless pain on the way to death, and blaming Elsie for smoking was much easier than blaming her for leaving me, as she was doing. To complicate matters, there is no question that I wanted her dead there and then – I wanted the pain to be over – but part of me didn't know if I could survive this. What was to become of me?

I should have helped her to die. It would have been the easiest thing in the world to put a pillow over that tiny face, to hold it down, and to let her go. What was the point of all of this suffering, when it was clear where it would end? I would never have taken the decision to help my mother die without consulting Jenny and the rest of the family; and I was also terrified of being convicted of murder. The fact is that I just didn't have the guts to take this on, and this is something I still regret. I am greatly admiring of Sean Davison, who helped his mother and others to die, and for the work done by Dignity South Africa dealing with the issue of compassionate death.[2] But I didn't have the guts to fulfil this final act of kindness to Elsie, and to us.

By this time Yvonne and sometimes her colleagues were visiting at least daily, and working closely with Alan and the doctors at Colinton, as well as with the oncologist, on morphine drips and other forms of pain care. We raised the idea with Yvonne of just giving Elsie too much morphine, but Yvonne was very clear that legally and morally she would do everything to make Elsie more comfortable (which she did), but she would not help her to die. As the painful weeks dragged on with Elsie in extremis, and all of us distraught, we communicated to Yvonne how hard this was for us to bear. She offered to admit Elsie to St Luke's inpatient facility for a time to give us a break, but we didn't want this. Not now, after all we had gone through. I don't think I was the only one feeling that I was failing at the last hurdle, but I did feel I was failing. I was grateful, though, that this was all happening over the summer break, so I didn't have too much work to do, and I wasn't going in to the office.

Yvonne was experienced in knowing when people were close to death, and on more than one occasion she called us together, the whole family around the deathbed, to say goodbye to this old woman we loved so much. But Elsie wouldn't die. She kept on and on into the next week and the next. She was barely conscious most of the time, but this perverse hanging on to life just carried on and on. This was no time for shouting loud, but there you have it. We had a number of stagings of Elsie dying with the family all around, and we did the heartfelt but textbooky telling her, 'You can let go now. We will be all right. We will always love you.' But the weak breath continued into the next day, the next and the next. Yvonne wanted this nice family, I think, to have the experience of the good moment of death, and she wanted Elsie to have the most gentle and dignified send-off possible, but it was not to be. On Elsie went, and so did we.

We did what we could – trying to be as kind as we could to Elsie and to ourselves, running away when we needed a bit of respite. The carers we had at the end were really lovely, and cared for Elsie so well and so gently we knew she was getting the best at all times. Pamie was there every day, as were Bev and Tony. We were lucky, and so was Elsie. One morning, with Elsie looking the same as she had done for days and days – dying but stable – Jenny and Ian and Louise and I went for a quick coffee in Woolworths in Cavendish Square, just to get away. For some reason we were in separate cars, and Louise and I went home first. When we got home, the lovely carer, Constance, said that she thought Elsie was now, at last, close to death. We contacted Jenny and Ian to come home, and sat with Elsie. She would take a few breaths, then nothing. Just when I was convinced she was dead, more raspy breathing. Eventually Constance said Elsie had died. Elsie had always spoken of having heard 'the death rattle' when her father died, but there was nothing like that. In a million clichéd death notices, people are spoken of as having 'died peacefully'. In some ways, I suppose, this was true of the last seconds or so of Elsie's life, but it was certainly not true of the past few weeks, which hadn't given us the sending-off, or Elsie the send-off, that the textbooks of good deaths called for.

And the timing. Having taken so long to die, Elsie couldn't wait for Jenny to get there in time. Unaccountably, and irrationally, I still feel guilty about this – as though somehow unconsciously I had manipulated this whole thing so that I would be the one who would win what after all was a trivial and silly fight – to be there at the side of the bed of a woman in extremis, and who, at that moment, didn't know she was dying. Jenny would never be so silly as to accuse me of such mean manipulation around our mother's death. But, irrationally, I accused myself. There is no question that to all of us the death was a release and a relief. Whoever tells you, though, that death magically stops all the nonsense of the living doesn't know what they are talking about.

Part III
Afterwords

14 | Death admin

The expression 'life admin' seems to be everywhere these days. It is even the title of a recent book by a savvy academic who understands the market.[1] I've never been very good at life admin and, embarrassingly, have to tell all my students that I have two response times to email: immediate or never, as I forget everything all the time unless I deal with it. Well, if life admin is a lot, death admin, though not as long-lasting, is even more work.

When my father died in 1983, he was buried in Johannesburg, where he lived and, as is the custom, a place next to his was reserved for his wife. I am not one for visiting graves or for believing that it is at the grave that one can find or speak to the dead person, but to Elsie it was very important to be buried next to her late husband. Long before she died I started liaising with rabbis in Cape Town and in Johannesburg. If she was to be buried in Johannesburg, we had to arrange for the body to get there, and we would have to have a rabbi from Johannesburg perform the burial, as was Elsie's wish. The Chevra Kadisha (Jewish Burial Society) were used to moving bodies around and they said that we could contact them. They did not work on the Sabbath but if Elsie were to die on a Saturday, we could leave a message for them, and they would pick up the body after the Sabbath. As luck would have it, Elsie did die on the Sabbath, and because we had had a difficult time with no visit from a medical doctor to confirm Louise's mother's death 18 months earlier, we knew to get the doctor in, even though it was after hours. Alan Wood's partner from

Colinton came, and he was businesslike and kind. We could send the carers on their way, off to the next privileged family going through death, but with the promise of a tea for them in a few weeks' time to thank them.

I phoned the Chevra to leave a message. Instead of getting the answering machine I got a very cross response from someone who berated me for calling on the Sabbath when I should have known better. No point in yes-butting. In the event, the men from the Chevra came when they could with their trolley. I didn't watch them putting Elsie on the trolley, but the sound of the wheels bumping over the concrete slabs in the garden didn't please me. She was gone. Her room was still full of medicines and ointments, pictures of my father and the grandchildren, bits and pieces of her. But the bed was stripped and bare, and it was time to pack her away. I don't know why I took a photograph of the dressing table full of things – I did this some time before she died – but I am very glad I did. In some ways this photograph speaks more to me of Elsie's illness and death than do photographs of Elsie herself.

We all flew to Johannesburg and stayed in the same bed and breakfast where Elsie stayed when she visited. Jenny and Ian had been extending and extending their tickets, as they had not planned to stay so long, and Jenny had to get back to work in Australia. I am so grateful that they just managed to stay for the funeral before having to fly off home. We all needed to be there. The funeral was low-key and quite pleasant. In the middle of the proceedings, a cell phone rang and the owner struggled to turn it off. We laughed. As it happened (and in confirmation of all my theories about the link between technology and the unconscious), the owner of the phone was someone who considered themselves very pious, disapproved of the Reform Shul, which was far too liberal theologically, and had been quite nasty to Elsie in the past. Elsie, being Elsie, had forgiven what I had thought was very bad behaviour and was on good terms with this person. But all of us chuckled at how Elsie would have laughed that of all the cell phones in the world not to have been properly switched off, it would be this one, in a House of God at the cemetery. The unconscious had spoken.

It was ages since I'd been in any religious service, apart from the Catholic funeral of Louise's mother the previous year, and I was pleased to see that the Reform Shul had moved a lot on issues of gender, allowing women to act as pallbearers, for example, so we all had a role in the proceedings. Jenny didn't want to speak, so only I spoke very briefly at the funeral, mainly thanking people, I think, but I have no recollection of what I said. It had been a good funeral, we were able to say good goodbyes to Jenny and Ian, and we returned home to life. There were issues of death certificates, closing of banking accounts, winding up Elsie's affairs. By the time Elsie died there was very little money left in her estate – we'd all agreed to spend what she had on life, on bringing the family together, and I never regretted this.

I like to tell everyone that Jenny and I fought over the will, and this is true. Elsie's instructions were very simple. Apart from a few very small bequests, everything was to go to Jenny and me, 50-50. Then the fights started, but not in the way you'd think. 'You take the money,' Jenny said. 'You did all the work.' 'No, you take the money. You had to be so far away.' 'No, you take it.' 'No, you take it.' And so on. I can't quite remember what we did in the end, and maybe things would have been different if there'd been more money to fight over, but, frankly, I don't think so. Elsie had rolled her eyes at Rabbi Greg's suggestions that she write an ethical will, but she'd clearly bequeathed something to us that was much more important than money. I remain so grateful to have my sister, and to have her love, even if I know in my heart, and on the basis of the best evidence available to me, that Winky loved me more than he loved her. I think we both knew that for people who are not living on the breadline, there are more important things to worry about than how much money you can cheat from your sibling. Elsie's life was full of compromise and lots of mistakes, as are all lives, but she'd done good by us. She's done good.

In many ways, I was completely unprepared for going through the long process of Elsie's dying, but in other ways, this was something to which my whole life was leading. I think those 11 and a half months of having Elsie with us, dying but mainly living, were in many ways the very worst time of my life, but also a time I feel deeply grateful for. As I write this, I am in that magic time of life where by many standards I am considered old (something I have no problem with – 'What's wrong with being old?' I hear my mother say) but physically well and with very few care responsibilities. I have been known to irritate my children when I say, 'I'm in the best time of my life – I am healthy, the parents are dead and the children are grown up.' But it's true, and there may even be some research to back up this idea.[2] It's not that long since Elsie died, and I honestly don't know how I managed it. But of course, it's just as true to say that I didn't manage it. These things come at us and, mostly, we survive them; not through any special moral qualities but through the fact of survival. One foot in front of the other, and one day after the other. And in my case, I had so much help. In so many ways, I wish Elsie's life had been different. I wish she'd had a career as a writer, I even wish she'd won the Nobel Prize. I wish she hadn't entangled me in her life so much – it wasn't fair. But I am so grateful for her, and I miss her.

For the first few months after her death especially, although I was relieved the ordeal was over and we had the house to ourselves, I would have moments, completely unbidden and seemingly random, of convulsive grief. I had dreams of being abandoned, of being left at school with no school shoes, of wandering around a foreign city with no idea how I'd got there or how I'd get home. Or was this home? My life carried on so much the same, as it often does for people who have the material resources and the work lives to carry on as before. But was I different? Was my life different? There is something odd about becoming an orphan in your 50s, losing the fantasy protective layer of the generation before, even when you know that the layer is tattered, old, ephemeral. But was I different? I think there was one way in which I was, in fact, profoundly changed, and not in the way I might have expected.

Unlike most of the people I knew growing up, and even as an adult, I had grown up in what was effectively a multi-generational household. I had a sense that there were old people who can live with you, and who could affect your lives. From experience, I knew that the self-contained nuclear family was a myth. In this I was different from Elsie, who had lived her whole childhood with cousins, aunts, uncles and various other hangers-on coming and going. I didn't have that, but I did have Granny and the Chicken. They were so out of the ordinary, so cartoonish in their bad behaviour, that I think in my mind they represented serious bad luck on my family's part and much less the reality of the need for care of the older generation. So somehow, they don't really count. There is also a lot of very sentimental writing (even academic research) on how wonderful it is to have grandparents around – grandma bakes wonderful pies with apples as rosy as her cheeks, and grandpa teaches the kids to whittle and to fish. I'm not saying that there aren't families like this, because there are, and good for them. But I have come to see that the biggest secret of all, it seems to me, is the secret that stares so many of us in the face – the secret that people get older and frailer, that they need more care, and they die.

I was struck during the whole time we were looking after Elsie by two reactions we got from many others. One was 'You are so wonderful.' I shouldn't mind this so much, because it is meant as a compliment, but I think we had limited choice unless we wanted Elsie to fall and to fall, and to spend the last year of her life in misery. We didn't really have an option. The second reaction was far more common. All sorts of people began to tell us about their own experiences with care, whether with dying relatives or with people with disabilities. I had honestly not known what people whom I saw regularly were dealing with. My friend the disability studies scholar Rosemarie Garland-Thomson often says that disability is nowhere till you see it, and then it is everywhere. The same is true, and I think for the same reasons, of care. We middle-class, successful people construct our world on the illusion that we are independent, when in fact we depend every day on others for our lives and well-being. Think of life without garbage collectors. We need them in order to get on with our lives. More than this, though, I think there is something we see as shameful when we give care its rightful placc in our lives, when we give it legitimacy. This goes, I think, both for our need to be cared for, and our need to care for others. We all love heroism and big dramatic gestures, we all idolise parents of disabled children, calling them 'selfless' and 'wonderful', but why do we have to make them so otherworldly?

I trained as a clinical psychologist in the early 1980s – somewhat to my shock, I realise that I have been a psychologist for almost 40 years, well over half my life. At the time I studied psychology as an undergraduate, the field of developmental psychology as it was taught to me dealt only with child development. We stopped thinking about development at adolescence. Erik Erikson, who won a Pulitzer Prize for his study of Gandhi's non-violence, had in 1959 written his *Identity and the Life Cycle*, examining human development across the lifespan,[3] but it took some time, in South Africa at least, for us to consider developmental psychology as the study of all of life. I was also taught, as a budding clinical psychologist, that there was not much point in trying to do in-depth psychotherapy with people in what has now come to be known as the 'second half of life'. This was because, the story went, the personality has already been formed by early adulthood, and older people are likely to be more rigid and resistant to change than are others. The irony of my having been taught this by a psychologist who was himself about 70 years old at the time, and very much still exploring life, was not lost on me. This neglect of most of life by my discipline as I was taught it angered me at the time, but since Elsie died, I'm even more angry. I am furious that the experience I had of trying my best to look after my dying mother, struggling, doing some things well but failing in other ways, was something my discipline hardly looks at. As I have given talks on these issues and spoken with dozens and dozens of people, the number of people who have said to me, 'I thought I was the only one who had to deal with this', has been staggering. I don't want to deny that there is something in the nature of caring for a sick or dying person that may in itself be isolating – life does just shrink when you are so focused on bodily needs, on whether someone has eaten, vomited, pooed. But there is something else at work here. This is the lack of a social space to speak about such things, to have this experience of care helped a bit by the knowledge that you are not the only one going through it. I have looked at a lot of lifespan developmental psychology textbooks recently, and generally they say very little, if anything at all, about the very common reality of the demands (and opportunities and pleasures) of care of people other than children, as part of development. Even feminist books looking at women's development often don't take care across the lifespan seriously.

I can give you a million academic explanations of why I think this is so, but I think they all boil down to ideas about people being individuals pursuing their individual life-goals. It's not for nothing that a life-goal for Jung, the founder of analytic psychology, is called 'individuation', or that Carl Rogers, who played an important part in popularising psychology and counselling in the USA, spoke about 'self-actualisation'. It's also important that in contemporary South Africa, following the example of Nelson Mandela and Desmond Tutu, there is a push-back against this individualism through ubuntu philosophy, with personhood being defined as something that happens in relationship – 'a person is a person through other people'. In general, though, and certainly through the discipline of psychology that I am part of, we just don't make public the reality of care issues for many, if not most people. This is part of why, after Elsie died, I decided to write this book. Mine is one story, and I am telling it for all the selfish reasons anyone would want to tell their own story, but also because I honestly believe that ordinary stories like mine need to be told. I'm pleased that there are now more and more books being written about dying, and some of these do talk about care, but there need to be more.

St Luke's, and Yvonne in particular, had been an enormous help to us, and Louise and I wanted to do something, apart from donating money, to try to begin to repay their care. As these things happen, we bumped into an old friend while walking our dogs in the park, who was now working at St Luke's. She asked us if we could do some work with the Spiritual Care team of volunteers. Louise was not free during the week because of work commitments, but I could make the time. I was lucky enough to spend quite a bit of time with a caring, insightful and generous group of people, from a range of religious and non-religious (including atheist) backgrounds, who allowed me to hear about their work, their joys and frustrations. One thing that became clear was that they worried, like so many people doing caring work, that their work was not visible, and was difficult to explain to others. This concern about invisibility was so familiar to me – about death and care, as I have mentioned, but also about other issues in care like the crucial but hidden role cleaners and security guards play in looking after people with mental disorders in psychiatric institutions. So we thought together about how to make the invisible more visible. One of the things we did, and something I am proud of, was to produce a beautifully illustrated little book on spiritual care work at St Luke's.[4] I was so lucky to have this chance to work with creative people (including my friend Barbara Hutton, who did the layout of the book) on a creative project. The book was not about Elsie, and it was not directly about Yvonne Jackman either – in the St Luke's system her formal role is that of a hospice nursing professional, and not of spiritual carer. But as I helped the carers put their ideas down and showcase their artwork, I had the chance to think through, and give appreciation for, some of the really good things about Elsie's dying process and how we were all looked after. Lucky, lucky me.

When I was director of the Child Guidance Clinic at the University of Cape Town (UCT) over 20 years ago, a colleague gave me a card with a Gary Larson Far Side cartoon showing a building labelled 'Crisis Clinic' on fire and floating in a river headed for sure destruction at the waterfall ahead. Clearly, Larson knows something about how organisations dealing with trauma become traumatised themselves, and how the organisations may come to reproduce, through their internal functioning, aspects of the very problem they are designed to improve. I have seen this many times in my professional work. Here are three examples.

One case was working with a group of teachers at a school for deaf children where we found that a major problem for the teachers was that they felt unheard by other teachers and by management. Another was in work we did supporting an organisation providing accelerated schooling for students who had been excluded during apartheid: all the staff were exhausted by the extremely fast pace at which they found themselves having to work. The third example was a health programme where there was a concern that patients were viewed not as whole people but as collections of symptoms; the nurses felt that they were viewed by colleagues just as a collection of clinical skills rather than as people in their own right.[5]

In my work for St Luke's, I felt the same familiar recognition of the organisation that deals with problems very well while also reproducing them internally. The spiritual carers, who were providing sterling support to families and communities in dire need, worried that their work could not be seen, could not be properly explained, and would not be seen as being of value in a world in which measurable outcomes are more highly valued. They spoke about how, from their point of view, the fundraising efforts of St Luke's (which they agreed were essential for their work to continue) were more highly valued than what they actually did for dying people and their families. I think part of why I worked so happily with the spiritual carers was that I had been through the experience of leaving the kingdom of the well and living in that strange, nameless and peculiarly invisible world of care. And this was exactly where they did their work. I wanted (and still want) our society, and my discipline of psychology, to become more open about the kind of experience that so many people go through.

A year to the day after Elsie died – on 15 January 2012 – I sat down to write this book. I knew I wanted to make visible to others what had become visible to me. Well, here's a piece of advice one would not expect someone of my background to need. Don't try to write a book about the loss of your mother at the very time you are in such grief for her, when it is just a year since she died, you are busy with the unveiling of her tombstone, and your father-in-law, like your mother before him, is living in your house very close to death. Big mistake, and an obvious one.

I'm not altogether surprised by my trying to do this, though. I always say that the only people who have to present themselves as big and powerful are those who feel small and powerless inside. We often forget that narcissism and all the self-aggrandisement that goes with it is not about self-love, but about the worry that if I don't puff myself up to be big and wonderful, nobody will notice me. The sheer omnipotence on my part of thinking I could knock off a book about my mother quickly and so soon after her death now tells me everything about how powerless I felt during her dying, and afterward, how without words to tell what had happened to me. Just like the St Luke's spiritual carers and many others, I was reproducing the very problem I wanted to address.

I had no choice but to put the book project aside and to allow it to percolate as a continual but barely perceptible hum under everything else I was doing in my personal and professional life, like the sound of an air-conditioner: you can tune it out sometimes but it is always there. When Louise read this part of my manuscript, she reminded me that for some psychoanalysts, especially in the Kleinian tradition, the concept of 'phantasy' (as opposed to 'fantasy') has been likened to a background hum.[6] The concept of phantasy, simply put, is that we see and experience the world through the organising lens of our past experiences. Everything I was seeing was to some degree or another structured by my experience of Elsie's death. The book was always there – and in fact my daughters Alison and Rebecca quite frequently asked when it would eventually be written – but it was also not there. This did wonders for my career, as it happens. Most people, in my experience, have helpful ways of avoiding writing. These may involve cleaning the kitchen, tidying the desk, eating muffins for energy and inspiration, deciding I just have to read these 45 articles before I can possibly write mine, and so on and so on. Like all writers and academics, I constantly live with the curse of procrastination, and in fact I am astonished that in all the talk at the moment about a mental health crisis among academics, there is so little discussion of how procrastination eats you from the inside and affects your mental health.

I don't think what was going on with my avoiding committing to writing this book was pure procrastination, however. Leaving aside the fact that I always have to be special – no garden-variety procrastination for me – I had to let my process of not writing this book teach me something, something I thought I already knew. Since Elsie died, I have been exceptionally productive academically, writing huge amounts, getting articles and other (edited and co-written) books out at a cracking pace. All of which had value, and lots of joy and pleasure, in themselves. But instead of cleaning the kitchen, instead of writing, reading to avoid writing, doing mountains of meticulous administration that somebody else could do (and complaining about it) to avoid writing, I had another avoidance at work. I was writing to avoid writing. I wrote and wrote things that were quite easy for me to write, so that I didn't have to face the problem of my not writing this book. It got to the point where I was publishing more in one year than many colleagues publish in an entire academic career (I kid you not). If I went any faster, I would, like the tigers in the Rudyard Kipling story I read as a child, chase around and around until I turned into a pool of butter.[i] I couldn't stop. And I was enjoying moving so much that why would I even think of stopping? But the hum kept humming, and the slight but barely perceptible discomfort of the grit in the shoe, or in the oyster, was there all the time. I could not dodge this one forever.

For all my wanting to understand absolutely everything (I think I'm like my mother in this), some things are mysterious. I honestly don't know how I came to break the impasse, but I am glad I did. The first thing I had to recognise, after years of writing bits and pieces of this book, both in my head and on paper, was that I needed help. I started to explore the idea of doing a degree in creative writing, and settled on applying through the English Department at my university. It was only

---

i 'The Story of Little Black Sambo' is, of course, rightly called racist, and I am no Kipling fan, but the image of rushing and rushing until the very structure of you disappears – until you fall apart – is something that speaks clearly to me.

during the first joint supervision meeting that I had with both my supervisors, Shaun Viljoen and Louise Green, that the full impact of what I was doing really hit me. I spend a large proportion of my professional life supervising PhDs and mentoring more junior academics, and I love this work. Now here I was, in Shaun's office, waiting for feedback from my supervisors on my draft dissertation proposal. As an academic, I am very accustomed to the often bruising process of receiving negative peer reviews on my work – I often say that being an academic is an addiction to humiliation, because no matter how senior and experienced you are, those hurtful negative reviews from people assessing your work, or deciding whether you should get a research grant, just keep on coming. But this felt (and was) different. I was the boy who didn't go to nursery school because his mother couldn't manage it, and then went to big school far too young. I was the teenager who ran away from home and started university much too early for my own good. I was always the little, little boy, the mama's boy, trying to be big, and convincing both myself and others that I was indeed big enough and strong enough to stand on my own two feet. And by a host of objective measures, I was big. I was good at being big, successful and someone in the world.

And here I sat in Shaun's office, with these two kind adults, both of them in terms of the university hierarchy objectively of lower status than I was, but nevertheless feeling terrified about what they would say, and far more vulnerable than I was comfortable with. As I listened to their kind, careful, but also trenchant analysis of my work, their comments infused with disciplinary knowledge and experience I didn't have, the tears got me. Since Elsie's death, I had become interested theoretically in questions of care. I had joined a Care Ethics network. I had taken every opportunity to proselytise the care ethics (and profoundly feminist) gospel that all human beings, all living things, are dependent on others, and we all need care. I wanted to be part of the fight, which I saw as an important fight, to make the care that we all receive all the time but often invisibilise, visible and recognised. I had made this the topic of articles and speeches – even of a talk to graduating students at Wits University. All good. But of course, for obvious reasons of my own history, there were ways in which I had resisted being cared for. For me, being cared for by my mother – my wonderful, wonderful mother, whom I miss so much to this very day – was tantamount to being engulfed in her own needs, to losing myself. I realised that even my decision never to tell my parents about my difficulties at boarding school was partly to protect them, but mainly to stop me from being washed away in a torrent of anxiety and concern – all offered in love, but to me a dangerous torrent nevertheless.

I loved doing my first PhD, which I completed as a young father, and I knew that I would never be crazy enough to do another one. As far as the certainty of that prediction goes, all I can say in my defence is that at that time I also knew for sure that I would never be bald, as I had so much hair. It's not possible to be more bald than I am at this stage of my life. No harm in getting things wrong. But there were two rather odd things about my first PhD – well, not about the PhD itself, which I remain proud of, but about the process. The first was that in the early stages I really didn't want to hear anything from my supervisor, Don Foster. I wanted to do everything on my own, without his help. Don read me well, backed off, and gave very helpful feedback at later stages. But yet again, as a young PhD candidate, I had run away from home and the help I could have got earlier on, which would have made life much easier. The second thing I did with that first PhD was even closer to home. At the time, I was married to Sally, my first wife, and we had two very young children. Sally was very supportive and helpful to my work. But throughout the process, I never told Elsie, who was in Johannesburg, that I was doing a PhD. You might think it would come up, and in any usual family it would. But I felt at the time that I would not be able to bear her anxiety, and her constant questions about my progress. Now, it is the job of any concerned parent, and certainly of any Jewish Mother, to worry over her child's progress and to ask how things are going. Most children – especially of Jewish Mothers – learn to deal with this concern, and even to welcome it in many cases. There are, after all, worse things than having people care about you. But in some ways, not for me. The first Elsie heard of my doing a PhD was when I received my results. She didn't know about the struggles I had had at boarding school, and she didn't know about the struggles that were an inevitable part of doing a PhD.

A PhD, like a barmitzvah, like dying, is a rite of passage. I had not fully allowed myself to go through the passage the first time – I didn't allow my supervisor fully to be my guide, and I didn't allow my surviving parent to experience the worry that parents of children doing PhDs are privileged to experience (and I know this privilege from the inside as both my daughters have PhDs and, boy, did I worry! And proudly worry…). In my mind, I had made my barmitzvah partly not about myself but about the memory of Jenny looking for the right dress. How unfair of me. Since Elsie's death, I had become an advocate for giving issues of care their due place in the world. But it took what felt like forever eventually to realise that if I really wanted to deal with what I had learned from looking after Elsie as she died, I needed to do something about allowing myself to be cared for. In that day in Shaun's office, I came to see that at last I was doing something care ethicists talk about: for care to be completed, it has to be received. As Louise says, there's a generosity in receiving. For a long time I had been mean to Elsie and others on this count.

I am not claiming a damascene moment of dramatic change here, and I resist with every fibre of my being the thought of all difficult experiences, like Elsie's death, being Things That Have Been Sent To Teach Us About Life. Spare me the humbug. It is also far from true that I am not, or have not been, capable of accepting care from others. I depend on, and have done for years, the support of many others, not least of them being Louise and my children. I'm still not fabulous at allowing too much opportunity for supervision – I am not a completely new person. But as I sit here 10 years almost to the day after Elsie moved in with us to live and die in our home, I know that something, however small, has changed in me. I wish Elsie was alive to see it, but, of course, if she were alive, it wouldn't have happened. Sad but also wonderful, when you think about it.

15 | How I lost my mother

How do you lose your mother? How do you lose anyone? It's not the same as losing spectacles or keys. I lose those constantly, and my family have learned to say, 'Don't panic. They are where you put them. Have you actually looked for them?' Well, I have actually looked for my mother, and I suppose that I can say that she is, if not a hundred per cent right, a hundred per cent here. And a hundred percent not here. I don't believe in life after death, I don't believe she's looking down on me smiling indulgently (or even furiously, or exasperatedly). But like everyone who has lost someone, and we all have or will unless we are very, very unlucky to be lost before everyone else, I have to deal with, and live with, memory.

When I lose my glasses or my keys, my family says, 'Think where you were when you last had them, and work from there.' Good, helpful advice. But where was I when I last had my mother? I can think of the day she died, but of course the longing and the loss started long before that. I joke with friends who have young children: 'Ruin them emotionally when they're young,' I say, 'or they will leave you.' And in fact I do believe that one of the greatest ironies of parenting is that our crowning success comes when our children can go off into the world and make their own lives, becoming adults. I went off into the world and did well, and for Elsie this was in many ways a great betrayal. And to be fair, although I never would have admitted this to her, I was actively betraying her. I wanted out, I wanted my life, and I made sure that, like Shakespeare's

Macduff, I was 'untimely ripped' from my mother, leaving us both scarred. In some ways, however, I had lost her long before that, when she needed me to be something other than her child. Psychoanalysis would, of course, say that every birth is a traumatic separation of infant from mother. You lost me at Day One, and I lost you.

Life, as they say, goes on. Louise's father David was still living in Johannesburg, and as far as we could see, he was really struggling. He had had a bruising and exhausting battle to do his best by his beloved wife, Rose, who had died of dementia under very difficult circumstances in April 2009. He had faced some family difficulties in addition to this, and we were concerned that he was depressed. Louise was caring for him by phoning him four times per day, but we thought it would be better, if he wanted this, if he came and lived with us. He decided to visit us over the December holidays the same year Elsie died, and we hoped he would decide to stay. We met him at the airport, and he looked thin and gaunt. He had a troublesome cough, for which he had seen his family doctor in Johannesburg a few times. The doctor had told David that he had a postnasal drip and, according to David, the doctor had also told him that he must not fuss over his health. Having met this doctor before, I had no doubt that David was accurate about what had been said to him. To us, though, he looked very ill indeed, and we did not like the sound of his having been coughing for months. Louise took him to see Dr Dani Cahill, who at that time was still working at our trusted Colinton Surgery. In the very first consultation, within a matter of minutes, Dr Cahill suspected that David had lung cancer. This was confirmed on further examination, and it was now Stage 4. If this sounds familiar, that's because it is.

They say that lightning never strikes twice, but both Elsie and David had been fobbed off by doctors, told effectively that they were imagining things, and both were seriously ill. Both eventually got excellent health care from wonderful doctors, but by then both were in Stage 4 cancer. If this is how the health of two elderly people with privilege can be handled – with disavowal, inattention and rank incompetence – I can only imagine how other people are treated. As had been the case with Elsie, there was a part of me that wanted to sue the doctors concerned, and perhaps we should have, but our focus was much more on the immediate issue of the best possible care going forward.

We dug in for the long haul. It was less than a year since Elsie had died. We had not foreseen that we would once again have the decision about having a sick parent living with us. There was no question, though, that we would do this. Although Louise had been very close to Elsie, and would have taken her in even if I had not been there, I did feel that this was a chance for me to repay her a bit. We were concerned that when we went back to work David would be lonely, so we got two small dogs to keep him company. When they arrived, the first thing they did was go to sleep under his bed, so they seemed to understand their role very well. In the event, David's health deteriorated dramatically and very quickly.

The unveiling of Elsie's tombstone was coming up, a year after her death, and we were due to go to Johannesburg for this. It became clear that David was now very ill, so Louise stayed with him. Thank goodness she did. A week later, and in fact exactly a year and a week after Elsie died, David died in our home, in the same bed where Elsie had died before him.

Not long after Elsie had died, Rebecca had been awarded a large scholarship to do her PhD in London. Shortly before she left, she and I, very unusually, had an enormous row, most of the details of which I honestly can't remember (repression is a wonderful thing), but it affected me deeply for months, and even years. It's really not that unusual for people who are about to be parted to have an argument just before the time of parting, and we can speculate that having the fight may be a way of making the parting easier. One thing I do remember very clearly from our argument was Rebecca's telling me that she felt that while I was very proud of her achievements (which I was), I kept myself at a distance from her and was not that interested in her as a person. I found this feedback devastating, but I have had similar comments from Alison, and I've really had to think about this.

I am very clear that I adore and admire my children with a ferocity and love I had not thought possible, so the problem was not that I didn't care enough. There was something else I was doing. And then it dawned on me. I don't know if this is how my children see it, but this version makes some sense to me. I had spent much of my life adoring but feeling swallowed up by my mother, and I was determined not to do the same to my children as was done to me. It wasn't fair. I added to this determination in the wake of my divorce. I believed then and believe now that other things being equal, parental divorce is not a kind thing to do to a child. I felt (feel) that I let them down. Whatever the rights and wrongs were with my divorce (and these things are always more complicated than they seem), I was one of the adults putting children through this. It wasn't fair. To complicate matters further, I felt so broken after the divorce and before I met Louise that all I wanted to do was grab my children to myself for comfort, and never let them go. I felt this powerfully, and for a very long time. But as the child of a woman who needed too much from me, who unwittingly but nevertheless unfairly made me into her little man at a very young age, I was determined not to do the same to my own children. I let them go, tried my best not to demand, and tried to convince them in every way possible that I was fine and happy, out there in the world doing fun things. I didn't want them to look after me. I treasure the good relationships I have with my children – and the good very substantially outweighs the bad – but I have to live with the feeling I have that each of them, in her own way, has felt at times that my attention was not on her; that, not to sugar-coat this, I in some way abandoned her. I am so lucky that I have come to know this in the context of what are mainly very close relationships with my children (I adore them and I believe that they adore me), but by not wanting to demand too much, I've given them reason to feel abandoned in some way. You can dress this up any way you like, but my feeling is that I've wounded them, even if in a small way. Where does my wounding come from? I don't know the full answer to this, but I am certain that at least part of the story is that I didn't want to inflict the same wounds on my children as my mother had inflicted on me. She couldn't bear to let me go, she couldn't see me as fully separate from her, so off I go to the other extreme and communicate to my own children that I am only too keen to let them go, to let them be separate and different from me. In the big picture of how we all get on and love one another, this is really not a huge issue, but it's real for me. I don't know properly how to ask my children for things, and it is a slow process of learning from them that I may ask, and that my needs will not engulf them as I felt engulfed. I am lucky and grateful that they are my teachers and helpers in this regard, as is Louise in no small measure. I have to learn fully the generosity of receiving.

I don't fully understand how, and when, I lost my mother. I am lucky and grateful that I don't have to write a book called *How I Lost My Children*. Unwittingly, and with the very best of intentions, I was working on that book for some time. It's inconceivable to me as I sit here that that book will ever need to be written, and I am grateful for that, but in trying not to engulf my children with closeness, I ran the risk of their feeling me to be far, far away. Like everyone else, I try my best, but it is partly a matter of profound luck, and a matter of the generosity and kindness of others, that the best I tried did not have catastrophic consequences. I don't like thinking about this, but it does help me be more understanding of Elsie. Some of her engulfing, smothering warmth to me, after all, may have been occasioned by her own experience of being the outsider, unwanted, the wrong person in her family. If I allow myself the luxury of thinking that I meant well with my children but over-compensated for my own wounds, I must allow the same for Elsie, who may also have been compensating. Closeness and distance, closeness and distance. So hard to find a good path through that.

In the Jewish religion, the unveiling of the tombstone is supposed to mark the end of the mourning period, the return to life as usual. It didn't feel that way for me. Louise was dealing with the terminal illness of her father, and so were we all. Rebecca had gone off to London to start her PhD, and in the three weeks that she was away, her step-grandfather had deteriorated very badly in health and was now terminally ill; and her beloved uncle from Zimbabwe (her mother's brother-in-law), who had come to Cape Town for a medical procedure, had died unexpectedly. Worst of all, one of her very closest friends, a young woman of her own age, had died tragically of a brain tumour. When Alison and I went up to Johannesburg for the unveiling, Rebecca flew to Cape Town for her friend's funeral. In differing ways, and to differing degrees, we were in the thick of it.

Thank goodness for Alison, who, apart from being a mourner herself and missing her Bobbe (this is Yiddish for 'Grandmother', and what we all ended up calling Elsie for years, as she wanted us to) terribly, supported me in my role as chief mourner. At the unveiling, as is the custom, I had to nominate two people to remove the cloth covering over the tombstone (to 'unveil') it. It was obvious that the first of those people would be Alison, but I had to make a decision about who to ask to be the second to undertake what is regarded as an honour. In the moment, the decision was not difficult.

Much to the distress of Elsie and other relatives at the time, quite a few years previously, her sister Ada had died under difficult circumstances. After her husband Louis died, Ada had decided to fulfil a long-held dream of going to live in Israel. She had been left well off by Louis, and she was convinced that she would not live very long, so she moved, on a permanent basis, into a five-star hotel in Tel Aviv. In the event she lived much longer than her money lasted, and this very wealthy woman, who had donated widely to charities and had always been exceptionally generous, now found herself a pauper. She moved into an indigent care facility where she did not even have her own clothes – residents were just given clothes available from a communal pile. There, uncomplaining and apparently happy, she lived until she died; she was buried in a pauper's grave with no gravestone of her own. I don't know the ins and outs of all the extended family fights that happened before and after Ada's death, nor the rights and the wrongs of it all. But among many in the family there was the view that my cousin Dinky, Ada's only child, who lived in London, should have done more to help Ada financially when she was alive and that she should have given her a more dignified burial. Dinky had disagreed with this, but as it happened, in memory of her mother she decided to return to South Africa and have a plaque placed on her father's grave, with an inscription for Ada. Dinky arranged for the sanctification of this plaque on the same day as Elsie's unveiling.

I wish to this day that Elsie had known about the plaque, because it would have given her such pleasure to think of her sister remembered in this way. Whatever fights there were in our family, and beyond, Elsie believed in reconciliation, and in taking any hand that was extended, even if there had been acrimony in the past. I had been close to Dinky when I was a teenager and we both lived in Johannesburg. There was no question in my mind that Elsie would have wanted me to give Dinky the honour of being the second unveiler.

Once I had made this decision, I saw what I read as the stony face of a distant relative but family patriarch. This man was much older than me, and he had had quite a rocky relationship with Elsie. He was also, I knew, a stickler for protocol and doing things by the book. Not only had I made what to Orthodox Jews was the scandalous decision to allow women to be involved in unveiling (this was for men only), but I had snubbed the person who should have by rights and tradition been first in line for the honour – the patriarch. If I had to make the decision over again, I don't think I would change it. For Elsie it was important to welcome somebody, like Dinky, who had faced criticism from the family, back into the fold, to mend broken bridges. I tried to be pleasant to the patriarch, and I tried on quite a few occasions to get in touch with him after Elsie died, because I think that is what she would have wanted. But he has never got back to me. I don't know if he is now officially on non-speaking terms with me (how would I?), but I do know that he has a history of not speaking to people who have slighted him or family members. I guess I'll never know. I don't especially want or need to see him again, but it was important for me to try to do what I think Elsie would have wanted me to do. So I tried. Maybe not hard enough, but I did try.

In some ways, this is such a trivial issue – I had not seen the man for years before Elsie's death and I don't think I would enjoy seeing him again. My worrying, till today, all these years later, that I may have offended him comes not from guilt about him, but from something that is important to me. So often, and at unexpected times, our family are in a situation in which we ask, 'What would Bobbe do?' Not infrequently, we imagine Elsie telling someone that she is 'a hundred per cent right' or nodding vigorously in agreement and then surreptitiously rolling her blue eyes at us. It's tender to think of her and remember her like this. I find myself talking in a cadence that is hers, hearing her voice through me, wagging my finger in a particular way, wanting to show Elsie that I, too, now have arthritic fingers just like hers, and there's nothing as good as an arthritic finger-wag.

The concept of haunting (very fashionable in current psychoanalytic circles) is often seen as something scary and chilling. As much as I was afraid of being engulfed by Elsie for a good deal of my life, not quite knowing where she ended and I began, I find being haunted by her in this way – finding myself speaking with her voice, wagging her finger, seeing with her eyes – comforting and warming. In many ways the 'What would Bobbe do?' question is the very opposite of the currently fashionable question so beloved by evangelicals, 'What would Jesus do?' I can just hear Elsie – I can really hear her – saying, 'Well, it's clear as day. What would Jesus do? He'd vote for Trump.' And those eyes would roll. She died long before Donald Trump became president, but I have no doubt in my mind that she would have been appalled, and would have found the business of rebutting anyone who supported Trump such, such fun. Shouting loud, fighting the fight.

So when we ask, 'What would Bobbe do?' what are we asking? I don't think we are asking for a moral legacy for the saintly department, and Elsie shared my irritation with the instant beatification of anyone immediately upon their death. Elsie had struggled through a lot of her life and did many things she shouldn't have, like all of us. But also, and especially in later years, she had such vitality, such ability at last to enjoy things, that a 'What would Bobbe do?' question is not about what the right thing to do is, but about the sheer joy of the struggle, the delight of being out there in the world, having opinions, arguing, changing your mind sometimes but working even harder to change the minds of others.

All legacies are mixed, the good with the bad, the things you wish had not happened, the losses, the scars that won't go away, along, if you're lucky like me, with the wonder of having known an exceptional person. And the struggle, the struggle – that's the essence of life. When I read 'What Would You Have Done?' A Problem Story by Elsie Cohen, 59 Abel Road, Johannesburg, I didn't at first realise that the first name of the hero was so similar to mine – identical to the second syllable of my name, in fact. Maybe part of me started a long time ago, maybe part of me, like Elsie now, will have some meaning into the future. In the meantime, since we are talking here about endings, allow me here to paraphrase the end of Elsie Cohen's Problem Story:

Leslie did the right thing …

What he did I leave to you, dear reader, to decide.

Notes

Chapter 3

1 *SA Jewish Report*, 7–14 February 2014: 14.

2 Devarim (Deuteronomy), 32:7.

3 Devarim (Deuteronomy), 32:6.

4 Philip Roth, *The Ghost Writer*, international edition (New York: Vintage, 1995), 100.

Chapter 4

1 Ena Jansen, *Like Family: Domestic Workers in South African History and Literature* (Johannesburg: Wits University Press, 2019).

Chapter 5

1 Megan Healy-Clancy, *A World of Their Own: A History of South African Women's Education* (Charlottesville: University of Virginia Press, 2014).

2 Nadine Gordimer, 'Treasures of the Sea', *Trek: A South African Literary Monthly* 14, no. 6 (8–11 June 1950): 8.

3 Mark Gevisser, *Lost and Found in Johannesburg: A Memoir* (New York: Farrar, Straus and Giroux, 2014).

4 Umberto Eco, *The Role of the Reader: Explorations in the Semiotics of Texts* (Bloomington: Indiana University Press, 1984).

Chapter 6

1 Sally French, 'Can You See the Rainbow? The Roots of Denial', in *Disabling Barriers – Enabling Environments*, ed. John Swain (London: Sage Publications, 2004), 69–77.

2 Rose Zwi, *Last Walk in Naryshkin Park* (Melbourne, Australia: Spinifex Press, 1997).

3 Rod Freedman, *Uncle Chatzkel* (2000). Documentary, 52 minutes. https://www.imdb.com/title/tt0267062/

4 Anne Frank, *The Diary of a Young Girl: The Definitive Edition*, ed. Otto Frank and Mirjam Pressler; trans. Susan Massotty (London: Penguin Books, 2012), 250.

5 Ari Shavit, *My Promised Land* (New York: Spiegel & Grau, 2013).

6 https://www.theguardian.com/music/2013/apr/14/justin-bieber-anne-frank-belieber. The Facebook post of the Anne Frank House was suitably restrained, reading: 'Last night Justin Bieber visited the Anne Frank House, together with his friends and guards. Fans were waiting outside to see a glimpse of him. He stayed more than an hour in the museum. In our guestbook he wrote: "Truly inspiring to be able to come here. Anne was a great girl. Hopefully she would have been a belieber." Tonight Bieber will give a concert at Arnheim in the Netherlands.'

7 Philip Roth, *The Ghost Writer*, international edition (New York: Vintage, 1995).

8 Nathan Auslander, *Hope: A Tragedy* (New York: Pan Macmillan, 2012).

9 Rachel McLennan, *Representations of Anne Frank in American Literature* (New York: Routledge, 2016).

10 Rachel Small, 'Simon Fujiwara's Distant Memory', *Interview* magazine, 28 June 2013. https://www.interviewmagazine.com/art/simon-fujiwara-studio-pieta-king-kong-komplex-andrea-rosen-gallery

Chapter 7

1 Susan Jeffers, *Feel the Fear and Do It Anyway: How to Turn Your Fear and Indecision into Confidence and Action* (London: Vermillion, 1987).

2 Curtis Sittenfeld, *American Wife* (New York: Random House, 2008).

3 Thomas Harding, *Legacy: One Family, a Cup of Tea and the Company that Took on the World* (London: William Heinemann, 2019).

4 Jung Chan, *Wild Swans: Three Daughters of China* (London: Harper Collins, 1991).

Chapter 10

1 John Bayley, *Iris: A Memoir of Iris Murdoch* (London: Gerald Duckworth and Co., 1998).

2 Robert Frost, 'The Death of the Hired Man'. https://poets.org/poem/death-hired-man

3 Michael Ignatieff, *Scar Tissue* (London: Chatto & Windus, 1993).

Chapter 11

1 James C Scott, *Weapons of the Weak: Everyday Forms of Peasant Resistance* (New Haven: Yale University Press, 1987).

Chapter 12

1 Deborah Moggach, *The Carer* (London: Tinder Press, 2019), 1.

2 Phil Baker, 'Fiction at a Glance: The Carer by Deborah Moggach', *The Sunday Times*, 21 July 2019. https://www.thetimes.co.uk/article/fiction-at-a-glance-the-carer-by-deborah-moggach-everything-you-ever-wanted-by-luiza-sauma-when-we-were-rich-by-tim-lott-rqzlh3zsb

3 Deborah Moggach, 'Winter 2019' (website posting). https://www.deborah-moggach.com/deborah-moggach-news/2019/11/18/winter-2019/

4 Atul Gawande, *Being Mortal: Illness, Medicine, and What Matters in the End* (New York: Profile Books, 2014).

5 Nicci Gerrard, *What Dementia Teaches Us about Love* (London: Allen Lane, 2019).

6 Marlene van Niekerk, *Agaat* (Cape Town: Tafelberg, 2004); Ena Jansen, *Like Family: Domestic Workers in South African History and Literature* (Johannesburg: Wits University Press, 2019); JM Coetzee, *Slow Man* (New York: Penguin Books, 2006).

7 Leslie Swartz, 'Race, Gender, and the Impossibilities of Care', *Medical Humanities* 38 (2012): 34–37; Leslie Swartz, 'Care and the Luxury of Trauma: A South African Story', *Palliative and Supportive Care* 13 (2015): 399–404.

8 Abigail Wilson and Leslie Swartz, 'Paid Carers Talk about Emotionally Charged Experiences in Caring for Dying People: A South African Study', *Journal of Palliative Care* 29, no. 4 (19 December 2019): 246–252.

9 Louise Frenkel, Leslie Swartz and Jason Bantjes, 'Chronic Traumatic Stress and Chronic Pain in the Majority World: Notes towards an Integrative Approach', *Critical Public Health* 28 (2018): 12–21; Louise Frenkel and Leslie Swartz, 'Chronic Pain as a Human Rights Issue: Setting an Agenda for Preventive Action', *Global Health Action* 10, no. 1 (August 2017): 1–8; Justine Evans and Leslie Swartz, 'Training Service Providers Working with Traumatised Children in South Africa: The Navigations of a Trainer', *Psychodynamic Counselling* 6, no. 1 (2000): 49–64; Kerry Gibson and Leslie Swartz, 'Politics and Emotion: Working with Disadvantaged Children in South Africa', *Psychodynamic Counselling* 6, no. 2 (November 2000): 133–153.

10 See Jason Bantjes and Leslie Swartz, 'What Can We Learn from First-Person Narratives? The Case of Non-Fatal Suicidal Behaviour'. *Qualitative Health Research* 29, no. 10 (August 2019): 1497–1507; Heidi Hjelmeland and Birthe L Knizek, 'Response to Bantjes and Swartz', *Qualitative Health Research* 30, no. 6 (May 2020): 942–943.

Chapter 13

1 See, for example: Maria Marchetti-Mercer, Leslie Swartz, Vinitha Jithoo, Nthopele Mabandla, Maxine Wolfe and Alessandra Briguglia (in press), 'South African International Migration and Its Impact on Older Family Members', *Family Process*; Leslie Swartz and Maria Marchetti-Mercer, 'Migration, Technology and Care: What Happens to the Body?' *Disability and Society* 34 (2019): 407–420; Leslie Swartz and Maria Marchetti-Mercer, 'Disabling Africa: The Power of Depiction and the Benefits of Discomfort', *Disability and Society* 33 (November 2017): 482–486.

2 https://dignitysouthafrica.org/

Chapter 14

1 Elizabeth F Emens, *The Art of Life Admin: How to Do Less, Do It Better, and Live More* (New York: Penguin Books, 2019).

2 Richard M Ryan and Edward L Deci, 'On Happiness and Human Potentials: A Review of Research on Hedonic and Eudaimonic Well-Being', *Annual Review of Psychology* 52, no. 1 (February 2001): 141–166; Terence C Cheng, Nattavuddh Powdthavee and Andrew J Oswald, 'Longitudinal Evidence for a Midlife Nadir in Human Well-Being: Results from Four Data Sets', *The Economic Journal* 127, no. 599 (February 2017): 126–142.

3 Erik Erikson, *Identity and the Life Cycle* (New York: WW Norton & Co., 1980).

4 Leslie Swartz, Barbara Hutton and Marius Brand, eds, *Opening a Window: The Story of Spiritual Care at St Luke's Hospice* (Stellenbosch: SunMedia, 2015).

5 See the following for our ideas on these issues, and some examples: Kerry Gibson, Leslie Swartz and Rob Sandenbergh, *Counselling and Coping* (Cape Town: Oxford University Press, 2002); Leslie Swartz, Kerry Gibson, Tamara Gelman, eds. *Reflective Practice: Psychodynamic Ideas in the Community* (Cape Town: HSRC Press, 2002).

6 See, for example, Robert Young's essays 'Melanie Klein I and II'. http://www.psychoanalysis-and-therapy.com/human_nature/papers/pap127h.html

Bibliography

Auslander, Nathan. *Hope: A Tragedy*. New York: Pan Macmillan, 2012.

Baker, Phil. 'Fiction at a Glance: The Carer by Deborah Moggach'. *The Sunday Times*, 21 July 2019. https://www.thetimes.co.uk/article/fiction-at-a-glance-the-carer-by-deborah-moggach-everything-you-ever-wanted-by-luiza-sauma-when-we-were-rich-by-tim-lott-rqzlh3zsb

Bantjes, Jason and Leslie Swartz. 'What Can We Learn from First-Person Narratives? The Case of Non-Fatal Suicidal Behaviour'. *Qualitative Health Research* 29, no. 10 (August 2019): 1497–1507.

Bayley, John. *Iris: A Memoir of Iris Murdoch*. London: Gerald Duckworth & Co., 1988.

Chan, Jung. *Wild Swans: Three Daughters of China*. London: Harper Collins, 1991.

Cheng, Terence C, Nattavuddh Powdthavee and Andrew J Oswald. 'Longitudinal Evidence for a Midlife Nadir in Human Well-Being: Results from Four Data Sets'. *The Economic Journal* 127, no. 599 (February 2017): 126–142.

Coetzee, JM. *Slow Man*. New York: Penguin Books, 2006.

Eco, Umberto. *The Role of the Reader: Explorations in the Semiotics of Texts*. Bloomington: Indiana University Press, 1984.

Eliot, George. *Middlemarch: A Study of Provincial Life*. Harmondsworth: Penguin Classics, 2005. Originally published in serial form, 1871–1872.

Emens, Elizabeth F. *The Art of Life Admin: How to Do Less, Do It Better, and Live More*. New York: Penguin Books, 2019.

Erikson, Erik. *Identity and the Life Cycle*. New York: WW Norton & Co., 1980.

Evans, Justine and Leslie Swartz. 'Training Service Providers Working with Traumatised Children in South Africa: The Navigations of a Trainer'. *Psychodynamic Counselling* 6, no. 1 (2000): 49–64.

Frank, Anne. *The Diary of a Young Girl: The Definitive Edition*. Edited by Otto Frank and Mirjam Pressler; translated by Susan Massotty. London: Penguin Books, 2012.

Freedman, Rod. *Uncle Chatzkel* (2000). Documentary, duration 52 minutes. https://www.imdb.com/title/tt0267062/

French, Sally. 'Can You See the Rainbow? The Roots of Denial'. In *Disabling Barriers – Enabling Environments,* edited by John Swain, 69–77. London: Sage Publications, 2004.

Frenkel, Louise and Leslie Swartz. 'Chronic Pain as a Human Rights Issue: Setting an Agenda for Preventive Action'. *Global Health Action* 10, no. 1 (August 2017): 1–8.

Frenkel, Louise, Leslie Swartz and Jason Bantjes. 'Chronic Traumatic Stress and Chronic Pain in the Majority World: Notes towards an Integrative Approach'. *Critical Public Health* 28 (2018): 12–21.

Frost, Robert. 'The Death of the Hired Man'. https://poets.org/poem/death-hired-man

Gawande, Atul. *Being Mortal: Illness, Medicine, and What Matters in the End.* New York: Profile Books, 2014.

Gerrard, Nicci. *What Dementia Teaches Us about Love.* London: Allen Lane, 2019.

Gevisser, Mark. *Lost and Found in Johannesburg: A Memoir.* New York: Farrar, Straus and Giroux, 2014.

Gibson, Kerry and Leslie Swartz. 'Politics and Emotion: Working with Disadvantaged Children in South Africa'. *Psychodynamic Counselling* 6, no. 2 (November 2000): 133–153.

Gibson, Kerry, Leslie Swartz and Rob Sandenbergh. *Counselling and Coping.* Cape Town: Oxford University Press, 2002.

Gordimer, Nadine. 'Treasures of the Sea'. *Trek: A South African Literary Monthly* 14, no. 6 (8–11 June 1950): 8.

Harding, Thomas. *Legacy: One Family, a Cup of Tea and the Company that Took on the World.* London: William Heinemann, 2019.

Healy-Clancy, Megan. *A World of Their Own: A History of South African Women's Education.* Charlottesville: University of Virginia Press, 2014.

Hjelmeland, Heidi and Birthe L Knizek. 'Response to Bantjes and Swartz'. *Qualitative Health Research* 30, no. 6 (May 2020): 942–943.

Ignatieff, Michael. *Scar Tissue.* London: Chatto & Windus, 1993.

Jansen, Ena. *Like Family: Domestic Workers in South African History and Literature.* Johannesburg: Wits University Press, 2019.

Jeffers, Susan. *Feel the Fear and Do It Anyway: How to Turn Your Fear and Indecision into Confidence and Action.* London: Vermillion, 1987.

Marchetti-Mercer, Maria, Leslie Swartz, Vinitha Jithoo, Nthopele Mabandla, Maxine Wolfe and Alessandra Briguglia (in press). 'South African International Migration and Its Impact on Older Family Members'. *Family Process.*

McLennan, Rachel. *Representations of Anne Frank in American Literature.* New York: Routledge, 2016.

Moggach, Deborah. *The Carer.* London: Tinder Press, 2019.

Moggach, Deborah. 'Winter 2019' (website posting). https://www.deborahmoggach.com/deborah-moggach-news/2019/11/18/winter-2019/

Roth, Philip. *The Ghost Writer*. International edition. New York: Vintage, 1995.

Ryan, Richard M and Edward L Deci. 'On Happiness and Human Potentials: A Review of Research on Hedonic and Eudaimonic Well-Being'. *Annual Review of Psychology* 52, no. 1 (February 2001): 141–166.

SA Jewish Report, 7–14 February 2014: 14.

Scott, James C. *Weapons of the Weak: Everyday Forms of Peasant Resistance*. New Haven: Yale University Press, 1987.

Shavit, Ari. *My Promised Land*. New York: Spiegel & Grau, 2013.

Sittenfeld, Curtis. *American Wife*. New York: Random House, 2008.

Small, Rachel. 'Simon Fujiwara's Distant Memory'. *Interview* magazine, 28 June 2013. https://www.interviewmagazine.com/art/simon-fujiwara-studio-pieta-king-kong-komplex-andrea-rosen-gallery

Sontag, Susan S. *Illness as Metaphor*. New York: Vintage Books, 1978.

Swartz, Leslie. *Able-Bodied: Scenes from a Curious Life*. Cape Town: Zebra, 2010.

Swartz, Leslie. 'Care and the Luxury of Trauma: A South African Story'. *Palliative and Supportive Care* 13 (2015): 399–404.

Swartz, Leslie. 'Race, Gender, and the Impossibilities of Care'. *Medical Humanities* 38 (2012): 34–37.

Swartz, Leslie, Kerry Gibson and Tamara Gelman, eds. *Reflective Practice: Psychodynamic Ideas in the Community*. Cape Town: HSRC Press, 2002.

Swartz, Leslie, Barbara Hutton and Marius Brand, eds. *Opening a Window: The Story of Spiritual Care at St Luke's Hospice*. Stellenbosch: SunMedia, 2015.

Swartz, Leslie and Maria Marchetti-Mercer. 'Disabling Africa: The Power of Depiction and the Benefits of Discomfort'. *Disability and Society* 33 (November 2017): 482–486.

Swartz, Leslie and Maria Marchetti-Mercer. 'Migration, Technology and Care: What Happens to the Body?' *Disability and Society* 34 (2019): 407–420.

Van Niekerk, Marlene. *Agaat*. Cape Town: Tafelberg, 2004.

Wilson, Abigail and Leslie Swartz. 'Paid Carers Talk about Emotionally Charged Experiences in Caring for Dying People: A South African Study'. *Journal of Palliative Care* 29, no. 4 (19 December 2019): 246–252.

Young, Robert. 'Melanie Klein I and II'. http://www.psychoanalysis-and-therapy.com/human_nature/papers/pap127h.html

Zwi, Rose. *Last Walk in Naryshkin Park*. Melbourne, Australia: Spinifex Press, 1997.

Acknowledgements

As an author, I am all too aware that authors themselves are in many ways the worst people to know what their books are about. With this caveat, though this book is about many things, for me it is centrally a book about the long trajectory of care. I grew up with the luck of privilege, which has shaped and enabled many things I have done; but I have also had the good fortune of having had two parents who, flawed as they were like all of us, cared for me and played no small part in my having had the happy life I have had. So my first thanks are to Elsie Swartz (born Cohen) and Alfred Mervyn Swartz not only for caring for me, but also for continuing to fascinate and guide me through my life, and in my writing. It's hard to say these things without sounding soppy, but I'm really lucky. I hope that some of the writing shows how much they gave to me.

My sister Jenny Alter has supported me in many ways for over 60 years, and remains my fierce ally and protector. My daughters, Alison Swartz and Rebecca Swartz, and my wife, Louise Frenkel, cared for my mother and they care for me. Bobbe was so proud of all of you, and loved you all so much, as do I. I am lucky to have such wonderful people in my life. I can never repay you all for what you mean to me, and I hope this book is a very small part payment. Thank you.

Our family is fortunate to live in a wider circle of care, and in this regard I am grateful for support in this work, and in so many other ways, to Ian Alter, Adam Alter, Dean Alter, Pamie Britt, Bev Dickman, Joshua Frank, Tony Frank, Susan Filtane, Gordon Inggs, Nick Reynolds and Sally Swartz.

Kay McCormick provided a remarkable amount of fine-grained and thoughtful input on the manuscript – far more than I had any right to expect. There is something fitting about my having been taught in English I by Kay in 1973 when I was 17, and her having helped me with my late (second) PhD and with this book. Reconnecting with Kay has been a joy of the year of writing the book.

Lisa Compton edited my first book and also edited *Able-Bodied*. She taught me about clear writing. She very kindly read the manuscript for this book and, as ever, gave wonderful, detailed and helpful comments.

This book started its formal life as part of a PhD in creative writing at Stellenbosch University. I am grateful to the university for permitting me to use the text as a basis for the book. I thank my supervisors, Shaun Viljoen and Louise Green, for their help and support, which have been more helpful and wide-ranging than they may know. More good fortune for me. The examiners of the PhD, G Thomas Couser, David Medalie and Sally-Ann Murray, all provided constructive and helpful feedback, which improved the version you have read here.

Stellenbosch University generously gave me sabbatical leave to complete this project. Thank you to my colleagues, teachers, students and support staff, all of whom have contributed to my being able to start, and finish, this book. Special thanks to Gaynöhl Andrews, Ursula Hartzenberg and Kungeka Ndila, all of whom have supported me and my work over the years. The Division for Research Development at Stellenbosch University, and the Social, Behavioural and Education Research Ethics Committee, have provided and continue to provide support to me as an experienced researcher in some fields, but also as something of a novice as a creative writer. Nicky Steenstra of the Postgraduate Education Office in the Faculty of Arts and Social Sciences offers more support than I deserve, as does Marleen Hendriksz of Stellenbosch University Library. Thanks as well to the many colleagues and friends inside and outside of the university who have helped me learn and think.

Over many years, and with this book, Jacqueline Gamble has provided wonderful editing support. Ilse Feinauer was kind enough to pass on a request for translation work to Eduan Naudé; I am grateful to them both. Lizette Rabe has been remarkably supportive of this project and through her kind offices, and those of Isabeau Steytler, I was lucky enough to meet with the late Elsa Joubert, who was generous with her time and interest.

Everyone at Colinton Surgery, and especially Alan Wood, supported all of us through my mother's illness and continue to support us now. This is health care at its best.

St Luke's Hospice offered support to us, as they do for many families dealing with terminal illness. Thank you to all of them, and especially to Sister Yvonne Jackman, who embodies what care is and should be. My work over the years with the spiritual care team at St Luke's and with Ronita Mahillal, the CEO, continues to enrich me.

This book is not obviously a book about disability, but I would not have written it in the way I have done without all the support and mentorship I have gained from many friends and colleagues all over the world in the fields of disability studies and disability rights. I should like particularly to acknowledge the influence on me of the late Alexander Phiri, who was my kind and patient teacher. He substantially influenced how I have come to understand care as a personal and political practice.

I am grateful to all the people who helped with care for my mother, including those named and not named in the memoir. I have chosen not to name the paid carers who were with us for the long haul, but I thank them all.

At a time of great uncertainty in the world of publishing, Roshan Cader of Wits University Press has been brave enough to take a risk with this book. Thank you to Roshan and to your whole team. Special thanks to Alison Lockhart and Alison Lowry. Alison Lowry was the external reader of my submitted manuscript, and I could not have hoped for a more insightful, supportive and constructive interlocutor. It is a wonderful feeling to have my work really understood. Her kindness, skill, attention to detail and light touch carried through into her improving my book considerably through her suggestions and editing.

There were many other people who helped me. Some read drafts and gave comments, some provided useful information and leads, some helped with the care of my mother, and others helped in a wide range of other ways. Thank you to Greg Alexander, Bev Angus, Jason Bantjes, Carol Barac, Hazel Broker, Avril Cowlin, Anneliese de Wet, Madie Duncan, Ronit Elk, Clarissa Graham, Jack Greenblatt, Shirley Greenblatt Luck, Megan Healy-Clancy, Margaret Hoffman, Ena Jansen, Amanda Jermyn, Sharon Kleintjes, Maria Marchetti-Mercer, Tony Naidoo, Michele Rogers, Rizwana Roomaney, Valerie Sinason, Monica Spiro, Sandra Swart, Lucia Thesen, Anna van der Riet, Louise Viljoen, Brian Watermeyer and Rahla Xenopoulos.

Thank you to the Oppenheimer Memorial Trust for financial support for this project, which is much appreciated.

Many others whom I have not named here have helped me with this work, and with many other parts of my life. As with all other acknowledgements, though, I must add the rider that although this book would not have happened without the care and help of others, the responsibility for it, and its faults, are mine alone.

Printed and bound by CPI Group (UK) Ltd, Croydon, CR0 4YY

09/06/2025

14685821-0001